CARAMEL KNOWLEDGE

Caramel Knowledge

To Roy & Judy:
A day without chocolate
is like a day with Anita Bryant!

PANTS PRESS

Minneapolis

Design/ J.W. Smith

Cover illustration/ Roger Boehm

ISBN 0-9614241-0-9

PANTS PRESS
P.O. Box 15287
Minneapolis, Minn.
55415

For my mother, Miriam Sicherman, who loved words, and my father, Sam Sicherman, who has always enjoyed a good story (and a good cigar). And for my kids, Joe and Dave Sicherman, who have listened to a whole lot of my stories over the years — and who still laugh at them.

Acknowledgments:

There are a zillion cookbooks, most of which I look through every week in my search for recipes to mangle ... umm ... to adapt to my very peculiar needs. I've found several cookbooks to be especially good references, and — although they hardly need this from me — I'd like to recommend them: Mastering the Art of French Cooking (Julia Child, Louisette Bertholle and Simone Beck), Best Loved Recipes of the American People (Ida Bailey Allen), of course The Joy of Cooking (Irma Rombauer and Marion R. Becker) and most of all, because of its completeness and its very good index, The Doubleday Cookbook (Jean Anderson and Elaine Hanna).

On a more personal level, my thanks to various folks at the Minneapolis Star and Tribune for various reasons: Some for encouraging me to put this book together; some for helping me to put this book together, and most for listening to me grouse while I put this book together. Special thanks to colleague Mary Hart for all three.

And special thanks, too, to Catherine Watson, Peg Meier, Terry Wigand, Ingrid Sundstrom, Susan Stan, Roxanne Kroll and Linda James — the "regulars" at my table — who continue to show up almost every week, no matter how strange the dinner I inflict upon them. (I know they're all women. They know it, too, and they keep asking me why I don't invite men more often. Listen, I'm divorced, it's my pâté, and I'll cry if I want to.)

Many of these same friends and colleagues also helped proofread these pages, as did colleagues John Addington and Lee Svitak Dean. I'm deeply grateful. They found all the mistakes that aren't here any more. I missed all the ones that still are.

And last and most special thanks to Jody Smith, who not only designed the book and conceived the idea of making "Caramel Knowledge" into a candy bar for the cover, but also acted as daily (sometimes hourly) consultant and liaison over details of design and production.

"You don't know who your friends really are until you spill a bag of garbage or try to write a book." — **Anonymous**

Introduction

Each of these very strange food columns has appeared in the Minneapolis Star and Tribune, so you've already had one opportunity to save them. This book is your second chance. (How many more do you think there will be?)

With the exception of three Austrian tortes, I have personally prepared every recipe in this volume in my own personal kitchen, and I sampled each of them with my own personal mouth.

And that's not all. As a bonus to qualifying purchasers, I have included (scattered here and there throughout the book and absolutely free of additional charge) 12 "Little Mysteries" — selections from my attempts in the newspaper to solve some of the nagging food-related questions that might keep you awake some night but that aren't worth asking anybody else.

(Am I a sport, or what?)

Contents

The Mock Food Meal

When I was a lad in Milwaukee, I took violin lessons. I don't know how that developed — I don't remember being wildly crazy about violin music. Maybe my parents heard the line about it being easier to run with a violin than with a piano.

Anyway, however it happened, there I was in grade school with a violin — not loving it, but getting along with it OK. Until, in what must have been my second year of lessons (I think I was in the fourth grade), the dreaded Recital in the School Auditorium was scheduled.

I was not, as you might imagine, thrilled by the prospect of standing out on the stage, by myself, in front of God and the first through sixth grades, with nothing but my violin to defend me. And when I found out what I was supposed to play, it became worse.

It was "Mockingbird Hill," which you might recall if you are as far up the hill as I am. It has a melody that goes up and down a lot, necessitating frequent moves from one string of the violin to another. At my level of proficiency this was, I knew, going to be a disaster.

As the days of practice wore on, my worst fears were confirmed. I stunk.

Everyone kept telling me I was doing fine. I knew I stunk.

On the big morning I waited nervously in the wings while classmates whose parents had subjected them to the trombone, clarinet and drums strutted and fretted their hour upon the stage and then (except for an occasional whimper) were heard no more.

It was my turn.

My heart was in my mouth, along with my stomach and several other internal organs. My violin teacher and the school principal, beaming, were starting to prod me onto the stage. I knew I was about to humiliate myself.

And then a remarkable thing happened — a thing that hasn't happened again more than three or four times in my life at such a critical juncture.

I refused.

I just would not go out on that stage and become a laughingstock. As memory serves, while the two adults stared at me, I walked out of the wings, down the steps and took a seat in the audience, still holding the violin. If I remember correctly, there was a scattering of grateful applause. I think it was one of the best moments of my life.

It also, you may have noted, appears to have nothing to do with food.

Well, not everything worth remembering has something to do with food. But, as you probably know if you have suffered through other articles I have written, I have acquired the power to weave the most tenuous filament of association into a cable that allows me to drag in four or five recipes and several columns of type.

Watch:

I remembered the "Mockingbird Hill" incident recently while looking at some old sheet music, and that started me thinking about mock apple pie, a dish made with Ritz crackers instead of apples. I don't know why anybody would feel the need to make apple pie with Ritz crackers, since there is seldom a great apple shortage, but if you want to do it you can.

That, and a conversation with some colleagues, started me thinking about other mock foods. A check through recent cookbooks didn't turn up many, so food mockery seems to be an activity no longer much practiced (except by vegetarians, who make lots of mock things with soybeans), but older cookbooks were, comparatively speaking, loaded with them.

I knew that mock foods used to be around, because I remembered mock chicken legs made with veal. It's sure no surprise that folks aren't serving many mock chicken legs any more, given the price of veal.

Quite a few of the other mock dishes that I turned up also involved veal, but I did find a number that didn't, and that could be made without taking out a second mortgage. Thus, history will record, was born the Mock Food Meal.

This appetizer is the only part of the meal that I made up. I did that for three reasons: I couldn't find any mock appetizers, this one sounded like it could be pretty good and the name is an outrageous spoonerism.

Actually, I figured, if it worked out this might really be a practical mock dish. Making guacamole depends on finding ripe avocados, and it has been my experience that the chance of finding ripe avocados in a supermarket is like the chance of finding the red jelly-beans left in a bowl on somebody's coffee table. If there ever were any, somebody else already got them.

You can plan ahead, of course, and buy your avocados long in advance so that they are ripe when you need them, but I don't know anybody who plans *that* far ahead. (You can eliminate this whole problem by buying frozen guacamole already made, of course, but you can buy entire frozen dinners already made, too. If you've read this far in an article about cooking, I assume that is not the kind of solution that appeals to you.)

So let's make guacamole with softened butter instead of mashed avocado.

Opinions were clearly divided on this one. Some folks found it too rich and a little greasy. Others (myself included) thought it was wonderful. You be the judge. Send your opinion to the Judge Avocado General's office.

Mockaguole

2 sticks (½ lb.) softened butter
½ to 1 small tomato
1 small onion
1 small clove garlic
2 tbsp. lemon juice (juice of 1 lemon)
1 to 2 tsp. chili powder
2 drops or more Tabasco sauce
3 to 4 tbsp. flour
5 or 6 drops green food coloring
Corn chips

Cream the softened butter in a mixer or food processor.

Chop the tomato and the onion and crush the garlic. Drain off juice, retaining only the solids. Add tomato, onion, garlic, lemon juice, chili powder and Tabasco to the butter and beat or process until well blended.

If liquid has separated out, pour it off. Sift in and blend the flour, as needed to make the mixture hold together. Add food coloring to approximate the amazingly unlikely color of guacamole.

Serve with corn chips. Serves eight to ten.

The next dish also required my intervention, although not as severely. (If you want classic mock dishes from cookbooks, you'll have to be just a little patient. They're coming.)

Mock turtle soup is about the only mock dish that lots of people have heard of. A natural to make, right?

Wrong. Guess what is the principal ingredient in every recipe I found for mock turtle soup.

No. Guess. Come on. Stop cheating by looking ahead.

Oh, all right. The principal ingredient in mock turtle soup is a calf's head.

I don't mind making things like mockaguole. I *like* making things like mockaguole. But I'm *not* cooking a calf's head.

So I improvised.

Mock Mock Turtle Soup

1 (10½-oz.) can beef bouillon
1 (10½-oz.) can beef consommé
½ to 1 lb. beef stew meat
Dash allspice
Dash thyme
3 cloves
6 peppercorns
1 small onion, sliced
2 tbsp. butter
2 tbsp. flour
½ c. tomato juice
Juice of ½ lemon (about 1 tbsp. lemon juice)
Salt, pepper to taste
¼ c. sherry

Pour the canned bouillon, consommé and two soup cans of water into a Dutch oven and bring to the simmer. While the soup is heating, trim all fat from the stew meat and cut the meat into ¼-inch-thick slices. Cut the slices into ¼-inch-wide strips. Add to the soup along with the allspice and thyme.

Tie the cloves, peppercorns and onion in a hunk of cheesecloth and add to the soup, or put them in a metal-mesh colander or strainer and suspend it in the soup. (One way or the other, we'll want to fish them out of the soup easily.) Cover and simmer the soup about 20 minutes.

Melt the butter in a large saucepan. Stir in the flour and cook, stirring, over medium heat, about one minute. Slowly add a few spoonfuls of the soup, stirring. Continue stirring in soup, a ladleful or so at a time, until the paste is quite thin, then pour the paste back into the large soup pot and stir in well.

Add tomato juice, lemon juice, salt and pepper. Simmer five minutes. When ready to serve, add the sherry and simmer two minutes. Serves six.

For the main dish, these days you might be tempted to get back at mock chicken legs made with veal by making almost anything that calls for veal (scallopine, wiener schnitzel, etc.) and substituting sliced turkey breast or deboned and flattened chicken breast for the veal. That's an excellent substitution, and I highly recommend it, but it's time we have some classic mock dishes.

How about "mock duck?" It's one I'd never heard of, frankly, but it cropped up in a number of older books — in two forms.

One involves an entire quarter of lamb, cut to look like a duck. ("Have the butcher prepare a forequarter of lamb for mock duck . . . .") Something tells me that a request like that wouldn't get you a very kind look at the meat counter these days.

Luckily, there's a second version of mock duck, made with a flank steak. That isn't cheap, but I bet you could do it with a round steak, too. The idea is to slit the steak almost all the way in half ("butterfly" it), fill it with a seasoned meat-and-bread mixture, and sew it up, tying off a bit at both ends, to resemble head and tail.

It doesn't *taste* like duck (and it doesn't really *look* like a duck, either). But it looks sort of halfway between a steak and a drawing of a duck. It is kind of fun, and various folks can be rude when they ask for parts of it.

Mock Duck

1½ lbs. steak (about 6 inches wide
    and 10 to 12 inches long)
1 tsp. salt
¼ tsp. pepper
¼ tsp. ginger
5 tbsp. butter, divided
½ c. bread crumbs
About ¾ lb. ground beef
1 small onion, finely chopped
1 or 2 tbsp. chopped parsley
Salt, pepper to taste
Paprika
½ c. water
1 (10½-oz.) can beef bouillon
Coarse thread for sewing

Trim off all fat from steak. Carefully slice it in half edgewise, but leave about an inch unsliced at one edge, so you can open it up like a book or a butterfly. (This isn't nearly as hard as it sounds if you have a sharp knife. If you don't, you're in a heap of trouble.)

Season the open (inside) faces of the steak with the salt, pepper and ginger.

Melt three tablespoons of the butter,

mix in the bread crumbs, ground beef, onion and parsley, and salt, pepper and paprika to taste.

Pat the mixture evenly over one of the inside surfaces of the steak.

Close the steak up and, making the stitches an inch or so apart, sew up the three open sides with coarse thread. (Trust me. Use coarse thread. Ordinary thread tends to break rather than to pull back out of the mock duck when you are getting it ready to serve.)

Tie coarse thread about two inches down around each of two corners of the rectangle separated by a long side, and tighten to form the "head" and the "tail."

Preheat the oven to 250 degrees. Combine the ½ cup of water and the canned bouillon and heat to boiling.

Meanwhile, melt the remaining two tablespoons of butter in a 9- by 13- inch pan on the top of the stove and sear the "duck" in it on all sides.

Pour in the hot bouillon mixture, add the duck and cover with foil. Bake about 1½ hours, until the "duck" is tender. Remove thread and serve. Serves four.

For the vegetable, I made some broccoli with mock hollandaise sauce.

I have to say something about mock hollandaise sauce. Folks might make some mock foods, like the Ritz cracker pie, I guess, just because they are kind of interesting. They might make others to substitute for an expensive or hard-to-find ingredient. And they might make still others because they offer shortcuts.

My guess is that mock hollandaise sauce, which exists in many, many forms in current cookbooks, is around because people believe that real hollandaise sauce is hard to make. Some of the mock hollandaise sauces *are* easier, but those sounded dreadful (adding some lemon to cream of chicken soup, for example).

Here's one that isn't half bad. It sure isn't hollandaise sauce, either — it has a kind of a flour gravy quality — and I think it's at least as much work as the real thing, if not more. What it has to recommend it is that it is based on a flour white sauce, so it is not likely to curdle, like real hollandaise, if you get the heat too high.

Mock Hollandaise Sauce

6 tbsp. butter, divided
2 tbsp. flour
¼ tsp. salt
Pepper
1 c. milk
2 egg yolks
1 tbsp. lemon juice

In a saucepan over low heat, melt two tablespoons of the butter. Stir in the flour, salt and pepper and heat, stirring, about one minute. Add the milk, a little at a time, stirring constantly, until all the milk is in and the sauce is smooth.

Beat the two egg yolks lightly, then stir in a few tablespoons of the hot mixture. Stir the diluted egg yolks back into the hot white sauce. With the white sauce over very low heat, and stirring constantly, add the lemon juice and the remaining four tablespoons of butter — one at a time, waiting for one to be almost fully incorporated before adding the next one. Makes about 1½ cups.

Even a mock meal has to have a dessert, right? But a *mock* dessert. Or two. First, a mock pumpkin pie recipe from a 1929 pamphlet for a popular breakfast cereal. It tastes like pumpkin pie, but so would almost anything if you put in ginger, cloves, nutmeg and cinnamon. The color is more tan than brown, so I would cover the surface with whipped cream. (No, not extruded plastic topping. Real whipped cream. Even for a mock meal, I draw the line there.)

Grape-Nuts Mock Pumpkin Pie

¼ c. boiling water
½ c. Grape-Nuts
2 c. milk, scalded
¼ c. sugar
4 tbsp. flour
⅛ tsp. ginger
¼ tsp. cloves
¼ tsp. nutmeg
½ tsp. cinnamon
2 eggs, well beaten
1 baked 8- or 9-in. pie shell
1 c. heavy cream, whipped

Pour boiling water over Grape-Nuts. Stir. Let stand 10 minutes, then add milk.

Combine sugar, flour, ginger, cloves, nutmeg and cinnamon. Add to Grape-Nuts mixture and cook in a double boiler, stirring and lifting (the Grape-Nuts tend to settle) until thickened — about five minutes. Stir a little of the hot mixture into the eggs, then pour the diluted eggs back into the hot mixture, stirring, and continue to cook and stir another two to three minutes.

Cool a few minutes, pour into baked pie shell and chill. Top with whipped cream.

Serves six to eight.

Now we come to the dish we have spoken about so much already: Ritz Cracker Mock Apple Pie. The recipe is from the Ritz Cracker box. This *looks* like apple pie, which really is kind of amazing. But it doesn't taste at all like it. If you were blindfolded, you'd say it was lemon pie. But unless some troublemaker points that out, folks are so convinced by how much it looks like apple that they tend not to notice that it tastes like lemon.

One guest said it tasted like apple pie to her — because her mother always made Ritz Cracker Mock Apple Pie. She did not know why.

Another guest had never heard of it before, and even through several discussions of it earlier in the meal he had not quite gotten the message about it. He knew there were Ritz crackers in the pie, but I'm not sure where he thought they were. He clearly thought the filling was apples. "No," I said, "it's Ritz crackers." "Yes, but what's the fruit?" "Ritz crackers."

Now do *you* get it?

Here's the point: Even if we someday run out of apples, we can still have apple pie — if we haven't also run out of lemon juice. (And Ritz crackers.)

Ritz Cracker Mock Apple Pie

Pastry for a two-crust 9-inch pie
36 Ritz crackers
2 c. water
2 c. sugar
2 tsp. cream of tartar
Juice of 1 lemon (2 tbsp. lemon juice)
Grated rind of 1 lemon
1 to 2 tbsp. butter or margarine
½ tsp. cinnamon

Roll out the bottom crust and fit it into a 9-inch pie pan. Break the Ritz crackers coarsely into the pastry-lined pan.

Combine the water, sugar and cream of tartar in a saucepan; boil gently for 15 min-utes. Add lemon juice and lemon rind. Cool.

Preheat the oven to 425 degrees. Pour the syrup over the crackers, dot with the butter and sprinkle with cinnamon.

Cover with the top crust, trim and flute the edges and cut slits in the top crust to let steam escape. Bake for 30 to 35 minutes, until the crust is crisp and golden. Serve warm. Serves six to eight.

Food That's Good for You

When I was growing up in Milwaukee, just as when you were growing up in Ashtabula or Punxsutawney or Fort Snelling, my little sweeties, it was customary for members of my family to encourage me to eat various things I didn't want to eat by telling me that they were good for me.

You know the kind of thing I mean. "You'll never grow up to be big and strong like your Aunt Ethel if you don't eat all your broccoli."

I don't know about you, my little sweeties, but when I was faced with something like veal breast I didn't care if it was good for me or rotten for me; I wasn't about to eat any.

My mother once got me to eat mushrooms in a manner I consider truly reprehensible. She cut them into some unrecognizable shape and put them into chop suey, where she didn't normally use them. When I asked what they were, she told me they were Chinese evergreens. I was dumb enough to eat them, and of course I thought they were great. I still hold that against her.

The aunt of one of my childhood friends was a relatively recent immigrant from Eastern Europe. She was clearly inclined to explain the merits of her cuisine but was hampered by limited command of English. She shortened her pleading with him to one rather forceful remark: "Eat! Is good. I made."

The thing about foods that people always insisted were good for you is that they were foods that kids didn't particularly like. I can't remember ever being told that spaghetti and meatballs or chocolate cake or peanut butter and jelly sandwiches were good for me (although they must have been — they made me what I am today), because I was perfectly willing to eat them without any extra advice.

It is a truth, not well recognized by the mothers of kids of my generation, that the more people insist that something is good for you the less you want to eat any of it.

My father, by contrast, never seriously wheedled at me to eat things. He apparently felt that it was necessary to say *something,* but it usually turned out to be something like "You'll love the lima beans. They give you curly pimples."

In honor, then, of Father's Day, and in acknowledgment that father did indeed know best (I still dislike veal breast but I'll eat lima beans any time), I modestly present a meal of things that people always say are good for you.

But in recognition that there may be children present and that boiled beets are still boiled beets no matter how much iron or whatever they give you, I have arranged to present those good-for-you foods in one degree or another of disguise.

I don't warrant that any of these recipes (except the dessert) will appeal any more to kids than does the food in its more traditional presentation, but I think adults might find them interesting.

Carrots, you will no doubt remember hearing, are supposed to give you good eyesight. I can attest to the truth of that contention. I was always able to spot carrots being prepared — even at very great distances — and to try not to be home when they were finally served.

I don't remember any more what is wrong with carrots from the kid point of view, but even now unadorned boiled carrots strike me as among the least interesting things you could put on a plate.

I know, however, that carrots can dare to be great. I've eaten great carrots.

So today I offer a highly unusual carrot recipe. I can't say that everyone will like it, but I'll probably make it again, and it got a definite "Hmmmm" from the two other folks on whom I tried it out.

The liquid in which the carrots marinate is usable again for other things (like mushrooms and green beans, and as a sauce for meats), so don't be appalled at how much of it there is.

The recipe is based on one in The Modern Art of Chinese Cooking, a nice book by Barbara Tropp. I fiddled with the recipe as is my wont, so if you don't like it don't blame her.

Oriental Carrot Appetizer

1 (10¾-oz.) can chicken broth
1 soup can water
1 (10-oz.) bottle (that's right, the whole bottle) soy sauce
⅓ c. Chinese rice wine (or substitute dry sherry)
5 coin-size slices of fresh ginger
1 green onion, cut into 3-in. lengths
1½ star anise, broken into 12 points
¼ c. sugar
½ lb. carrots

This recipe requires marinating time.

Prepare the sauce: Put the chicken broth, water, soy sauce and wine in a saucepan. Slap the ginger slices and the onion pieces on a cutting board with the flat side of a heavy knife (to release the juices) and add them to the liquids, along with the broken pieces of star anise and the sugar.

Bring to a boil and simmer, stirring occasionally, for about an hour. Strain the sauce and use it to prepare the carrots.

Trim and peel the carrots. Cut them on a sharp diagonal into slices about ¼ inch thick (try to make them the same thickness, so they all get done at the same time).

Bring the sauce to a simmer and add the carrot slices. Cover and simmer 15 minutes, stirring once or twice. Turn off the heat and let the carrots steep 30 minutes covered and another 1½ hours uncovered.

Strain the used sauce through wet cheesecloth, pour it into a jar and refrigerate or freeze it for use with other vegetables or over meats. (It will keep in the refrigerator for a week.)

Put the carrots in a shallow bowl (careful — they break easily). They can be eaten warm or be refrigerated overnight (covered with plastic wrap) and eaten cold. If you choose the latter alternative, which gives them a more unusual texture, just before serving them invert them into a serving bowl so that the sauce that had settled to the bottom is now prettily on the top.

Serves two to three as a warm vegetable or five to six as an appetizer. Afterwards you'll be able to read the recipe in the dark.

Beets have earned a firm place in the I-don't-want-any parade. (What kid cares how much iron he gets? In fact, I don't care either.) This recipe, adapted from Sunset's Easy Basics for Good Cooking, beets a lot of others for tanginess — I liked it quite a beet.

Mustardy Beets

4 tbsp. softened butter
1 tbsp. tarragon vinegar
1 tbsp. Dijon mustard
1 (16-oz.) can diced beets

Beat together the softened butter, vinegar and mustard. Set aside.

Drain the beets, reserving one or two tablespoons of the beet liquid. Put the beets in a saucepan with the reserved liquid, cover and heat through until the liquid is just about fully evaporated. Add the mustard mixture and heat, stirring, just until it has melted and coated the beets.

Serves four. Gives you so much iron that your epitaph can say "Rust in Peace."

For the main course, of course, an intelligent person has no choice but to serve fish, it being so widely known as a brain food.

Fish was also widely known in my childhood circles as a *disgusting* food, so it would surprise my mother to know that I am actually recommending it to 579,847 of my closest friends.

To be honest, what I'm really recommending is the sauce. Some years back, when I was working ever-so-briefly in France, my colleagues took me to dinner at a hotsy-totsy restaurant, where I ate the best sauce-with-fish it has ever been my pleasure to get outside of. It was described as a beurre rouge (red butter), and I resolved to duplicate it upon my return to these shores.

Alas, most cookbooks did not list such a sauce, and the only one I found that did so described it as another name for lobster butter, whose ingredients include the coral or eggs of various shellfish. My refrigerator has never been deeply stocked with the coral or eggs of various shellfish, so I never made beurre rouge.

Then, quite recently, I found another — and much simpler — recipe for beurre rouge. "Ho, ho," I said to myself (or words to that effect). This new recipe is merely a variation of beurre blanc (white butter), which is a reasonably common sauce and quite simple. Red wine is substituted for the white wine and/or vinegar in the beurre blanc and voilà (or, as we say over here, there you go): Beurre rouge.

That struck me as so simple an idea that I made no advance preparation at all when I intended to serve it.

None.

At the last minute I discovered that I hadn't even bought any red wine.

I had some white wine to serve with the fish (wine for thy stomach's sake of course — another good-for-you food), but trying to make red butter with white wine didn't seem likely to be very productive.

As a desperate substitution, I used some tawny port that I had on the basement stairs. The result was quite sweet and not red. I would call it beurre khaki, but it actually went rather nicely with the fish (if you like sweet sauces).

On a retest with Burgundy, the beurre rouge turned out to be very nice indeed, and a somewhat better accompaniment to fish than beurre khaki — but not what I remembered. The next time I have a refrigerator full of shellfish coral, I'm going to give that one a try. In the meantime, here's the easy version, which I really do recommend (and the fish is excellent, too).

Poached Sole with Red Butter

Fish:
4 fillets of sole
Lemon juice
Salt
White pepper
3 tbsp. butter
1 c. dry vermouth
½ c. water
Sauce:
1 shallot
3 tbsp. red wine
¼ lb. unsalted butter

Preheat the oven to 350 degrees.

Wash the fish in water with a little lemon juice in it. Dry it well and sprinkle lightly with salt and white pepper.

Fold the fish fillets in half lengthwise and arrange them in a buttered baking dish. Butter a piece of waxed paper the size of the dish.

In a small saucepan, melt the three tablespoons of butter and add to it one tablespoon of lemon juice, a dash of salt and pinch of white pepper. Add the vermouth and water and bring to the boil. Spoon the hot liquid over the fish fillets and cover them with the piece of buttered wax paper (buttered side down).

Put the dish in the oven for 15 minutes, then remove the fish to a warm platter and serve with the sauce.

To prepare the sauce, put half a tablespoon of water in a small saucepan to see what that much liquid looks like. Discard the water and dry the pan.

Chop the shallot very finely. Put it in the small saucepan with the wine and boil until there is about half a tablespoon remaining. Reduce the heat to very low. Cut the butter into 8 pieces and stir them in, one at time, adding one just before the previous one is fully gone, to make a smooth, creamy sauce. (If the first pieces of butter become liquid instead of working into a sauce, the burner is too hot. Turn it VERY low, like I said. The sauce should be creamy, not greasy.) Strain out the bits of shallot, if you're fussy, season with salt and white pepper and serve with the fish.

Serves four. You certainly won't be sorry you tried this one. Not only does it taste good, after you've eaten it you'll be so smart you'll be able to perform astounding feats of brain power — like guessing the number of times the letters s, m, a, r and t appear in this article. (The answer is at the end, for those of you who just won't eat fish for *any* reason.)

One more good-for-you vegetable, please. Everybody knows what it's going to be, right? If you're a little slow this morning, I'll give you two hints:

It's green.

It's icky.

No, not okra. I'm not that mean. Spinach.

I must admit that I've already passed along my favorite spinach recipe.

Ordinarily I would say that it's not my fault if you haven't been attentive. I can't keep printing the same recipes over and over, just waiting for you to notice them and cut them out. But just for you sweeties who've bought this book, you'll find it with the SPAM recipes. Leave out the SPAM if you like; it's great either way.

This substitute is quite good. It is blessed with lots of butter and a very nice covering of béchamel sauce and cheese.

Altogether a grown-up version of the food that gives you big muscles, so let's give it a French name.

La Favorite de Popoeil

<u>Spinach:</u>
2 (10-oz.) pkg. frozen chopped
    spinach
9 tbsp. butter, divided
3 eggs
½ c. heavy cream
½ tsp. pepper
½ tsp. salt
<u>Sauce:</u>
1 small carrot
1 c. milk
1½ tbsp. flour
1 slice onion
1 clove
1 bay leaf
2 sprigs parsley
Pinch of nutmeg
¼ c. grated Parmesan cheese

Preheat the oven to 350 degrees.

Prepare the spinach according to package directions. Rinse, drain and squeeze the spinach until it is dry. In a large frying pan, sauté the spinach in four tablespoons of the butter until the spinach has fully absorbed the butter.

Beat the eggs. Blend in the cream, pepper and salt. Stir the mixture slowly into the spinach.

Brown four more tablespoons of the butter in a pan and stir into the spinach.

Butter a 1½-quart oven-safe casserole or mold and fill it with the spinach.

Put the casserole in a pan of hot water and bake about 30 minutes.

While the casserole is in the oven, prepare the sauce:

Pare and slice the carrot. Heat the milk in a small saucepan.

In another pan melt the remaining one tablespoon of butter over low heat, and stir in the flour. Continue to cook, stirring, for two minutes, then slowly add the hot milk, stirring. Add the sliced carrot, the onion, clove, bay leaf, parsley and nutmeg. (If you don't have one or two of the seasonings, go ahead anyway; it'll work out just fine.) Simmer the sauce 10 minutes and strain out the solids.

When the casserole is cooked, pour the sauce over it (or unmold it onto an oven-safe platter and then cover with sauce).

Top with grated cheese and run briefly under the broiler to brown.

Serves six. (Try to keep from smashing furniture with one hand when you've finished eating your helping.)

Now we come to dessert. If you've been holding your breath, afraid I'd ruin dessert by adding cod-liver oil, you don't know me very well. There are still a few things in life that are sacred. Outdoor baseball may not be one of them, but *nobody* messes around with dessert in my house.

I did want to do something at least a *little* good for you, though. I remembered getting anguished letters after I made bread pudding with chocolate sauce, wondering why I hadn't simply made chocolate bread pudding. Well, OK, that's a perfect excuse to make something with bread crusts, which are alleged to give you curly hair or something. Actually, I used the rest of the bread, too.

▶

Chocolate Bread Pudding

3 c. milk

3 (1-oz.) squares unsweetened
    chocolate

1 (1-oz.) square semisweet chocolate
    (optional)

½ c. sugar

2 eggs

1 tsp. vanilla

2 c. (packed) bread crusts and
    whatever other parts of the
    bread you care to contribute, cut
    or torn into 1-in. pieces

Heat the milk and chocolate, including the extra ounce of semisweet if you want it *really* chocolate, in a double boiler until the chocolate is melted. Combine the sugar and eggs and beat until just blended. Slowly add the chocolate mixture to the eggs, stirring constantly. Add the vanilla.

Grease a 1½-quart baking dish and put the bread cubes in it. Pour the chocolate mixture over the bread and let it stand 20 minutes. Preheat the oven to 350 degrees.

Stir the pudding, set the baking dish in a 9- by 13-inch pan and add hot water to the pan until it is about an inch deep. Bake the pudding 45 to 50 minutes (check near the end to make sure there's still water in the pan), until the blade of a knife comes out clean. Eat, and wait for your hair to curl. Serves six.

This article has been subjected to a computer analysis, which revealed that, not counting this sentence, it contains 3,783 occurrences of the letters s, m, a, r and t; the analysis also revealed that the writer needs professional help.

Little Mystery #1: Pimientos

How does the pimiento get into the olive?

Solution: A spokesperson for Lindsay Olive Growers, Lindsay, Calif., said that until recent years it was mainly done in Spain, by hand. The pimiento was punched into the pitted olive with a little pin.

Now we're in the age of mechanical stuffing, he explained. The pimiento is ground into a paste, a jelling agent is added to the paste and a pimiento ribbon is formed, which hardens into a jelled strip, called a tape. The tape is rolled up and fed into a machine that pits and stuffs the olives in essentially one operation:

A coring knife comes in from one end and cores out around the olive pit, producing a large opening. Then a small punch pin comes through from the other end and punches out the pit. The pimiento tape is inserted into the large hole and cut off.

Pimiento *tape?* Isn't that the pits?

A Dark View of the Chocolate Fad

We're a nation of trend-followers.

Ten years ago, the only people in America drinking Perrier and eating croissants were effete snobs and Frenchmen held here against their will; now there are umpteen kinds of sparkling water available at Red Owl, and everybody with an oven is turning out fat crescent rolls.

Taco salad is threatening to replace the restaurant grilled-cheese sandwich.

There are parts of Minneapolis in which you can't go two blocks without stepping on a quiche.

Until now, I watched these trends with indifference or resignation. So what if the croissant, once a hard-to-find treat but always wonderful, is now more common than the cinnamon roll but often lousy?

So what if you can't find a nice bottle of cream soda at the store because of all the imported mineral water?

Indifference or resignation, I repeat, until now.

Now the trendsetters, the despoilers of delight, the waterers-down of wonder, have begun to hit where I live.

They're messing around with chocolate, and I suppose they won't be happy until it's in everything we eat, much more expensive and not very good.

The dilution has already begun. A flood of promotional material for a "chocolate cookbook" arrived in the office recently, gasping and groaning about the wonderful recipes to be found therein. It offered three examples, two of which used cocoa, not chocolate. (That's if memory serves correctly; it might have been all three — I was so put off that I threw the stuff away.)

Yes, cocoa is a perfectly nice ingredient, and plenty of people like it fine. But it's not chocolate. I'm afraid this kind of thing is the harbinger of much more to come. Food technologists have long-ago substituted cocoa and inexpensive artificial flavors for chocolate in lots of apparently chocolate items in grocery stores. (A hint is the word "fudge" in the name instead of "chocolate." If it says "chocolate" there's got to be *some* chocolate in there, although the principal flavor ingredient is often cocoa and the chocolate is down with the BHA, BHT, mono- and diglycerides, giving a whole new meaning to the phrase "below the salt.")

How many of the chichi chocolate items that are on their way will be worth eating?

We now have "devil's food" Twinkies (with no chocolate in them) and fancy gold-foil-wrapped chocolate bars that are no better than the cheaper ones they're edging out.

Mark my words: It will get worse. Bill Blass is already putting out "designer chocolates" (whatever *that* means), and there are outrageously priced confections covered with "white chocolate," which has about as much flavor as wallboard.

It could turn ugly, too. You could waltz into your neighborhood drug store one day to buy a few Hershey's Special Dark bars and be met by a guy built like a McCormick reaper, who will smile at you through steel teeth and tell you that the free ride is over and that they're gonna cost you five bucks apiece.

That probably won't happen, but even if the gentrification of chocolate remains civilized, I greatly resent it.

I was eating chocolate before it was being advertised in The New Yorker or written about in Time magazine. Lots of you were, too. But now there are others in the market — people who don't really love the stuff like you and I do but who wait in line to buy fashionable Godiva chocolates at $17.50 a pound, depriving you and me of the chance to get them for the $8 or $9 they probably would have cost under more-limited demand.

Not everything that rides the crest of the chocolate wave is terrible, of course. Sandra Boynton, the woman who draws the chocolate-consuming hippos that grace (if that is the word) calendars and T-shirts, probably would not have been able to interest publishers in her wonderfully funny little book, Chocolate — the Consuming Passion, had chocolate not become such a hot item.

(A sample of Boynton, on carob: "Some consider carob an adequate substitute for chocolate because it has some similar nutrients [calcium, phosphorus], and because it can, when combined with vegetable fat and sugar, be made to approximate the color and consistency of chocolate. Of course, the same arguments can as persuasively be made in favor of dirt.")

If Boynton gets rich on her marvelous book, that's great. But I object to many of the others who are seeking to make a chocolate mint, because I know what's going to happen. See, as those of you who find my words going directly to the heart (or perhaps to the stomach) already know, the world can be divided into two classes of people:

■ Those who *really love* chocolate. (People I have seen described as "chocolate-intensive personalities.")

■ Those who hate it, don't care for it or like it well enough but would sometimes just as readily eat some strawberries. (Everybody else.)

Because those in the first category are already buying all the chocolate they can carry, it is those in the second category at whom the trendy merchandising is being directed. Those second-category folks don't like chocolate all that well, so the stuff that's coming, however fancy its design or wrapper, is likely to be less-than-satisfying to the real chocolate person.

For those of you in the first category, my brothers and sisters in a dark but delicious bond, I feel the least I can do in these times of trouble is to pass along some recipes to cherish as the world crumbles blandly around us.

Others be warned: These aren't recipes for the faint of taste. My partner, Kate Parry, whose preference in chocolate runs to things the color of package-wrapping paper, would hate every one of them. On the other hand, there is already plenty of "chocolate" stuff for you folks, and more on the way. Have some Fudge Sticks or something.

Note: Just because it might be contributing to the trend, I don't subscribe to Chocolate News, a newsletter for chocoholics. I hear, though, that it's not bad (even though it is printed on brown, chocolate-scented paper). Maybe I should. Do you suppose I could deduct it on my income tax?

We should have lost a fair number of cocoa, carob and "white chocolate" fans by now, so I'll assume I'm talking only to hard-core (or should it be soft-center?) chocolate lovers.

This is my opportunity to go for broke — to pass along some really intense chocolate stuff.

That puts me in something of a dilemma. A few of my favorites have already been in the paper, some time ago. I don't want to run second-string recipes just because better ones have already appeared. On the other hand, you've paid your money for the paper, and you shouldn't be getting stuff we already gave you. This isn't the Ann Landers column, after all. (I'm not being completely selfless in this regard; when my grandchildren compile the posthumous Compleat Works of Al Sicherman, I don't want them to think I cheated because I used the same recipe twice.)

Here's a compromise. I'll reproduce an all-time great or two, which will be clearly identified, and I'll try out a few new things, too. OK?

Note: Many of these recipes call for semisweet chocolate in one-ounce squares. Those who prefer their chocolate a little sweeter (and a little cheaper) might substitute chocolate chips.

In an article I wrote a while back about dipping things in semisweet chocolate, I tried dipping potato chips. They were truly marvelous. I knew that chocolate and salt combined nicely, but the crispness of the potato chip added another dimension.

Recently a colleague mentioned that his mother-in-law makes chocolate-covered popcorn. I didn't need to hear another word; I know a winning idea when I hear it. It also appealed because, I figured, you could pour the chocolate into a bowl of popcorn and do the coating just by tossing it with a couple of large spoons. Hand-dipping is messy any time; in the summer it's really dreadful.

If you make chocolate popcorn in the summer you must keep it refrigerated, but that's a small sacrifice. A small warning: Don't grab a handful to eat a little at a time. (It melts in your hand; not in your mouth.)

After I brought the popcorn into the office, the colleague's wife phoned to say that her mother's version isn't messy. But it's made with cocoa and milk. We don't want to hear about that right now, do we?

Chocolate-Covered Popcorn

½ c. or so (your standard batch)
    unpopped popcorn
Oil for popping
Salt
8 (1-oz.) squares semisweet chocolate

Line a couple of baking sheets with waxed paper.

Pop the popcorn however you normally do that. Salt and pour into a large bowl. As best you can, remove any "OMs." (I'm trying not to be sexist. The Popcorn Institute in Chicago, which calls them what everybody else calls them, also calls them spinsters — not much better.) You don't want the unpopped kernels in there because once they're covered with chocolate they're hard to see, and you might hurt a tooth if you bite one.

Melt the chocolate and pour it over the still-warm popcorn. Toss thoroughly, using two very large spoons. Using the spoons, spread the coated popcorn onto the waxed-paper-covered pans and cool in the refrigerator until the chocolate has set. Break apart any big clumps before you pour the chocolate popcorn into a bowl to serve.

This is among the best desserts I've ever eaten, and I think it's one of the two or three best I've made. It has been in the paper before. So what? It's dense, creamy and very, very rich. It's also rather easy to make, although quite expensive. Lots of folks will find it much too rich and not sweet enough.

The heck with them.

Others, hearing the cholesterol-laden list of ingredients, will want to file a complaint with the American Heart Association.

What can I say?

(Note: After this article appeared in the newspaper I improved the recipe, and that modified recipe appeared in a much later article. Because you, dear book reader, deserve only the best, what follows is the improved version.)

The original recipe, Chocolate Regal, is from Maida Heatter's Book of Great Chocolate Desserts — a wonderful book. I made that recipe approximately a zillion times and I love it, but let's be frank: It had (gasp!) a butter-seepage problem. No matter how much you softened the butter beforehand, some would weep out of the batter while the cake was in the oven and while it was cooling. You could catch the butter with pans and paper towels so it didn't make a mess, but that was a bother, and the loss of butter didn't improve the cake one bit.

This method produces a somewhat creamier cake (the whole thing has always been like incredibly rich fudge anyway) and no mess, so I figured I should rename it.

I think the change is significant enough to make a new name legitimate, so let's give it a legitimate-sounding name.

Chocolate Legal

¾ lb. (3 sticks) unsalted butter (no substitute)
16 (1-oz.) squares semisweet chocolate (or 2⅔ c. chips)
1 c. milk
Pinch of salt
7 egg yolks (6 if using extra-large or jumbo eggs)
Heavy cream, whipped, for topping

Melt the butter over low heat and allow it to cool to room temperature.

Preheat the oven to 350 degrees. Cut a round of waxed paper to fit the bottom of a 9-inch springform pan. Butter the sides of the pan and one side of the waxed paper. Place the paper in the pan, buttered side up.

In a saucepan over very low heat, heat the chocolate, milk and salt, stirring constantly, until the chocolate is melted. You will note that at every step the batter for this cake smells even better than it did at the last one. Pour the mixture into the large bowl of an electric mixer.

Beat on low speed, just to smooth out any bitsy lumps of chocolate. Let stand four or five minutes, to cool slightly. With the mixer running at low speed, add about a seventh of the melted butter (a shy one-fourth cup) and beat at low speed only until the butter is fully absorbed. Then add an egg yolk and beat, at low speed, just until the mixture has fully absorbed it. Don't raise the speed of the mixer, because we don't want to beat in any air. It's not supposed to be a fluffy cake; it's supposed to be a fudgy lump of goo.

Continue to alternate additions of butter and egg yolk until all are used up, scraping the bowl with a rubber spatula and beating after each addition only until incorporated. When the mixture is smooth, pour it into the prepared pan.

Set the pan on a cookie sheet (despite my wonderful improvement it might still weep a bit).

Put the whole thing in the oven (not near the top).

Bake for 25 minutes. It will be soupy in the middle and look like a mistake, but unless you forgot to turn the oven on, it is done.

The cake will not have risen so as you'd notice.

Allow it to cool on a rack, then refrigerate a few hours, until firm. It may be kept refrigerated a day or two.

When ready to serve, cut around the side of the pan with a small, sharp knife and release and remove the side of the pan. Cover the dessert with a flat plate and invert.

Carefully (it takes a bit of doing) pry up and remove the bottom of the pan and the waxed paper.

Decorate with whipped cream. (I like to make a simple lattice pattern that lets the dark, dark chocolate show through.) Serves 12.

Some time ago, I got a letter from Deborah Weiland recommending this cake, which is quite similar to the Chocolate Regal/Legal but also contains a significant flavor boost from strong coffee.

Weiland's recommendation, in part: "This is a cake that will bring you to your knees."

Actually, to be perfectly honest, it bounced me off the ceiling. I ate a big piece about 10 p.m. and, between the chocolate and the coffee, I wasn't able to get to sleep until 4:30 the next morning.

It's great, but eat it early.

Mocha Fudge Cake

1 c. plus 2 tbsp. very strong brewed coffee
18 (1-oz.) squares semisweet chocolate, chopped
2¼ c. sugar
2¼ c. (4½ sticks) unsalted butter
9 eggs
Topping:
1½ c. heavy cream
¼ c. confectioners' sugar
½ tsp. vanilla

Note: Weiland says about the coffee: "I grind the amount of espresso beans I would use for about two large cups [and make the 1⅛ cups of coffee from that]. This is important. I believe instant anything or ground regular coffee have no place in this cake."

Preheat oven to 250 degrees. Line a 9-inch springform pan with heavy aluminum foil and butter the foil lightly but thoroughly with unsalted butter.

Combine coffee, chocolate, sugar and butter in a large saucepan. ("The feeling of using more than one box of butter in one recipe," Weiland writes, "is indescribably lovely.") Stirring constantly, heat to 130 degrees.

Lower heat and whisk in nine eggs. (I beat them very lightly first, to make them easier to whisk in.) Pour into the prepared pan and bake 2 to 2½ hours. When it is done the top looks a little crisp and the sides are cracking. Cool, cover and refrigerate overnight or up to a week.

When it cools, the center of the cake falls a little. Since the cake will be inverted, you might first want to cut away the ridge around the edge. (Anyone who thinks you throw this crispy chocolate stuff away should stop reading right now. Of course you eat it, as your reward for having made the cake.) Several hours before serving, invert the cake onto a platter and remove the foil. Whip the heavy cream with the confectioners' sugar and the vanilla until it is thick enough to spread. Frost the cake with half the whipped cream, then, using a pastry bag with a star tip, pipe rosettes all over the top.

Serves 12 or more.

Here's a nice little item that's reasonably easy to do and rather attractive, too. Unlike half the things being served in restaurants that are called chocolate mousse but are nothing more than chocolate (or maybe even cocoa) pudding, this has beaten egg whites and all the real stuff.

Chocolate Mousse Parfaits

3 (1-oz.) squares semisweet chocolate
3 eggs, separated
2 to 3 tbsp. rum, brandy, orange
     liqueur, etc.
1 c. heavy cream

Melt the chocolate in a double boiler or in a saucepan over very low heat. Beat the egg yolks until they are thick and creamy. Stir a bit of melted chocolate into the egg yolks, then stir the egg yolks into the rest of the chocolate. Stir in the liqueur.

Whip the egg whites until they are stiff and fold them into the chocolate mixture.

Whip the cream until it is stiff. Spoon thin layers of chocolate and cream into serving glasses, finishing with cream. If the first layer of cream sinks, set the remaining chocolate into the freezer for a few minutes, stirring occasionally, until it gets a bit firmer. It's nice to make the top layer of cream a little fancy, so if you have a pastry bag, you might use that.

Or just fold the whipped cream into the chocolate mixture. The effect is not quite as elegant as layers but is lighter-looking. (Don't be misled — it's just as good.) Serves four to six.

Another repeated recipe, Chocolate Soufflé, was in this article when it appeared in the newspaper, but the article from which it was repeated is in this book, too. You'll find the recipe on page 25. (It's the one called Good Chocolate Soufflé. Don't try the one marked "not recommended." It's not recommended.)

Here's a quickie version of the Chocolate Legal/Regal, or if you add coffee, Mocha Fudge Cake. It's not as good as either, but it takes only half an hour, start to finish. I found it in a book by Emalee Chapman called, with slight exaggeration, Fifteen Minute Meals.

Rich, Rich Chocolate Dessert

6 tbsp. unsalted butter
6 (1-oz.) squares semisweet chocolate
     (or, for a slightly sweeter
     version, 1½ [4 oz.] German's
     Sweet Chocolate bars)
2 tbsp. brown sugar
2 tbsp. granulated sugar
3 tbsp. flour
2 tsp. instant coffee powder (optional)
2 eggs, at room temperature,
     separated

Preheat the oven to 450 degrees. Butter a 6- to 8-inch oven-safe sauté pan or skillet. Melt butter and chocolate in a double boiler or in a saucepan over very low heat. While chocolate is melting, stir in both sugars. When butter, sugar and chocolate are fully combined, stir in flour (and coffee, if you like). Remove from heat.

Beat the egg whites until they stand in soft peaks. In another bowl, beat the egg yolks and stir the chocolate mixture into them, a little at a time.

Fold in the egg whites and spoon the mixture into the buttered pan. Bake for 10 to 12 minutes. The outer edge is like cake; the inner part is like a melted chocolate bar. It's quite good cold, if you're willing to wait. Serves two or three.

Next a recipe supplied by a colleague, who got it from a friend, who got it from somebody else, who got it who-knows-where. The first time I made it, each of the four layers developed huge humps, and they looked like bathmats. The cake tasted fine, so I did it again. The result was much improved, and that version of the recipe is reproduced below. The cake is very densely chocolate. So is the frosting.

Chocolate Poem

Cake:
10 (1-oz.) squares semisweet
    chocolate
1½ c. (3 sticks) butter
12 eggs
3 c. confectioners' sugar
1½ c. cake flour
Frosting:
6 (1-oz.) squares unsweetened
    chocolate
½ c. butter (I used unsalted)
4 c. confectioners' sugar
2 tsp. vanilla
⅔ c. heavy cream
Decoration:
Chocolate curls, almonds

Preheat the oven to 350 degrees. Grease and flour four 8- or 9-inch layer-cake pans. Melt the chocolate and butter together in a large saucepan.

Note: The following mixture gets to be quite voluminous; it comes near the top of the large mixer bowl. You might want to make it in two parts.

Beat the eggs until they are lemon colored. Sift the confectioners' sugar and add gradually to the eggs. When all the sugar is in, beat the eggs for 10 to 15 minutes. (If your mixer gets very hot, give it a brief rest.)

Sift the flour three times. With the mixer on low speed, add the flour to the egg mixture, and beat slowly until it is fully blended. Fold in the chocolate.

Pour into the four prepared pans and bake 25 minutes. The cake will test done with a toothpick well before that. Don't be fooled. If you take them out too soon, the layers will be like bathmats. (Trust me.)

While the cake cools, prepare the frosting:

Melt the chocolate. Cool. Cream the butter until it is light and fluffy. Add the confectioners' sugar and the chocolate alternately, a little at a time, beating after each addition. As liquid is needed, add the vanilla and then the cream, a little at a time. Use about a cup of frosting to frost the first, second and third layers, and use the rest for the top and sides. Decorate with semisweet chocolate curls and almonds.

The writer has laid in a supply of semisweet chocolate; he is not coming out until Bill Blass goes away.

A Healthy Meal

I should learn when to say no.

When a friend asked me to help him move his oak roll-top desk into a third-floor walkup, I should have said no.

When I was asked to drive nine kids, all under ten years old, to a movie (in my five-passenger car) I should have said no.

And when it was suggested that I put together a healthy meal as a response to what was sure to be a devastating analysis of my dietary habits (arranged by colleague Kate Parry for an article on three folks' food consumption), I should have categorically refused.

I didn't refuse because it really sounded like a good-enough idea: Take the office glutton (me) and have him demonstrate that a healthy meal can be just as appealing and tasty as the disgustingly rich meal he really wanted to eat.

It didn't work.

As I write this I have not yet seen what the experts had to say about my food preferences, but I know the kind of thing it's likely to be. Nice as they probably are, these are the kind of folks who exist to tell you that you're doing something wrong.

Everybody likes to tell you that you're doing something wrong, of course. My partner Kate has been positively beside herself waiting for the experts' opinion of my intake. And when I asked her what sorts of things she thought I might eat for this experimental healthy meal, it was as though I had opened a floodgate of diet information.

The worst of it is that this information is so depressing. I might not eat the most balanced diet in the world, but I really don't think that, even if I decided to improve it, I need to rip it apart and start from the ground up. I've been staying alive on it quite nicely so far.

But consider the following exchange with Ms. Parry after I had examined some of the books she offered me (I admit I sought her out in the cafeteria, where she was hiding from me):

Me: "Gee, this is miserable. Nothing really works. Even skinless chicken has almost as much cholesterol as beef. And something that's low in cholesterol may still have lots of calories."

Kate: "You're making it too hard. You can *have* some fat. You can *have* some cholesterol. You can *have* two eggs a week."

Two eggs a *week?* I left the room.

What surprised me most in my very brief research was the difficulty I had in finding some just-plain healthier menus. Our department gets lots of cookbooks and diet books, and I figured it would be but a few minutes' work to page through them until I found a reasonably appealing meal that was low in all the things it should be low in and balanced in all the things that should be balanced.

Well, Kate claimed to have such a book at home, and our boss said she had one, too. And the day after my noble experiment Kate thought of one that we have at work. But the bulk of the "get-healthy" books on our shelves tend to emphasize one aspect or another of diet: lowering calories, lowering cholesterol, lowering salt, lowering carbohydrates, and (it seemed to me) on and on.

Piecing together a meal out of that maze was, to put it mildly, no fun. I'm not a menu planner to begin with. If I were, I might already be planning healthy menus. Instead, I just pick up what I need for whatever appeals to me as a main course, and then I think of things that I might like to eat along with it. My only considerations are flavor, texture, color and maybe temperature, in that order.

When I had to sit there and actually consider the nutritional makeup of every lousy item I planned to cook, I got really irritated, and I began to snap at my colleagues. It was like having to find out who built the bus I was planning to ride to work, or establishing the fiber content of my chair cushion before I sat down.

But, as Horton the Elephant observed, a promise made is a debt unpaid, so I pitched in.

There were, it seemed to me, three ways to approach the business of designing a healthy meal:

■ I could take the kind of meal I normally eat (I should point out that I don't normally eat preserved meats as often as I did in the period examined by the nutrition experts, but my father had just sent me a four-foot summer sausage), and attempt to duplicate it in a healthier way. I might try to make hollandaise sauce with soy lecithin and polyunsaturated oil instead of egg yolks and butter, for example. I decided that would be ludicrous. It certainly wouldn't taste as good, and it bordered on (if it didn't cross over into) food faddiness instead of healthy eating.

■ I could make a very plain meal that wouldn't appeal to me — broiled fish with a teaspoon of butter, lots of plain vegetables with lemon juice. But that sounded depressing — more like hospital or health-farm food than I wanted to consider.

■ I could try to find some appealing-sounding recipes in the healthy cookbooks. That seemed least likely to be a disaster, and I didn't want a disaster. I really wasn't setting out to prove that the only thing I can enjoy eating is deep-fat-fried fat.

I had a brief run-in with Ms. Parry over a promising-looking book that offered French gourmet cooking for good health. She didn't like the authors' credentials — one is a food writer, the other a lawyer; neither is a nutritionist or medical doctor.

That over (I gave up), I picked out some recipes from a low-cholesterol guidebook, checked them against a calorie and carbohydrate table in another book to make sure they weren't too awful, and ran the whole thing past the basic-food-groups chart in still a third book.

Here's what I decided to have:

Eggplant casserole deluxe, featuring eggplant, polyunsaturated oil, onion, celery, garlic, spices, tomato sauce and tomato paste, green pepper, mushrooms, a lot of spaghetti and some bread crumbs. It sounded fairly good, although I wondered at the presence of the very large amount of spaghetti — but this was a cholesterol-cutting book and spaghetti has no cholesterol.

Cold green beans, with a low-cholesterol Italian dressing consisting of wine vinegar, polyunsaturated oil and spices. The eggplant casserole looked to me pretty much like a complete meal, but I felt it needed a side dish. I'm not a lettuce-and-tomato person, so this would do for salad as well as for an extra vegetable and something tangy. Left to my own devices I would have used a vinaigrette made with olive oil, which, I learned, is apparently the opposite of polyunsaturated (but *real good.)*

Between those two items I certainly had enough for a meal. Not a seven-course feast, to be sure, but a perfectly adequate meal — except for dessert.

Now I must explain that, although I like to eat well, as far as I'm concerned it isn't the main course that can make or break a meal; it's the dessert. And I just couldn't bring myself to have any of the highly touted fruit desserts that I kept running across in these books. Fruit is a dessert in the same way a glass of Welch's grape juice is an aperitif.

OK, I said to myself, you're just not going to have a scrumptious dessert tonight. You'll live. Settle for something tolerable, and then quit.

Raspberry gelatin struck me as a reasonable choice — no cholesterol, relatively few calories, pleasant enough to look at, reasonably sweet and a whole lot better than eating an apple. (If you don't appreciate the vast difference between fruit for dessert and fruit gelatin for dessert, see me later.)

Whipped cream on top would have made it a whole lot better, but that was clearly out of the question, so I decided to see whether yogurt can be whipped — or at least spritzed in curly spirals out of a pastry tube.

Reenter Ms. Parry.

Kate: "You're supposed to make healthy foods that are *appealing.* Does that dessert appeal to you?"

Me: "Not a lot, but . . ."

Kate: "Well, then, why don't you have some fruit?"

Me: "%&¢#!"

[The curtain must descend briefly to cover an exchange in which I ranted almost senselessly about fruit.]

Our boss, attracted by the noise, came over and joined Kate in trying to convince me that there were plenty of wonderful, healthy things I could have for dessert. I think she was also trying to keep me from throwing something at Kate. I kept muttering that I'd rather have Jell-O.

Finally somebody found a diet book that appeared to be full of amazingly gooey items.

I smelled a rat.

Pointing to a recipe for a soufflé with chocolate and Grand Marnier, I shouted, "All right, then, I'm making *THIS!"*

I fully expected Kate to find some reason to rule it out. Instead she looked at the recipe and noted with pleasure that a serving of the soufflé had half the calories of a serving of ice cream. I noted back, louder, that it was a serving half as big as a serving of ice cream and that I was beginning to think this whole thing was a lot of hooey.

Thus primed for a healthy meal or a heart attack, whichever came first, I went home to cook.

Thanks to the milk in the soufflé, the meal would contain something from every food group but meat. If I felt the need afterward, I reasoned, I could have a slice or two of summer sausage.

The eggplant casserole turned out OK, after I simmered down enough to make it, but the flavor was strangely thin — quite possibly there was too much spaghetti, or too little salt, or both. (I almost never salt food beyond what's in the recipe — not a health concern, I'm just not fond of salt and don't keep it on the table.) My best guess, though, is that some butter, or the fat from the meat that I would normally have included, would have spread the flavor more fully to the spaghetti.

The green beans and slim Italian dressing were all right, too, but again just a little underflavored.

I would, nonetheless, make both of those recipes again, unchanged if I had to, or punched up a bit with more flavorful oils and/or fats.

A side note: A spokesperson for the Department of Food Science and Nutrition at the University of Minnesota is quoted in a recent news release from the Institute of Food Technologists as saying that fats in the diet are important sources of nutrients and are responsible for many of the characteristic flavors, aromas and textures. "They are also," she continued, "the most concentrated sources of food energy in the diet . . . ."

Right on! Sounds like a recruiting poster for the Grease Corps.

Oh, all right. Honesty compels me to add the rest of that quote: Fats are also "responsible for some of the dieter's problems." Mutter, mutter.

Anyway, on to the chocolate and Grand Marnier soufflé, which turned out to be a serious mistake.

The recipe called for a choice of egg substitute or egg yolks and for either semisweet chocolate or carob chips. In the interest of science I'm willing to use an egg substitute instead of wonderful egg yolks, but lips that touch carob shall never touch mine, so I stuck with the semisweet chocolate.

It turned out not to make much difference. I make a soufflé very much like this one in every other regard. To roughly the same volume of milk, eggs, cornstarch and liqueur in this recipe, mine uses 3 ounces of unsweetened chocolate and 9 tablespoons of sugar. This one uses 1½ ounces of semisweet chocolate — the equivalent of 1 ounce of unsweetened chocolate and 1½ tablespoons of sugar.

Had I noticed that in advance, I would have picked something else to make. The result, as you might expect, was drastically underflavored. So much so that my boss, to whom I brought a sample, said it had no chocolate flavor at all.

Kate liked the flavor.

The color, given the lack of chocolate, was an unappealing light gray-brown.

The other problem is the use of egg substitute for egg yolks. Commercial egg substitute is 99 percent egg white. The substitute suggested in the cookbook is about 75 percent egg white. In neither case is there enough oil, emulsifier — or whatever is so yolky about egg yolks — to give a soufflé any body. This one shot up out of the bowl like it had been inflated with a service-station air hose, but it collapsed to a puddle when I took it out of the oven. It was fully baked all right, but very, very limp. I suppose it would have behaved more nicely had I used egg yolks instead of the substitute. Given how it tasted, I don't care to find out.

When all is said and done, and even before all is said and done, I'd much rather have a good bowl of Jell-O than a pale imitation of a rich dessert.

An hour after I was done with dinner, I had a chocolate bar.

Sorry.

The recipes for Eggplant Casserole Deluxe and Italian Salad Dressing are from Cholesterol Counter, a nice little book by Elizabeth Weiss and Rita Wolfson. The authors do not appear to be nutritionists or medical doctors, but their book contains a cholesterol chart that seemed to satisfy Ms. Parry.

Eggplant Casserole Deluxe

1 eggplant (about 1¼ lb.)
¼ c. polyunsaturated oil
1 onion, chopped
1 rib celery, chopped
1 clove garlic, minced
1 tsp. salt
¼ tsp. pepper
½ tsp. basil
¼ tsp. oregano
2 tbsp. red wine
2 tbsp. tomato paste
2 (8-oz.) cans tomato sauce
1 lb. spaghetti or vermicelli, cooked
    according to package directions
    and drained
1 green pepper, seeded and chopped
¼ lb. fresh mushrooms, cut in thirds
    vertically
1 tbsp. minced parsley
2 tbsp. bread crumbs

Wash the eggplant but do not peel it. Cut off the stem end and discard it. Slice the rest into half-inch cubes (cut into half-inch slices, then cube the slices).

Heat the oil in a Dutch oven. Add the eggplant cubes, onion, celery and garlic and sauté until the onion is translucent and the eggplant is lightly browned.

Add the salt, pepper, basil, oregano, wine, tomato paste and tomato sauce. Stir to mix well, bring to a boil, cover and simmer over low heat for 10 minutes.

(This is a good time to cook the spaghetti, too, in a separate pot.)

Into the eggplant mixture stir the green pepper, mushrooms and parsley and simmer another five minutes.

Preheat the oven to 350 degrees.

Grease a large casserole dish with corn-oil margarine (or some more polyunsaturated oil), and layer a third of the cooked spaghetti over the bottom. Top with a third of the eggplant mixture. Repeat twice more, using up all the spaghetti and eggplant mixture. Sprinkle the bread crumbs over all.

Bake uncovered for 20 minutes. Serves three to four (I'd say more like five or six) as a main dish, six to eight (or ten) as a side dish.

Italian Salad Dressing

2 tbsp. wine vinegar
5 tbsp. polyunsaturated oil
1 clove garlic, peeled
¼ tsp. oregano
Paprika to taste
Salt, pepper to taste

Shake all ingredients together in a jar. Refrigerate for two or more hours, to allow flavors to blend. Before serving, remove the whole garlic clove.

Makes a scant half cup. Serve over tossed green salad (or chilled green beans, cucumber slices or anything else, for that matter).

This chocolate and Grand Marnier soufflé recipe is from a book written by a woman who is decribed as a registered dietitian. It is a terrible recipe anyway.

Grand Marnier Chocolate Soufflé

(NOT RECOMMENDED, but maybe you have a friend with no taste)
1 tbsp. cornstarch
¾ c. prepared nonfat milk
¼ c. semisweet chocolate or carob pieces
3 tbsp. Grand Marnier (or other orange liqueur)
½ c. egg substitute, or 3 egg yolks, beaten
4 egg whites, at room temperature
½ tsp. cream of tartar
½ tsp. low-calorie margarine

Combine cornstarch and milk in a saucepan and stir until cornstarch is dissolved. Bring to a boil, lower heat and cook, stirring constantly, until thickened. (Actually, it thickens *before* it boils. Let it boil a minute, stirring constantly.)

Add the chocolate and the liqueur, remove from heat and stir until the chocolate melts. Cool slightly and mix in the egg substitute or egg yolks, one tablespoon at a time or one yolk at a time. Set aside.

Preheat the oven to 350 degrees.

Beat the egg whites at low speed until they are foamy. Add the cream of tartar and beat at high speed until stiff, glossy peaks form. Stir a fourth of the egg whites into the cooled chocolate mixture to lighten it, then gently fold in the remaining whites.

Grease a 1½-quart soufflé dish or six individual dishes with the margarine and turn the mixture into the dish(es). Bake individual soufflés for 15 minutes or large soufflé 35 to 40 minutes, or until set and puffy.

Serve immediately. (Or, better, don't serve at all.)

This is the chocolate soufflé I usually make. I would prefer one bite of this one to six barrels of the one on the left. (To be absolutely honest, I would really prefer no dessert at all to any amount of the one on the left.)

Good Chocolate Soufflé

9 tbsp. sugar, divided
1 tbsp. cornstarch
⅔ c. whole milk
3 (1-oz.) squares unsweetened chocolate
3 tbsp. coffee liqueur (or 3 tbsp. strong, sweet black coffee)
4 eggs, separated

In a saucepan, mix six tablespoons of the sugar with the cornstarch. Add a very small amount of the milk and stir to make a paste. Slowly, and stirring to avoid lumps, add the rest of the milk.

Bring to boil over medium heat, stirring constantly. Reduce heat and cook, stirring, one additional minute. Add the chocolate and stir until it is melted. Stir in the coffee liqueur or coffee. Allow the mixture to cool for five minutes. Preheat the oven to 350 degrees. Lightly butter a 1½-quart soufflé dish. (You could use a diet margarine, I suppose, as a gesture.)

Beat the egg yolks lightly. Add a few tablespoons of the chocolate mixture to the egg yolks, stirring. Now stir the egg yolk mixture into the chocolate mixture. Set aside.

Beat the egg whites, gradually adding the three remaining tablespoons of sugar, until the whites hold peaks and are firm but not dry.

Gently fold the whites into the chocolate mixture and pour into the soufflé dish. Bake 35 to 40 minutes. Yum!

The 9-by-13 Cookbook

Whenever there's a popular new appliance, there is always a cookbook or two written especially to go with it. There have been mini-deep-fry cookbooks, blender cookbooks, hamburger-cooker cookbooks, food-processor cookbooks, crepe-pan cookbooks, and on and on. I modestly propose one more specialty cookbook — one that should have been produced some time ago.

Welcome to the wonderful world of 9- by 13-inch pan cookery!

As you get accustomed to using your new pan, you'll wonder how you ever got along without it. There's hardly a category of food — be it appetizer, main course, vegetable or dessert (or even soup, if you are truly desperate) — that cannot be prepared in the versatile 9- by 13-inch pan.

Your 9- by 13-inch pan requires no electric cords, special tools or lessons. Operation is simplicity itself. Just fill it up and watch it work!

Before you use your new 9- by 13-inch pan, you'll want to familiarize yourself with it. Note that it is about 9 inches wide and approximately 13 inches long.* Sometimes the pan is referred to as a "9-by-13-by-2." That, you'll soon discover, is because it's about 2 inches deep.

In Europe, this pan is referred to as the "33-by-23-by-5." Can you guess why?

On the following pages are numerous recipes designed to take advantage of the versatility of your new pan. The 9- by 13- by 2-inch pan is so good at so many things that some have called it "the kitchen in a seventh-of-a-cubic-foot." Even Craig Claiborne recommends it.

Wondering what to make first with your new 9-by-13? Just let your imagination run wild! The many uses of the adaptable 9-by-13 will delight your family and make you a big hit at the . . . .

Oh, dear reader, I can't keep this up. I take off my hat to Mable Hoffman, and all the others who crank out these specialty cookbooks, but keeping up that manic enthusiasm is too much for me.

If the truth were told, there's only one cookbook I ever really wanted to write, one for the slow cooking pot, and that's just because I wanted to use this title: The Betty Cooker Crockbook.

But as long as I got us started on 9- by 13-inch pans, let's go ahead and make some things in them. A couple of quick asides, and then we'll get to the recipes.

Just in case you measured your oblong pan and came away puzzled, you should know that not every "9- by 13-inch pan" is indeed 9 inches wide and 13 inches long. In fact, after a brief but exhausting survey, I conclude that hardly *any* 9- by 13-inch pan is 9 inches wide and 13 inches long. There

---

*Note to owners of 8- by 12-inch pans. You'll find that most software for the 8-by-12 is upward-compatible to the 9-by-13. Minor adjustments may be necessary; consult your dealer for details.

probably are some; I couldn't find a single one.

A brand-new Ekco pan measures 7⅞ inches by 12¾ inches; others of different ages and manufactures varied, mostly under but some over, by as much as half an inch. A 1974 bakeware brochure produced by Wear-Ever Aluminum says that the American Home Economics Association and the American National Standards Institute set up standard sizes for bakeware, but it notes that "a manufacturing tolerance of plus or minus ¼ inch is allowed." It doesn't even hint at the reason.

Surely in this day of microcomputers and space shuttles, we can produce a 9- by 13-inch pan that is a whole lot less than ¼ inch off. It isn't, after all, like the boxes of crackers whose "contents may settle in shipping." If the pan measured 13 inches long when it left Ekco, it would measure 13 inches long when it reached you (unless it reached you at a velocity approaching the speed of light).

(It isn't often that one gets to invoke the Lorentz-Fitzgerald Contraction in a food article, but it isn't often that one's boss is on vacation, either.)

Actually, I suspect that the pan-dimension phenomenon is related to lumber, a field of endeavor in which a two-by-four is more like 1½ by 3½.

Incidentally, the area of a nominal 9- by 13-inch pan is 117 square inches and that of two 8- by 8-inch pans is 128 square inches — about the same — so the 9-by-13 holds a double recipe of any bar cookie intended for an 8-by-8. The area of two 9-inch round pans is about 127 square inches, so any cake recipe intended for two of those could as well be made in one 9-by-13.

One other thing, if your 9-by-13 is

glass (Pyrex, for example), or glass-ceramic (CorningWare): A spokesperson for Corning Glass said that "because, in a conventional oven, glass and glass-ceramic dishes absorb heat faster than metal pans, baking temperature should be 25 degrees lower for glass materials." Got that? OK, let's cook!

You could have baked this appetizer on cookie sheets. But the 9-by-13 does a splendid job and isn't as big. (There's no advantage to that, but it is true.)

Cheese Appetizers

3 tbsp. butter or margarine
1 c. (4 oz.) shredded Cheddar cheese
1 tsp. steak sauce
½ c. flour
Dash of salt
1 tsp. paprika
2 tbsp. sesame seeds (optional)
12 smallish pimiento-stuffed olives
12 toasted pecan halves

These can be prepared ahead of time and refrigerated, unbaked. Cream butter, beat in cheese and steak sauce. Combine flour, salt, paprika and sesame seeds. Blend into butter-cheese mixture until there is no dry, uncolored flour remaining.

Put about a teaspoon of dough in the palm of one hand. Drop an olive or pecan half into it and mold the dough around it, adding a bit of dough if necessary to enclose the olive or pecan half sparingly but completely. (You could use all olives or all nuts, but giving guests a choice is always nice). When ready to serve, preheat the oven to 400 degrees. Place dough balls in an ungreased 9- by 13-inch pan. Bake for about 12 minutes, until they are golden brown. Makes 24.

Here's a vegetable that's just made for the roomy interior of a 9- by 13-inch pan. The cookbook in which I found it suggests that it makes a delicious poultry stuffing, too. It *is* the kind of thing that would substitute marvelously for mashed potatoes. ("Which would *you* rather have, Mr. Tompkins? Mashed potatoes . . . or Rice and Sweet Potato Casserole?" "I'd have to say the Rice and Sweet Potato Casserole." "How about *that,* Mrs. Tompkins?" "Well, I guess it's Rice and Sweet Potato Casserole, then. I wish *he'd* make it, though.")

Rice and Sweet Potato Casserole

(From the American Family Cook Book)
1½ c. coarsely chopped celery (about 2 ribs)
1½ c. chopped onion (about 2 medium onions)
½ c. butter
2 c. uncooked quick-cooking rice (about one 7-oz. pkg.)
2½ c. chicken broth (two 10¾-oz. cans), divided
2 tbsp. brown sugar
1¾ tsp. salt
½ tsp. pepper
1 tsp. ground coriander (optional)
¾ tsp. rosemary
¼ tsp. ground ginger
2 eggs, lightly beaten
1 (18-oz.) can vacuum-packed (not syrup-packed) sweet potatoes

Chop the celery and onion. Melt the butter in a five-quart Dutch oven. Stir the celery, onion and rice into the hot butter and cook over low heat, stirring constantly, about ten minutes, until the rice is pale yellow. Reserve ½ cup of chicken broth. Stir in the remaining broth (about two cups) and the brown sugar, salt, pepper, coriander, rosemary and ginger. Cover the pot and bring the mixture to boiling.

Lower the heat and simmer, stirring occasionally, about 15 minutes or until the rice is tender. Uncover, remove from heat and allow to cool. Preheat the oven to 325 degrees. Mix the lightly beaten eggs with the remaining half cup of chicken broth, and blend into the rice mixture.

Cut the sweet potatoes into ½-inch pieces (you can do that fairly well while they're still in the can), add them to the rice and toss gently. Grease a 9- by 13-inch pan and turn the rice mixture into it. Bake for about 25 minutes, until the top begins to brown. Serves eight to ten.

When talk turns, as often it does, to the 9- by 13-inch pan, one of the first main-course dishes that comes up is lasagne. Here's a nice, flavorful version.

Lasagne

1 lb. Italian sausage
1 medium onion, chopped
1 clove garlic, crushed
1 tbsp. dried basil
½ tsp. salt
1 (16-oz.) can whole tomatoes, with liquid
1 (8-oz.) can tomato sauce
1 (6-oz.) can tomato paste
1 (8-oz.) pkg. lasagne noodles
3 c. (24 oz.) creamy cottage cheese
½ c. (3 oz.) grated Parmesan cheese
2 tbsp. parsley flakes
2 beaten eggs
1 tsp. salt
½ tsp. pepper
1 lb. sliced Mozzarella cheese

If necessary, remove sausage meat from casings.

Slowly brown the sausage and onion in a skillet until the sausage is broken up and well cooked and the onion is translucent. Drain fat from pan.

Add garlic, basil, salt, tomatoes and liquid, tomato sauce and tomato paste. Stir, cutting the tomatoes into chunks with the edge of the spoon.

Simmer uncovered for 30 minutes, stirring occasionally.

Meanwhile cook the lasagne noodles according to package directions. Drain, rinse in cold water and drain again.

Preheat the oven to 375 degrees. Combine the cottage cheese, Parmesan cheese, parsley flakes, eggs, salt and pepper.

Put half the noodles in a 9- by 13-inch pan. Spread with half the cottage-cheese filling.

Top with half the Mozzarella cheese and half the meat sauce.

Repeat: noodles, cottage cheese, Mozzarella and meat sauce.

Bake about 30 minutes. Let stand ten minutes, to firm and cool slightly.

Makes 12 servings.

Here's something straight out of 1950s Sweet-Sixteen parties, but it remains very tasty.

It would make excellent picnic fare if your oven is close enough to the picnic that the dish could arrive hot. (Wrapping in many layers of newspapers helps, and it also helps get rid of newspapers.)

The flavor is pretty tomatoey-mustardy. If you'd like to tone down that Coney Island aura a bit without losing the tang, add some soy sauce. (Taste before topping with the cornbread batter.)

Cornbread-Topped Bean and Bratwurst Bake

(Adapted from the Pillsbury Family Cook Book)
1 lb. cooked bratwurst (or frankfurters), cut into ½-inch pieces
2 (1-lb.) cans baked beans
½ c. ketchup
½ c. water
1 tbsp. prepared mustard
Soy sauce to taste (optional)
Cornbread:
¾ c. sifted flour
1 tbsp. sugar
1½ tsp. baking powder
1 tsp. salt
⅔ c. corn meal
1 egg, lightly beaten
⅔ c. milk
¼ c. cooking oil
⅓ c. finely chopped onion (1 small onion)

Preheat oven to 400 degrees. Combine bratwurst, beans, ketchup, water, mustard and soy sauce in 9- by 13-inch pan.

Sift flour, sugar, baking powder and salt into a mixing bowl. Stir in the corn meal. Add the egg, milk, oil and onion, stirring only after all are added and only enough to fully combine.

Spoon the cornbread mixture over the beans. (It won't cover fully; you want to make dollops over each portion, rather than try to make an even layer. If you prefer a whole, even layer of cornbread, make a double recipe of cornbread batter. That'll give you more than you need.)

Bake for about 40 minutes, until the cornbread is golden brown.

Every nationality that ever sent

anyone down in the mines seems to claim that pasties are its own. Let's avoid that controversy by attributing these tasty meat turnovers to a group that surely predates most claimants — everybody else got the recipe from them. So did Pillsbury, in whose cookbook I found this version.

Sumerian-Akkadian Pasties

1 lb. round steak
1 c. cubed raw potatoes (about 1
    medium baking potato)
½ c. chopped onion (1 small onion)
½ c. chopped celery (less than 1 rib)
½ c. chopped carrots (about 1 carrot)
¼ tsp. pepper
2 tsp. salt, divided
3 c. sifted flour
1 c. (2 sticks) butter or margarine
About ½ c. cold water
Milk (for wash)

Cut the steak, uncooked, into very small dice (about ¼ inch on a side — they'll be tough if you make them too big). Combine the steak, potatoes, onion, celery, carrots, the pepper and half of the salt in a large bowl. Refrigerate.

Prepare the dough: Sift the flour and the remaining one teaspoon of salt into a bowl. Using two knives or a pastry blender, cut in the butter or margarine until it is the size of peas. Stir in just enough water to make the dough hold together. If time permits, refrigerate dough for an hour or two.

Preheat the oven to 450 degrees. Divide dough into eight pieces. Roll each out into a circle on a generously floured surface. The circle should be 6 or 7 inches in diameter.

Put a portion of the meat mixture (around half a cup) on one side of each circle. Brush the edges of each circle with water, fold and crimp shut with a fork. Punch a few small holes in the top, to let the steam out.

Put the pies into two ungreased 9- by 13-inch pans. Brush carefully with milk. (Try not to let the milk spill onto the pan, where it will burn and stick.)

Bake at 450 degrees for ten minutes, then lower temperature to 350 degrees and bake 40 to 50 additional minutes.

Serve hot or cold. Makes eight.

It's when we come to dessert that the 9- by 13-inch pan really shines (figuratively speaking, because unless you're a compulsive cleaner, your new 9- by 13-inch pan won't literally shine all that long). From the host of bar-cookie recipes, I have selected a rich, firm mocha brownie. I topped it with cinnamon-flavored cream-cheese frosting, but you could certainly use a more traditional chocolate frosting (with liquid coffee instead of other liquid, if you like).

Mocha Brownies

(From the Farm Journal book,
    Homemade Cookies)
4 (1-oz.) squares unsweetened
    chocolate
⅔ c. butter or margarine
4 eggs
2 c. sugar
2 tsp. vanilla
1½ c. sifted flour
1 tsp. baking powder
½ tsp. salt
¼ c. instant coffee powder
1 c. chopped nuts (optional) (I think
    they'd be a distraction)

Melt chocolate and butter together over very low heat, stirring constantly. Set aside to cool. Beat the eggs. Gradually beat in the sugar until the mixture is light and fluffy. Add the vanilla. Stir in the chocolate mixture and mix well.

Preheat the oven to 350 degrees.

Sift together the flour, baking powder, salt and coffee powder. Stir into the first mixture. Fold in the nuts, if used. Pour into a greased 9- by 13-inch pan. (What else?) Bake 30 minutes. Cool, frost if you like, then cut into squares.

The mocha brownies are good just plain, but this frosting is very nice:

Cinnamon Cream-Cheese Frosting

1 c. confectioners' sugar
2 (3-oz.) pkg. cream cheese
1 tbsp. milk
1 tsp. vanilla
½ tsp. cinnamon

Cream together the sugar and cream cheese. Add the milk, vanilla and cinnamon. If too thin, firm up with additional confectioners' sugar. Frost the brownies after they're cool.

Here's a nonbaked summery dessert for the 9- by 13-inch pan, distilled from many similar recipes. I really didn't expect much of this one, particularly since it is so much like so many others that are fine but not breathtaking, but it went over *really* well.

Frozen Chocolate-Mint Cheesecake-Mousse Stuff

½ c. butter
1½ c. graham cracker crumbs (12 double crackers)

1 tbsp. sugar
1 (6-oz.) pkg. chocolate chips
1 (8-oz.) pkg. cream cheese
¾ c. sugar, divided
1 tsp. mint extract
2 eggs, separated
1 c. heavy cream

Melt the butter. Combine graham cracker crumbs, melted butter and the tablespoon of sugar. Press onto the bottom of a 9- by 13-inch pan, and up the sides if there's enough.

Melt the chocolate chips over very low heat. Soften the cream cheese in the large bowl of an electric mixer. Add the melted chocolate, half a cup of the sugar and the mint extract. Beat well.

Put the egg whites into the small bowl of the mixer. Set aside. Add the egg yolks to the chocolate mixture and beat.

Clean the beaters with soap and water. Beat the egg whites with the remaining one-fourth cup of sugar until soft, syrupy peaks form. Fold into the chocolate mixture. Scrape the mixer bowl clean of egg whites, but don't bother washing it or the beaters. Whip the cream and fold it into the mixture.

Pour over the crumb crust and freeze. Serves 10 to 12.

Popovers (and Bagels)

I used to think popovers were hard to make. Or tricky. Or something.

When I was growing up in Milwaukee, there was a restaurant that drew people from as far away as Wauwatosa just on the strength of its popovers. Since nobody in possession of his faculties would even drive around the block to get scrambled eggs, mashed potatoes or toast, as far as I was concerned, it followed as the night the day that popovers were not as easily made.

Then there were the few occasions when my grandmother made popovers. She chose to make them only for company meals, people would rave and rave about them (they *were* big and light and golden), and she always gave the impression, without saying so outright, that their success had been a near thing — due only to skill, luck and living right.

So when I made my first batch some years ago and they all popped very nicely, I was extremely surprised.

I was a little less surprised when they worked the next time, and I'm no longer surprised by them at all. In fact, I think it's almost impossible to make a popover that doesn't pop. I'm sorry, Grandma, but your secret's out: Popovers are a snap.

Easy as they are, and good as they are with a big chunk of butter melting down inside them, I hadn't made popovers in quite a while. Then one night a few weeks ago, while I was in the middle of making an unholy number of crepes, it occurred to me that there was something awfully familiar about the recipe: Equal amounts of flour and milk, lots of egg and a little melted butter.

A quick look at a popover recipe confirmed my suspicion: Crepes and popovers are made from essentially the same batter.

Well, now.

Besides being a source of powerful wonderment (how can the same batter make something both high and puffy and something perfectly — even desperately — flat?) this revelation made me wonder once more about the possible fallibility of popovers. Is there some ghastly mistake one can make with a popover to confuse it into thinking that it's a crepe?

How, in other words, does a popover turn into a flopover?

Although there are a lot of popover recipes, the batter does not vary much from one to another. What does differ is the *method* of preparing them. So I decided to try as many of those variations as I could.

(As a contrast in texture, I decided to make some bagels, too, which I'd never done before. They rise, all right, but they're firm.)

The differences in popover instructions are many. Older recipes call for lengthy beating of the batter. Newer ones caution not to beat it more than a minute. Some recipes call for putting the greased pans or custard cups into the hot oven to preheat them before adding the batter. Others don't bother with preheating the pans, and some even insist that the pans and batter go into a stone-cold oven.

That brings us to oven temperature.

The start-stone-cold method suggests turning the oven to 400 degrees and baking for 50 minutes. (If pop-overs were at all tricky I can't imagine how this method would be generally successful, given the differences in ovens and the amount of time it takes one to heat up compared with another.) More conventional techniques are 450 degrees for half an hour then 15 minutes at 350 degrees, or an even 400 degrees for 40 minutes.

I'll cut a long story short. They all work. Every #$%&! popover I made — and I made a lot of them — popped and looked beautiful.

However, there is the matter of greasing the pans. And here there *are* differences. Sometimes popovers won't come out of the pan (or out of the custard cups). When that happens it doesn't make much difference how great they look, because by the time you rip them out, leaving the bottoms stuck in the pan, they don't look so good anymore.

You can use a little oil, a lot of oil, a little margarine, a lot of margarine, or a little or a lot of vegetable shortening.

I have concluded, after hours of greasing and baking, that the best method, whether for pans or for cups, is to use a great deal of solid vegetable shortening (Crisco, or whatever). A great deal. Enough that you can't see the bottom through the white. Leave an extra glob of it in the middle of the bottom of each cup, where the sticking problem is worst. For that added measure of protection, as they say in deodorant commercials, spread some on the top of the muffin pan between the cups, and around the rims of individual custard cups. That way the big puffy tops won't stick, either.

But the most significant thing you can do to eliminate sticking, if you're using muffin tins as opposed to individual custard cups, is to use bright, shiny ones. My old muffin tins, which have been around the block and have acquired that well-used, coffee-bean color, gave me much more trouble than one I bought more recently that is still silvery.

Here is a popover recipe, with variations, every one of which works.

Popovers

1 c. sifted flour
3 eggs
1 c. milk
2 tbsp. melted butter

Put the sifted flour in a large bowl. In a smaller bowl, beat the eggs lightly. Add the milk to the eggs and mix well. Add the liquid gradually to the flour, beating with a mixer or wire whisk to incorporate it. Beat in the melted butter.

You can beat this mixture just long enough to make it smooth (less than 30 seconds) or beat it four or five minutes. It doesn't make any difference.

You can preheat the oven to 450 degrees, 400 degrees or not preheat it at all. It doesn't make any difference, except for how long you'll wind up baking the popovers.

Grease the pans or custard cups *very* heavily. Pour the batter into 12 cups, or if you prefer bigger, meatier popovers (as does my colleague, Mary Hart), pour it into six cups.

If you didn't preheat the oven, turn it to 400 degrees and bake the popovers for 50 minutes. If you preheated it to 450, bake the popovers for 30 minutes, reduce the temperature to 350 and bake for another 15 minutes. If you preheated it to 400 degrees, bake the popovers for 40 minutes. If you put the batter into six cups instead of 12, bake for an additional 15 to 20 minutes.

Here are some variations that do make a difference:

Fry four or five slices of bacon until crisp, drain and crumble them and add them to the finished popover batter.

Or add to the finished batter half a cup or more of grated cheese, an extra shake of salt and a little pepper or cayenne.

These are both very nice.

While whomping up my fifth or sixth batch of popovers, and not looking forward to them very much, it occurred to me to find out whether I could make one big popover instead of six or 12 little ones.

So I rubbed a lot of shortening into a soufflé dish (a regular 1½-quart baking dish probably would work as well) and poured in the whole batch of popover batter.

It puffed up beautifully around the sides. After about an hour, I pulled it out of the oven. It wasn't bad, but it was much heavier than a popover. More like Yorkshire pudding (the batter for which, amazingly enough, is much the same as for crepes and popovers).

I'd serve the giant popover, with gravy available, as an appealing substitute for mashed potatoes.

Recalling a British lunch specialty called Toad in the Hole (which is like Yorkshire pudding with sausages in it), and never being one to let a good thing alone, I decided to see what would happen if I put some leftover-type-stuff in the popover-soufflé-pudding. It worked very well indeed.

Endless variations on this one are clearly possible:

Popleftover

¼ to ½ lb. leftover ground beef, fried, crumbled and drained
½ c. or more leftover mixed vegetables
½ tsp. or more Worcestershire sauce
1 recipe popover batter

Combine the cooked ground beef, the vegetables and the Worcestershire sauce.

Heavily grease a soufflé dish or 1½-quart baking dish. Put the meat-vegetable mixture in the bottom of the dish and gently pour the popover batter over it.

Bake at 400 degrees for about one hour. A lovely crust forms, and the meat and vegetables wind up distributed throughout the rather heavy batter.

Leftover or canned gravy, if available, would be nice but not necessary.

I didn't try this with individual popovers (I won't be able to look a popover in the face for months), but I bet it would work.

Bagel dough is NOT the same as crepe/popover/Yorkshire-pudding batter. As substantial as the popleftover is, it's still light and airy compared with the bagel.

But, I was surprised to learn when I made my second batch of bagels (the first recipe wasn't very good), bagels do not *have* to be hard as rocks. Fresh from the oven, these bagels were dense, all right, but they yielded pleasantly when chewed, in the manner of a raised doughnut. Not as easily, mind you, but they did yield.

Some folks may actually prefer the cement-doughnut style. I'm sure these bagels would acquire that texture if left out for a day or two.

The bagels, like so many other

things that nobody makes at home, are fun to make at home. Kids would like doing it. *I* liked doing it. You even get to pick out toppings, like sesame seed or poppy seed or bits of onion. A Gentile friend insisted on topping one with red and green sugar. Wrong.

Bagels

(Adapted from the International Jewish Cook Book)

3 c. flour
½ tbsp. salt
5 tbsp. sugar, divided
2 (¼-oz.) pkg. active dry yeast
⅔ c. lukewarm water
3 tbsp. oil
1 egg
4 qt. water
1 egg yolk
1 tbsp. cold water
Optional toppings: Poppy seeds, sesame seeds, caraway seeds, sea salt or coarsely chopped onion; NOT red and green sugar

Sift together into a large bowl the flour, salt and two tablespoons of the sugar. Dissolve the yeast in half the lukewarm water and stir well. Add the oil and the rest of the lukewarm water to the yeast.

Beat the egg and add it to the yeast mixture. Make a well in the center of the flour and stir in the yeast mixture, gathering up all the flour. Mix well and knead three or four minutes, until the dough is smooth and firm. Cover it with a cloth and let it rise in a warm place for one hour.

Turn the dough out onto a floured board and knead it well, until it becomes somewhat elastic.

Divide the dough into 12 equal portions and shape each, rolling between your palms, into a smooth roll about 5 inches long and ¾ inch in diameter. Dip one end in water and pinch the two ends together firmly. Place the rings on a floured board, and even them out into circles as perfect as possible.

Let them rest, covered, for 10 to 15 minutes, until they show signs of starting to rise.

Bring the four quarts of water to the boil in a five-quart Dutch oven or wider pan. Add the remaining three tablespoons of sugar and wait for the water to return to the boil. Then add six bagels, one by one, using a slotted spoon.

When all the bagels are in the water and it is once more boiling, reduce the heat to minimize boil-over, wait for the bagels to rise to the surface if they did not do so immediately, and let them boil for three minutes.

Turn them over and allow them to boil three minutes more.

Meanwhile, preheat the oven to 400 degrees and lightly oil two baking sheets.

Remove the bagels from the water with a slotted spoon, drain them briefly on paper toweling (watch out — if you leave them too long they'll stick), and transfer them to one of the baking sheets.

Repeat this process with the other six bagels.

Beat the egg yolk with the tablespoon of water and brush onto the tops and sides of the bagels. Sprinkle, if you like, with your choice of topping. (An assortment is always nice.)

Bake for 25 to 30 minutes, until they are crisp and turning golden brown.

Follow-Up

In last Sunday's Food section, it was alleged that it is almost impossible to make popovers that don't rise beautifully. Monday morning, the person who so foolishly made that statement (he should have remembered that all generalizations are false, including this one) arrived at his desk to find there a bag of things about three-quarters of an inch high and weighing what seemed to be about a quarter of a pound apiece. Attached was this note: "My husband made these with your no-fail popover recipe."

A quick consultation established that the only respect in which the gentleman, Lynn Christine, had departed from the recipe appeared to be that the lightly beaten eggs had instead been whipped in the Cuisinart. The author of the popover article had attempted what he thought to be every possible variation — oven temperature, amount of batter in each cup, etc. — to see what prevents popovers from rising. He hadn't thought of that.

(Oh, I cannot keep up this third-person pretense any longer. That author, dear reader, that author was me.)

I went home and tested Christine's approach to egg-beating. It made no difference at all. The popovers were fine. So I made another batch, in which I attempted, viciously, to *make* them flop. I opened the oven door for five minutes just as the popovers were starting to rise. Then I slammed it. They worked, too. I made another batch, in which I added half-again too much flour. Those were heavy, and didn't rise nearly as well as they should, but they did rise.

Next morning on my desk was another batch of low, dense flopovers from Christine, along with a detailed description of his approach. It was an eye-opener for me about what the people at General Mills and Pillsbury call "recipe tolerance." Folks substitute and fiddle with recipes, even when they don't think they're doing so, and a good recipe must permit a wide variation in ingredients and cooking techniques.

The popover recipe called for eggs, milk, flour and butter. It didn't say so, but it as-

sumed that standard ingredients would be used — large eggs, whole milk, all-purpose flour and real butter. Christine, it turns out, had used jumbo eggs (about 20 percent larger than large eggs), one-percent milk (which contains one-fourth of the butterfat of whole milk), unbleached spring-wheat flour (I don't know *what* that does) and margarine. The last substitution is probably perfectly safe in most recipes, the question of flavor aside. But I was sure that, between the eggs, milk and flour, Christine had gone too far.

Then I read what he *did* with the ingredients. The recipe called for adding the milk to the eggs, stirring that mixture gradually into the flour and then adding the melted butter. Christine (who is, according to his wife, a good cook and makes tricky things like soufflés without difficulty) beat the eggs in the food processor, added the milk and margarine and spun that mixture around, then added the flour and spun that just until it was mixed.

Well, I can tell you, I was pretty smug. Between substituting for every ingredient and changing the method, I said to myself, no wonder Christine's popovers didn't work. I was going to conclude this follow-up with the standard advice Mary Hart uses on these occasions: "If it didn't work the first time, try following the recipe." I went home and made them his way, except for the spring-wheat flour, which I couldn't find at my neighborhood grocery.

They worked.

So I called around, found some unbleached spring-wheat flour, and made another batch, slamming the oven door viciously as they started to rise.

They came out fine.

Negotiations the next day with Christine's wife, Faith, who is a computer systems coordinator at the paper, produced this suggestion on her part: She would ask

Christine to make another batch, using my ingredients and method. He did. It flopped.

Maybe it has something to do with the moon. We'll explore this further, I'm afraid, next week. In the meantime, Christine has volunteered to test any other "no-fail" recipes.

More Follow-Up

Regular readers will recall that we have been dealing, for the past few weeks, with the problem of the short, squat popover. (Irregular readers might consider adding some fiber to their diets.)

To review, I made the mistake, two weeks ago, of writing that it is almost impossible to make popovers that don't pop up. Overbeating or underbeating don't matter, I alleged, nor do oven temperature or preheating, nor does whether or not you preheat the empty pans. In every case, I wrote, your popovers will pop. Whereupon Lynn Christine, the husband of a colleague, produced several batches of popovers that could have served as hockey pucks.

The faithful among you will remember that I established, through intense retesting, that although Christine hadn't stuck precisely to either the ingredients or the method suggested in the newspaper, none of his variations made any difference.

I tried all his popover techniques and I slammed the oven door on them besides. Mine worked. He tried sticking to my recipe. His flopped.

In the interest of giving an accurate impression, I should point out that, when the original article appeared, I got many calls and notes from folks who had made the popovers and were successful. I even got a letter from Carolyn and Henry Mar, in Brookings, S.D., saying that the Popleftover, the giant popover I had suggested as a way to use up odd bits of food, had succeeded and done wonders for some capon scraps.

I also got, however, a letter form Debbie Michels, of Columbia Heights, who said that she's been making Betty Crocker's popover recipe successfully for years. She tried mine and it bombed.

And Glenda Wright, of Minneapolis, wrote to say that until six months ago she would have agreed that popovers are fool-proof. But last year she made a batch that flopped, and so has every batch she's made since — using the same recipe and the same containers as she's always used.

I also got a hint from Renee Burrows, of Loretto, who says that, although popovers do pop with other oven-temperature arrangements, she gets her best results by putting them in a cold oven, setting it for 450 degrees and baking them for 40 minutes. Useful information, but the Christine mystery lingered.

That's where it all stood until a week ago when, muffin tin in hand, I invited myself to the Christines' to make popovers.

Now, Christine is, if I may steal a phrase from P.G. Wodehouse, as pleasant a fellow as ever bit a sandwich. But after our early phone conversations I was beginning to think that his cooking technique might be the problem. After his third failure it developed that he had never sifted the flour. I couldn't believe that so small a thing would cause his problem, but we'd eliminated almost everything else, so I resolved to stand over him with a bludgeon and make sure he used the #$% sifter. I even brought my sifter along.

And I brought my oven thermometer, too, on the theory that if they were cooked at too low a temperature his popovers were perhaps setting before they could rise.

I can't stand much more of this, so I'll cut it short. He and I each made a batch of popovers. We both followed the recipe exactly, sifting and all, and put both batches into a preheated oven at 400 degrees (confirmed by thermometer).

Both batches *worked*.

Could the problem have been the sifting? It seemed very unlikely.

I was quite discouraged, but a welcome break was provided by Faith, Lynn's wife, who prepared a very nice free dinner. (Who says there's no such thing?)

After dinner, Lynn and I made one more batch of popovers each, neither of us sifting the flour. Mine went into a cold oven (the method he had been using, and which I had already tested successfully) and his went in after the oven had come up to temperature. Both of those batches worked too!

I absolutely don't get it. What had happened to make all of his previous efforts flop? And what had changed since then?

We are down, now, to a thin straw indeed. He says that the eggs he used for all three batches that flopped had been in the refrigerator for a few weeks. I have set aside some eggs, and I'll make another batch of popovers with them in three or four weeks, to see if they'll bomb. Stay tuned.

In the meantime, we do have one hint, confirmed in a letter from Mrs. Dennis Kramer, of Elk River. Popovers do NOT rise very well in nonstick pans. Each of the two batches that Christine made under my watchful eye was split between two six-cup pans, one a regular metal muffin pan and one a pan with a nonstick surface. In both batches, the popovers in the nonstick pan were lots lower than their counterparts in the traditional pan.

And even without that information, the evening was not a total loss from the point of view of the popover. Faced with two more batches of popovers after supper, Faith suggested that we spoon some of her chocolate mousse into them.

They were WONDERFUL! Ice cream would be a very nice second choice.

There's a spoilsport in every crowd, though. When I enthused about this discovery later to a friend, predicting that the chocolate-mouse popover would sweep the country and that 8-foot plastic popovers would soon be seen revolving on poles atop franchise restaurants, she gave me a withering glance and said, "You've just invented the cream puff."

Still More Follow-Up

This is the last failed-popover theory for a while:

Esmé Evans, Minneapolis, wrote to offer what she calls Evans's Theory of Relative Competence: Every time you figure out how to cook something new reasonably well, you cease being able to cook something you thought you had mastered.

She bets that Lynn Christine, who produced some of the worst-looking popovers ever to defile a table, must have "just learned how to make coulibiac or pithiviers or something else wonderful and therefore used up his competence quotient for the month."

"There was a year or two there, a while back," Evans wrote, "when every cake I made fell. I couldn't figure out what was the matter; I was using the same oven, same recipes, same ingredients, same everything, and yet the cakes, which looked fine when I tested them with a broomstraw, would heave great sighs of exhaustion and sink into weary little leatherlike puddles.

"Later on I realized that there was something fishy going on, and it had nothing to do with my abilities in the kitchen. What had happened was that I had just learned how to make baklava, and was impressing friends and coworkers with the results of my new skills. Needless to say, I had overdrawn my competence account, and the cosmic kitchen accountants decided to use my cake-making ability to cover the overdraft.

"The same thing happened when I started to make good pie crust; I suddenly lost all ability to separate eggs. It got so that I was unable to make a lemon meringue pie unless my husband was around to separate the eggs for me.

"I must say, things seem to have settled down lately, and I have no more than an average number of smushed cakes and yolk-flecked, unbeatable egg whites. And I still seem to be able to whomp out a reasonably tasty pie crust. I assume I can still make baklava, although I won't know for sure until next weekend, when I plan to make it after a year's hiatus. If it's awful, I'll let you know."

We'll be waiting.

Final Follow-Up

Special note for readers of this book:

That's as far as I carried the Popover Predicament in the newspaper. By the time we got to Evans's Theory of Relative Competence I had had the course, weariness clouded my mind, and soon I had completely forgotten my promise to try using old eggs.

But for you, as long as you've already spent this much time on it, let me add a last — and possibly useful — bit of information.

When I realized, in looking over this peculiar bit of material, that I had never tried to make popovers with aged eggs, I took a carton of eggs that had been in my refrigerator a while anyway and moved it to the back, to ensure that I wouldn't accidentally use them up. A week after the "use-by" date on the end of the carton had expired, making them more than a month old, I made a batch of popovers. (Sorry I didn't wait longer than that. But I wanted to find out whether popovers can be made with old eggs, not whether popovers can be made with rotten eggs.)

To end a *very* long story, these popovers rose, but not very darn far. They weren't hockey pucks, but they were sort of muffins. The inside texture, while quite yielding, was uniform dough, not the yawning cavity one expects to find in a popover so that he can get more butter into it. They were not popovers.

So. While I don't want to say this is *the* reason that popovers might not work for some people (because I don't want any mail from people who have just made half-inch-high black-hole popovers using eggs just wrung from the chicken), I will tentatively offer the possibility that it is *one* reason that popovers might not work for some people. After all this work, I don't want to wind up with egg on my face. Even fresh egg.

Using Up Parsley

Not long ago I was having breakfast at a restaurant counter, musing idly about whether I needed a new left-front tire, why I haven't made a million dollars and where babies come from, when I began to notice that the fellow next to me, who was placing his order, sounded like he was undergoing something like the Minnesota Multiphasic Personality Inventory.

Piecing it back together, the conversation between him and the person behind the counter went something like this:

"I'll have the No. 4 breakfast and coffee."

"How do you want your eggs?"

"Over easy."

"Bacon or sausage?"

"Sausage."

"Links or patties?"

"Links."

"Toast or muffin?"

"Toast."

"White or whole wheat?"

"Whole wheat."

"Regular or decaffeinated coffee?"

"Regular."

"Cream or sugar?"

"Sugar."

It seemed absolutely endless. But as I turned it over in my teeny mind I thought of several further questions that would represent only a logical extension of the process, and that some hapless customer might well encounter one fine day:

"Sugar or sweetener for your coffee?"

"Saccharine sweetener or Nutra-Sweet sweetener?"

"Cream, milk or non-dairy coffee whitener?"

"Butter or margarine on your toast?"

"Jelly or marmalade?"

"Apple jelly or cherry jelly?"

The whole thing could add up to rather an unpleasant experience for somebody who was having difficulty making decisions.

Then I thought of one option that I'd bet *nobody* — not even the most breathlessly eager teen-age Burger-King-ette — will *ever* offer. And it's one I'd dearly love to be asked:

"Do you want us to throw sprigs of parsley all over the top of your food for no particular reason?"

No, I don't.

Don't misunderstand. I don't hate parsley (although there are many, I'm sure, who like it more than I do). It's just that, even in this age of varied choice, just about everybody thinks it's a neat idea to throw parsley on a plate of just about anything.

I'm sure, too, that there are some folks who eat the parsley that decorates their plates in restaurants. But I'm even surer that a whole lot of parsley goes right back to the kitchen with the dirty dishes.

What a tremendous saving restaurants could make if they switched to reusable plastic parsley for those who don't care to eat theirs.

("Real parsley or artificial?")

I'm told that parsley is a natural breath-freshener, and that perhaps that is the origin of the custom of tossing it onto plates of food.

I dunno.

I do know that if you ate all the

parsley that comes your way if you dine out very much, you might be kissing sweet a lot of the time but you'd probably have little green things stuck to your teeth a lot of the time, too.

A better suggestion is to save up all that parsley and use it to make something intentionally parsley-laden, like the recipes that follow.

No, serious-minded readers, I don't really mean that you should collect parsley in your pockets or purses and take it home.

That was just me engaging in one of my wild, zany bits of food humor. The only reason I said that was to end the introductory part of this article with a nod toward the recipe portion that follows.

Maybe, to avoid difficulty and misunderstanding, I should do that with more openness and honesty. I'll try.

That's all I have to say about parsley. Here are some recipes:

(Hmm. Honest, but awfully flat. Let me try something in between.)

Even if you don't frequent restaurants with UPS (unnecessary parsley syndrome), you might occasionally buy a big bunch of parsley at a supermarket, use the little bit that your recipe called for and wind up watching the rest of it wilt — or worse — in your refrigerator's produce compartment. Doctors call it Green Accumulation in Crisper-Keeper (GACK). Here are some recipes to help you use up a bunch of parsley before that can happen.

First, of course, a dip. You can vary the amount of parsley a great deal — to accommodate how much parsley you have.

Variable Parsley Dip

1 c. sour cream
1 bunch parsley, washed and chopped (or any lesser amount, for that matter)
1 tbsp. oil
1½ tsp. or more crumbled dried basil
1 clove garlic, crushed
½ tsp. or more salt
Pepper

Combine all ingredients. Serve with chips, crackers or raw vegetables. Serves eight.

That makes getting rid of parsley almost too easy. Let's move up one step in difficulty, or you won't respect parsley in the morning.

Parsley Soup

2 leeks
1 medium onion
2 tbsp. butter
2 bunches parsley
3 (10¾-oz.) cans chicken broth
Salt, pepper

Wash the leeks thoroughly and cut them into 1-inch chunks (use only the white part and the bottom half of the green part). Wash the chunks. (Leeks acquire an amazing amount of grit inside them.) Chop them coarsely. Chop the onion coarsely.

Melt the butter in a Dutch oven and sauté the leeks and onions until the onions are translucent.

Wash and chop the parsley, including a few chopped stems. (Maybe I should have said this before: When chopped parsley is not going to be cooked, don't include the stems. They're twiggy. When the parsley is going to be cooked, it is a fine idea to include a few stems here and there.)

Add the parsley and the chicken broth, plus two soup cans of water, to the leeks and onions. Cover and simmer for 10 minutes. Pour through a strainer (into a second pot — we're keeping the broth because we're making soup; pay attention). Put the solids into a food processor or a blender (add a few tablespoons of liquid if necessary) and whomp them around until they're nicely puréed.

Return the purée to the broth by pressing it through the strainer, to remove any unpuréed bits. (If it's going to be mostly smooth it should be fully smooth.)

Add salt and pepper and heat to serving temperature. Serves six to eight.

It's true that there's fairly little that parsley *doesn't* go with nicely. That's probably why most folks don't really notice the sprig of parsley on their plates at restaurants — it doesn't actually clash with much.

But there are some things with which it goes especially well, and lamb is one of them.

This leg of lamb is an expensive little item, but it's awfully good, so don't be sheepish about serving it.

Parsleyed Leg of Lamb

1 bunch parsley
2 sticks butter, 1 of them softened
3 tbsp. dried basil, crumbled
1 (4- to 5-lb.) leg of lamb
8 medium onions
Salt, pepper
½ c. white wine
½ c. dry white vermouth
¼ c. water
2 tbsp. cornstarch

Wash and chop the parsley, including a few stems. Combine the parsley, the softened butter and the crumbled basil. Trim fat from the lamb.

With a sharp knife make six or eight deep cuts into the lamb, some on every surface but all widely separated. Force a large spoonful of the parsley mixture into each cut. Spread the remaining mixture over the top of the lamb.

Melt the other stick of butter and pour it into a roasting pan or a 9- by 13-inch pan. Preheat the oven to 300 degrees.

Peel the onions but leave them whole. Put the lamb in the pan with the melted butter and surround it with the onions. Season all with salt and pepper and cover tightly. (If using a 9- by 13-inch pan, cover tightly with aluminum foil.)

Bake for 30 minutes, then raise oven temperature to 375 degrees, remove the cover and brown for another 30 minutes.

Pour the wine and vermouth over all, reduce the temperature to 300 degrees again, cover the pan and bake one more hour (total, two hours). This will leave a four-pound roast done past pink, and a touch of pink in a five-pound roast. Adjust time up or down, depending on how you like your lamb.

When the lamb is done, remove it to a serving dish and surround it with the onions. Stir the water into the cornstarch in a cup. Skim the fat from the cooking liquid (if you must, but it's very tasty) and pour the cooking liquid into a medium saucepan. Stir in the dissolved cornstarch and cook briefly, stirring, until the gravy has thickened.

You can make the gravy a few minutes early, if you like, by pouring or spooning off most of the cooking liquid before removing the lamb from the oven. Pour some gravy over the lamb and onions and serve the rest of the gravy separately. (I made the gravy a little early and forgot to serve it altogether. That was really too bad, because it was wonderful! I ate it over bread for days afterward.)

Serves six to eight.

Parsleyed potatoes is a possibility, but that hardly needs a recipe. So how about some pasta? That gives us a chance to get in some much-needed olive oil and garlic.

Linguine with Parsley and Garlic

1 lb. linguine
½ c. olive oil
2 cloves garlic
1 bunch parsley, washed and chopped
Salt, pepper

Prepare the linguine according to package directions. Drain. Meanwhile, heat the olive oil in a saucepan over medium heat. Crush the garlic, add it to the oil and sauté very briefly — just until it begins to color. Don't let it darken or it will get bitter.

In a large bowl, toss the pasta with the oil, garlic, parsley, salt and pepper.

Serves six to eight.

For dessert . . . no, I didn't make anything with parsley for dessert. But I did make something green, mostly because it sounded good but partly to convince my guests (briefly, but it was fun) that I *had* made a parsley dessert.

What I served were little castles of tiny cream puffs, filled with lime custard and partly coated with thin, crackly-hard caramel.

Nummy!

You could skip the caramel part if you want, but I like it a lot.

Amusing Green Dessert

Puffs:
¾ c. milk
6 tbsp. butter
¾ c. sifted flour
⅛ tsp. salt
3 eggs
Filling:
1 c. sugar
6 tbsp. cornstarch
2 c. water
Pinch of salt
4 egg yolks
3 tbsp. butter
⅓ c. lime juice or juice of 2 limes
1 lime rind, grated
About 3 drops of green food coloring
Caramel:
2 c. sugar
⅔ c. water
2 tbsp. corn syrup
Whipped cream, for garnish

Make the puffs: Heat the milk in a medium saucepan. Stir in the butter, cut into chunks. Bring the milk to the boil. Reduce the heat to low-medium. Thoroughly stir in the sifted flour and the salt, and cook, stirring, until the mixture forms a ball and cleans the side of the pan. Remove the pan from the heat.

Stir in the eggs one at a time, being sure each egg is completely absorbed before adding the next one (or it gets really messy).

Preheat the oven to 425 degrees. Grease a cookie sheet.

With spoons or a pastry bag, poot out small ball-shaped mounds of the dough onto the cookie sheet. They should be something like 1 or 1¼ inches across. You will want to get 40 of them (five each for eight people), so judge accordingly as you move through the batter. Wet a fingertip with water and smooth down any very jagged peaks, which would otherwise burn.

Bake 15 minutes at 425 degrees, then turn the pan, lower the temperature to 375 degrees and bake 15 more minutes.

Remove them from the oven and let them cool a minute or two.

If you're going to fill the puffs with a pastry bag, poke a small hole in the bottom of each with a sharp knife and return them to the oven for five minutes to dry.

If you don't have a pastry bag, slice the top of each puff open about ⅓ of the way down — trying, if possible, to leave a hinge of dough still holding the cap to the rest of the puff. If you lose, you lose, but make the effort. Don't discard any caps that came off completely because we need to close those puffs after they're filled. Return the opened puffs to the oven for five minutes to dry.

Prepare the filling: In a saucepan over low heat, combine the sugar, cornstarch, water and salt. Cook, stirring, until the mixture thickens and eventually boils. Reduce heat to very low, cover, and cook 10 minutes, stirring occasionally.

Beat the egg yolks, and stir in a few spoonfuls of the hot mixture. Stir the diluted egg yolks back into the hot mixture. Cook, stirring, another three minutes.

Remove the mixture from the heat and stir in the butter until it melts. Add the lime juice, lime rind and food coloring.

Cool the mixture and, no more than a few hours before serving, fill the puffs, replacing any loose caps. Refrigerate the filled puffs. (Warning: They may get soggy if you keep them in the refrigerator for an extended period.)

If you like, you can stop here and serve the filled puffs in bowls with whipped cream over them or on the side.

Or you can go the extra mile and make the caramel: Grease a cookie sheet and get the serving plates or bowls ready, too.

Combine the sugar, water and corn syr-up in a saucepan. Stir to dissolve the sugar, then cover the pan and bring to a boil over high heat without any further stirring. Once the boiling has gone on for three minutes, remove the cover but do not stir. Continue to boil for about 10 more minutes, until the syrup reaches about 300 degrees and has begun to color. (It's hard to see the color when it's boiling, so you might lower the heat when the temperature is about 300. Don't let the color get at all dark, or the syrup will taste burnt.)

As soon as the light color is reached, remove the pan from the heat, and, working rapidly — but carefully to avoid burning fingers in hot syrup — dip the top of each puff into the syrup and set it, dipped side down, on the greased cookie sheet.

After all 40 puffs are dipped, put four in a square, with the flat syrup "cap" up, on each serving dish. Lightly dip the bottom of the fifth puff in the syrup and position it on top of the other four. Serve with whipped cream on the side. Serves eight.

During dinner, one guest kept ducking into the bathroom to make sure she didn't have parsley in her teeth.

It occurred to me later that the appetizer dip should have contained parsley, sage, rosemary and thyme, so I tried it. (One cup sour cream; one bunch parsley, chopped; and half a teaspoon each of sage, rosemary [crumbled] and thyme. I also tossed in a clove of garlic, crushed, and salt and pepper.) I thought it tasted like turkey dressing but a friend liked it, so I decided to include it but not prominently. Anybody who finds it here will know that I wasn't crazy about it. I don't want anybody turning green.

A Digital Dinner

Well, it's almost April. I don't like being the person to tell you this, but you've got less than three weeks to finish up your income-tax returns.

So why are you sitting there on a Sunday morning wasting time with the Food section when you've got work to do?

You just don't want to do it right now, do you?

That's understandable if you owe money — putting it off until the last minute makes sense in that case.

But even lots of people who have a refund coming still haven't gotten out the bottle of aspirin and last year's mound of miscellaneous scraps of paper and *done* it.

Maybe it's because chasing numbers around the dining-room table simply isn't your idea of a fun way to spend the afternoon. Perhaps you need something to put you in the mood.

Precisely why I am here.

In the same way that lots of people like to crack their knuckles before they begin to type or play the piano, some of us may need a little special warmup to get the old 1040 flowing.

I suggest cooking with numbers.

(What did you *think* I'd suggest in the Food section? Playing tennis?)

There are quite a lot of numerical foods, so this won't be a difficult exercise. Here, for example, is a small selection of numerical goodies that I didn't use:

A.1. Sauce
Nine-Grain Bread
Fourtune Cookies
Seven-Layer Salad

Three-Minute Eggs
Thousand-Island Dressing
7-Up
Octopus
Nine Lives (if your cat dines with you)
Doughnuts, Bagels or Cheerios

There's also Mont Blanc, but even I will grant that that's a little obscure. Only people who read headlines in the sports pages think of blank as a number. They think of it as a verb, too.

To hold our investigation to a reasonable list, I decided to restrict myself to foods named with single numerals (or digits, if you like) — the integers from 0 to 9. That way we won't have to deal with 1,000 Year Eggs, Millefeuille ("thousand leaves" — the French name for what we call the Napoleon) or millet.

For lack of a better term, I'm calling my choices digital foods. That way we can sound stylishly computerized. If you want to carry that electronic idea further, you could throw some chips — chocolate, butterscotch or peanut butter — into one of the recipes, but I don't think that's necessary.

Because I've been kind of busy lately, I didn't try recipes representing all ten digits.

Here's what we eight:

Two-na Appetizer
Three-Bean Salad
Six-Legume Soup
Fettucine with Five Cheeses
Petits Fours

Having already chosen to make the

Fettucine with Five Cheeses, I came across something else nice while shopping, so I decided to toss it in. *Quince jelly* (on toast points).

Fourgive me if you can.

So. As they say in the analyst business, let's begin at the beginning.

This appetizer is slightly adapted from one in Best Loved Recipes of the American People, by Ida Bailey Allen. I picked it because it looked nice, but it deserves better billing than that. The little canapes were very good indeed — and when folks had gone home and I was cleaning up, I ate several of the leftovers cold. They weren't bad that way, either.

So the extras didn't go for (ahem) naught.

Two-na Appetizer

3 tbsp. butter
3 tbsp. flour
½ tsp. salt
Pepper
1 c. milk
½ c. finely chopped Brazil nuts
2 tbsp. chopped green pepper
2 tbsp. chopped onion
½ tsp. Worcestershire sauce
1 (6½- to 7-oz.) can tuna
8 slices bread
Pimiento strips (optional)
Slices of Brazil nuts

Melt the butter in a saucepan, blend in the flour, salt and pepper. Let cook a minute or so over low heat, then gradually stir in the milk. Continue cooking and stirring until the sauce is thickened and smooth.

Add the chopped nuts, green pepper, onion, Worcestershire sauce and tuna. Set aside.

Toast the bread and cut into wedges, strips, triangles, diamonds or whatever pleases your little heart.

Just before you plan to serve them, spread the tuna mixture on the toast shapes, place them on a cookie sheet and run them under the broiler a minute or two (or more, until they are heated through).

Garnish each with a strip of pimiento, if you like, and a slice of Brazil nut.

Makes 24 or so, depending on how small you cut the toast shapes.

Next comes the salad, a traditional American favorite that needs no introduction. This version is from The Doubleday Cookbook.

The only reason I'm introducing it is to mention that tastes in this matter do vary.

Some found the salad just what the arithmetic teacher ordered; others would have preferred it with a bit more vinegar. I won't try to make that decision for you (that's just not my number).

Three-Bean Salad

1 (16-oz.) can cut green beans
1 (16-oz.) can wax beans
1 (15-oz.) can kidney beans
2 ribs celery
1 medium green pepper
1 medium onion
1 small (or ½ large) dill pickle
    (optional)
3 tbsp. sugar
1 tsp. salt
⅛ tsp. pepper
½ c. olive oil
6 tbsp. vinegar (or more, he noted
    acidly)

Drain all three cans of beans well. Use a sieve. An awful lot of liquid remains in the beans if you just invert the can to drain them, and it dilutes the flavor of the dressing.

Chop the celery and green pepper. Cut off about three slices of onion, break them into rings and chop the rest of the onion. If you're including the pickle, chop it finely (or finally).

Combine beans, celery, green pepper, onion, pickle (if you're using it), sugar, salt, pepper, oil and vinegar. Stir well, cover and refrigerate several hours for flavors to blend.

Serves six.

Now to the nice, thick soup. The recipe on which this one is based is from Vegetarian Gourmet Cookery, by Alan Hooker, and was called Seven-Bean Soup.

It included kidney beans. Since we just *had* kidney beans, I decided to leave them out.

And since, on subjecting the recipe to the minute scrutiny that prudence demands (and patience tolerates) it became apparent that two of the remaining beans were peas, I felt justified in renaming it altogether.

Besides, I was already back from the grocery store before I realized that both salad and soup were based on beans. I figured that, with the soup renamed, the combination wouldn't seem quite so much like I was on some kind of bean toot.

This is an ideal recipe for using up the little half-bags of dried beans and peas that are collecting in your cupboard. If you don't have such a collection, this is an ideal recipe for starting one.

Six-Legume Soup

¼ c. dried yellow split peas
¼ c. dried green split peas
¼ c. dried Great Northern beans
¼ c. dried lima beans
¼ c. dried pinto beans
¼ c. dried garbanzo beans
1 large onion
1 medium green pepper
1 rib celery
1 carrot
1 clove garlic
2 tbsp. butter
2 bay leaves
¼ tsp. marjoram
¼ tsp. basil
1 tsp. salt
Pepper
4 beef bouillon cubes (or 4 tsp. beef
    bouillon granules)
1 c. chopped ripe tomato (or 1 8-oz.
    can tomato sauce)
¼ c. ketchup

Thoroughly wash and pick over the peas and beans, discarding anything that doesn't look like a pea or a bean. Put them in six cups of water in a Dutch oven and bring to the boil. Continue to boil two minutes, then remove from the heat, cover and let stand one hour. Skim off surface.

Return to low-medium heat and cook about 1½ hours, until they are tender.

Chop the onion, green pepper, celery and carrot and put in a large saucepan. Crush the garlic and add it and the butter. Add five cups of water and bring the whole thing to the boil. Continue cooking 20 to 25 minutes until the vegetables are tender.

Drain and retain the bean cooking liquid. Add the vegetables and their cooking liquid to the beans, and add the bay leaves, marjoram, basil, salt and pepper. Crush the bouillon cubes and add them (or use bouillon granules), and stir in the tomatoes (or tomato sauce) and the ketchup.

Simmer for half an hour or so, adding bean liquid as needed to achieve the kind of consistency you like.

Fish out the bay leaves if you're any kind of person at all, and serve. Makes about eight servings.

Fettucine has a way of cropping up (and getting misspelled) in lots of recipes these days. Here's another one. This one's pretty good. It is slightly adapted from one in Cooking Great Meals Every Day, by Richard Sax.

This recipe, too, calls for an assortment of things you probably don't have sitting around, but they have the advantage of being cheeses and subject to being used easily in other dishes (or just being eaten, as the produce folks say, "out of hand").

Fettucine with Five Cheeses

1 lb. fettucine
3 tbsp. unsalted butter
1 c. grated fontina cheese
1 c. grated Parmesan cheese
¾ c. ricotta cheese
¼ c. crumbled gorgonzola cheese
¼ c. grated Romano cheese
2 tbsp. milk
½ c. heavy cream
1 tbsp. brandy (optional)
Salt, pepper

Heat a large pot of salted water to boiling. Stir in the fettucine and cook according to package directions.

Meanwhile, melt the butter in a saucepan over low heat. Add the cheeses and heat, stirring, until they are just melted. Stir in the milk and the cream (stop short of the half cup if the sauce is getting thin). Add the brandy, if you like, and salt and pepper to taste.

Drain the fettucine, put in a large bowl or several individual bowls and pour the sauce over it. Serves four to six.

Now comes dessert, and none too soon.

What with two-na, three-bean salad, six-legume soup and five-cheese fettucine, I've been waiting for it for a total of sixteen.

I've always loved petits fours. When I was growing up in Milwaukee and would, like other kids, occasionally get a quarter or 50 cents to spend, while other kids would get squirt guns or jacks or barrettes, I would go to the bakery a few blocks away and buy a petit four or two. (That would be a petit eight.)

They are so *pretty* and so *good!*

The name is really a generic for all kinds of little oven goodies, but one kind has come to corner the market, as it were. The standard petit four — imagine such a phrase! — is little pieces of rich cake (typically genoise, the French sponge cake), dipped in a fruit glaze and then coated with a firm, shiny icing and decorated (with a flower of frosting, perhaps, or a candied violet or some such). Sometimes the cake is cut apart and a gooey filling inserted before the glaze and frosting are applied.

These were surprisingly easy to make.

Not easy, mind you, but not as dreadfully difficult as I had thought they might be. The recipe is adapted from The Doubleday Cookbook.

Petits Fours

<u>Cake:</u>
3½ tbsp. butter
4 eggs
¾ c. sugar, sifted
1 tsp. vanilla
1 tsp. grated lemon rind
¾ c. sifted cake flour
<u>Optional filling</u> (enough for about
    half the petits fours):
1½ tbsp. unsalted butter
½ c. cream
4 oz. semisweet chocolate
<u>Glaze:</u>
1½ c. (1 18-oz. jar) apricot preserves
⅜ c. water
<u>Icing:</u>
7½ c. confectioners' sugar (about 2
    lb.)
7½ tbsp. light corn syrup
7½ tbsp. water
<u>Optional decorations:</u>
Candied violets
Chocolate jimmies
etc.
    or:
<u>Frosting for decorating:</u>
1 tbsp. water
1 c. confectioners' sugar
Food colorings

Prepare the cake: Preheat the oven to 350 degrees. Grease a 9- by 13- inch pan, line the bottom, sides and ends of the pan with waxed paper and grease the waxed paper. Set aside.

Melt the 3½ tablespoons of butter in a small pan over very low heat. Allow the foam to subside and gently pour the clear part of the butter into a teacup or something else handy, leaving the milky residue in the pan. What you have in the cup is about three tablespoons of clarified butter.

Bring an inch or two of water just to the simmer in a saucepan. Turn the heat to low to keep it from boiling. Put the eggs, sugar, vanilla and lemon rind in a large mixer bowl and set it on top of the pan of simmering water, so that it does not rest in the water. Beat the mixture with an electric mixer at low to medium speed, or, if you're a glutton for punishment (and authenticity), use a wire whisk. In any case, beat until it foams and volume is almost doubled.

Take the mixer bowl off the heat and beat with a mixer at high speed several minutes until the batter becomes very thick. (It should flow off the beaters in a single wide ribbon that stays on the surface briefly before it dissolves.) Add a third of the flour and fold gently. Fold in a third of the clarified butter. Repeat until all the flour and butter are folded in.

Pour the batter into the prepared pan, tipping the pan to spread the batter evenly and tapping it on the countertop to break any bubbles. Bake 20 to 25 minutes until the cake tests done with a toothpick and springs back when touched.

While the cake is in the oven, prepare the optional filling if you're going to use it: Put the butter and the cream in a saucepan and bring the mixture to the boil over low to medium heat. Add the chocolate, stirring until it is melted. Pour the mixture into the small bowl of the mixer and cool it in the refrigerator until it is like honey.

When the cake is done, cool it in its pan on a wire rack 10 minutes, then loosen the edges, invert the cake and remove the pan. Gently peel off the waxed paper, then turn the cake right side up onto the rack and allow it to cool completely.

When it is cool, trim away the dry, hard edges (and eat them as your reward for getting this far; they're pretty good). Cut the cake into small diamonds, rectangles, parallelograms, circles or whatever. A variety of shapes makes a more attractive presentation. Don't make them large. A couple of dainty bites is all they ought to be good for. One inch by two or so is a fine size for the rectangles and parallelograms, for example. A few especially tiny circles (use the center of a doughnut cutter) are nice, too.

If you're going to be filling some petits fours, slice those in half now. Check on the filling mixture in the refrigerator and when it is thickened, whip it with the electric mixer until it is light and spreadable. Spread it on the bottom halves of the petit fours that are to be filled and put the tops back on them. Lick the bowl. (Nice, huh?)

Prepare the glaze: Heat the apricot preserves and water in a saucepan over low heat, stirring, until the mixture begins to bubble. Keep going two or three more minutes, then remove it from the heat and push it through a wire sieve. Discard or eat the stuff that remains in the sieve. Let the strained preserves cool slightly.

The next step sounds harder than it is. We're going to dip the petits fours in the apricot glaze so that the glaze covers the tops and all four sides. Set some wire racks over cookie sheets. Spear one of the cakes from the bottom with a large two-tined meat fork (start with the unfilled ones, to get the hang of it, and to keep chocolate filling out of the glaze that goes on the unfilled ones). The petits fours stay on the fork better if you insert it at an angle.

Dip each cake almost all the way in, so top and sides are covered, and then ease it off the fork, onto a wire rack, undipped side down and an inch or more away from other dipped cakes. (The cookie sheet is to catch the drips.) Let the cakes stand about an hour, uncovered, to allow the glaze to set.

When ready to ice the petits fours, put clean cookie sheets under them. Prepare the icing: Bring some water to the simmer in the bottom of a double boiler. Turn the heat down to keep it at a simmer. Sift the 7½ cups of confectioners' sugar, and put it and the corn syrup and the 7½ tablespoons of water into the top of the double boiler. Heat, stirring, until the sugar dissolves and the icing is quite smooth. Take the double boiler off the heat, but keep the icing over the hot water to keep it liquid.

Now comes another part that sounds tricky but isn't: Using a large spoon or ladle, pour enough icing over the top of a petit four so that it covers the top and runs down and covers all four sides. (Move the ladle around to get sides that aren't getting enough on their own.) Don't figure on coming back to give them a second coat to cover missed spots; that would look patchy. Don't worry if it looks like there might not be enough icing; the stuff that runs or drips off onto the cookie sheets can be scraped up and gently reheated in the double boiler to cover the remaining petits fours.

Let the petits fours dry another hour, then decorate them and transfer them to a serving plate (or transfer them first and then decorate them). To decorate, use candied violets, chocolate jimmies or whatever, and/or prepare decorative frosting:

Blend the tablespoon of water into the cup of confectioners' sugar (adjust so frosting is thick but not dry). Divide into small bowls and color some green, some yellow, etc., for making simple flowers. Load the frosting into a pastry tube and have your way with it. (Or use a bunch of envelopes, cutting off a tiny tip of the corner to pipe thin lines, a wider slit [pinched almost shut] to shape leaves, and so forth.)

Store in a cool, dry place where you can't get at them until you are ready to serve them. They're wonderful.

When the writer polished off the last of the petits fours, he had a Three Musketeers bar.

Binkies and Bostess Bupcakes

I was thinking the other day, while eating a Twinkie, about the recent Hostess advertising campaign that featured the slogan "Freshness never tasted so good." Lest I give the wrong impression, I should point out immediately that I *like* Hostess Cupcakes, Twinkies, Ding Dongs, Ho Hos and the rest. I eat a lot of them.

But, I reflected, I've never thought of them as fresh. I've thought of them as great-tasting, wonderful junk.

It is true that unlike, say, Cool Whip, which you keep in your freezer but is claimed to "taste fresh as homemade," the Hostess products really are made relatively soon before you eat them. According to a Hostess spokesperson, the "sell before" date stamped on the package should be no more than 4 or 5 days from the date the product comes out of the oven.

Nonetheless, I wouldn't normally call a cupcake baked on Monday "fresh" on Friday. If you really wanted a *fresh* Twinkie, I've said to myself almost every time I heard that "freshness never tasted so good" commercial, you'd have to make it yourself.

So I decided to try to do just that. You can't make Twinkies, of course, or Ding Dongs, Ho Hos or Hostess Cupcakes, because those are product names owned by ITT Continental Baking Co., Rye, N.Y. But you could make something rather like them — say Binkies, Bing Bongs, Bo Bos and Bostess Bupcakes.

Although the items I'm suggesting are imitations, they aren't mock products like the mock apple pie made with Ritz Crackers instead of apples. If you can make your own, you can not only make them fresh, you can make them realer than the things they're imitating — with lots of real chocolate instead of so much cocoa, and with whipped cream instead of sweetened whipped shortening.

That way, freshness would taste very good indeed.

Note: Don't use aerosol whipped cream to fill any of these items. It contains *much* more gas than home-whipped heavy cream, and it deflates very quickly. (Eight ounces of cream whips into a pint at home; seven ounces of aerosol cream produces a quart.)

I decided to tackle what seemed to me to be the most difficult item, the Binkie, first. Making the cake batter wouldn't be hard (I chose a sponge cake recipe, slightly altered, from The Joy of Cooking). But the Binkie, to be successful, has to look like a Twinkie, and I'm not aware of any pans with that shape.

So I made some Binkie molds. That turned out not to be very difficult after all, and the Binkies, if I say so myself (and I do), were stunning.

Real whipped cream tastes *lots* better than the standard filling, and, in addition, the filled Binkie is very, very light.

After I ate my first Binkie, I ate a Twinkie (which, I repeat, I have always enjoyed) and there was absolutely no comparison.

Binkies

(Requires a pastry bag)
Lots of aluminum foil
3 eggs
1 c. sugar
¼ c. boiling water
1 c. sifted cake flour
1½ tsp. baking powder
1½ tsp. vanilla, divided
¼ tsp. salt
1½ c. heavy cream (you might not use it all)
2 tsp. confectioners' sugar

Prepare nine Binkie molds as follows (it sounds hard, but it's not):

For each mold, tear about a 9-inch piece of 12-inch-wide aluminum foil. Fold it in half first one way and then the other. You wind up with a piece of foil about 4½ inches by 6.

Grease one side with solid shortening or margarine. Bend up the longer sides to form the folded foil into a U-shaped trough (6 inches long, about 1½ inches across the rounded bottom and maybe 1½ inches high). Lift *in* one end of the bottom, then turn the ends closed. Repeat with the other end, forming something like a little bathtub.

Mash the bottoms of the bathtub ends smooth, then fasten the tops of the ends (the head and the foot of the bathtub rim) together by firmly folding the overlapped edge down a little. Making nine of these won't take you ten minutes.

The Binkie recipe makes about 18, so you'll use the molds twice. Rather than trying to regrease the crumb-laden molds after the first use, flatten them out, grease what had been the outside and use that as the inside for the second batch.

OK? Molds in place, panel? Then let's go ahead and make Binkies!

Preheat the oven to 325 degrees.

Separate the eggs, putting the yolks in a large mixing bowl and the whites in a small one. Beat the yolks until they are very light. To the beaten egg yolks, gradually beat in the sugar, then the boiling water.

Resift the sifted cake flour with the baking powder, and gradually add the combination to the yolk mixture, beating until the mixture is well blended. Beat in one teaspoon of the vanilla. Set aside.

Wash the beaters carefully — there must be no egg yolk on them. Add the salt to the egg whites and beat them until they are stiff but still glossy. Stir a spatulaful of the egg whites into the yolk-flour mixture to lighten it, then lightly fold in the remainder of the whites, incorporating them well but gently.

Pour about two heaped tablespoons of the batter into a Binkie mold. The batter will flow, perhaps slowly, into the corners. When it has evened out it should be about half an inch deep (it rises rather a lot during baking).

Because getting the size just right is important, you might try filling and baking one mold first to see whether you are using the right amount of batter. Too little produces a Binkie too short to have enough space inside for filling; too much produces a Binkie that's perfectly fine for eating but looks kind of like a bus.

To bake, arrange four or five Binkie molds snugly in a loaf pan and bake in the 325-degree oven about 15 to 20 minutes, until one or two minutes *after* they test done with a toothpick. The top probably will not look very brown.

Allow the Binkies to cool for a few minutes. Using a sharp knife and flexing the molds, gently free the sides of the Binkies and invert them over a cooling rack. If they don't drop out easily, gently peel the foil away from the Binkies (not vice-versa).

Before the Binkies have cooled, use a toothpick as follows to make the holes in the light sponge cake that will hold the whipped cream:

Pierce the flat bottom of each Binkie (the side that was up while it was baking) three times — in the middle and halfway toward each end. Wiggle the toothpick around in a circular fashion to enlarge the cavity (but keep the entrance hole as small as you can). Don't go in so far that the toothpick is in any danger of coming out the other side.

Pour the heavy cream into a small bowl, stir in the confectioners' sugar and the last half teaspoon of vanilla, and beat until very stiff. (You might wind up having some of it left, but there are worse things than having leftover whipped cream.)

Fit a pastry bag with your smallest nozzle and fill the bag with the whipped cream. Inserting the nozzle fairly deeply, force the cream into each of the holes in the Binkies until it just begins to come back out.

Eat, smacking lips.

Makes about 18 Binkies.

As with all treats containing whipped cream, any Binkies not eaten immediately should be refrigerated. But if they have been refrigerated, they are best if they are allowed to warm for half an hour or so before serving.

If left uncovered long, even in the refrigerator, the outsides of the Binkies get rather crunchy — an undesirable trait in a Binkie — so they should be kept in plastic bags.

They'll get moist in the bags after a few days, so that's about as long as you can keep them.

Next, on to the easiest of the things I attempted, the Bostess Bupcakes. That they were relatively easy does not, however, mean that they were less than wonderful.

In fact, they were fantastic.

In addition to the whipped cream, they contain chocolate. To my mind, this gives them a real edge over the Binkies.

It isn't difficult to make a cream-filled cupcake. You can start with any cupcake recipe you want, including one made with cake mix.

But I wanted to make one that would be at least as good as the Hostess version (which is really pretty good.)

In my search for the proper Bupcake batter, I was guided by several concerns:

■ It must be dark, like the original.
■ It must be moist, like the original.
■ And it must use only real chocolate (unlike the original).

After two false starts, I found the recipe I wanted. It is another cake recipe from The Joy of Cooking, and, as the young man says in the Hillshire Farm commercial, I wouldn't change a thing.

Bostess Bupcakes

4 (1-oz.) squares unsweetened
    chocolate
1 c. milk, divided
1 c. brown sugar
2 eggs plus 1 egg yolk
½ c. butter
1 c. white sugar
¼ c. water
1 tsp. vanilla
2 c. sifted cake flour
1 tsp. soda
½ tsp. salt
Filling:
Raspberry jelly (optional)
2 tsp. confectioners' sugar
½ tsp. vanilla
1½ c. heavy cream (you might not use
    all of it)
Frosting:
2 (1-oz.) squares unsweetened
    chocolate
1 tbsp. butter
¼ c. hot water
⅛ tsp. salt
1¾ to 2 c. confectioners' sugar
1 tsp. vanilla
Decorative icing:
¾ c. confectioners' sugar
2 to 3 tsp. milk

Preheat the oven to 325 degrees. Put the chocolate, half a cup of the milk, the brown sugar and one egg yolk into a small saucepan.

Cook over very low heat, stirring constantly, until it has thickened. If it begins to boil, get it off the heat — it has cooked enough. Set the mixture aside to cool.

In a large mixing bowl, beat the butter until it has softened. Sift in the white sugar gradually, continuing to beat, until the butter-sugar mixture is light and creamy.

Separate the two whole eggs, putting the whites into a small mixing bowl. Beat the yolks, one at a time, into the butter-sugar mixture. In a cup, combine the water, the remaining half a cup of milk and the vanilla.

Resift the sifted cake flour with the soda and salt and add to the butter mixture in thirds, alternating with thirds of the milk mixture. Beat the batter after each addition until it is smooth. Stir in the chocolate mixture and mix until well blended.

Clean the beaters thoroughly. Beat the egg whites until they are stiff but still glossy. Stir a spatulaful of the whites into the chocolate batter to lighten it. Then lightly fold in the remaining whites, incorporating them well but gently.

Fill well-greased cupcake or muffin tins just a little more than half full. Bake between 12 and 15 minutes, turning the tins once for even baking, and remove them when a toothpick tests absolutely clean. If in doubt, give them an extra minute. They'll tear if they're not fully done. Allow them to cool in the pans for five minutes, run a knife around each Bupcake, invert the tins and stand Bupcakes right-side-up to cool.

When they are cool, use a sharp knife to slice off a bit of the top — a sliver about the size of a 25-cent piece. (Some cooks would take off the whole top, but this would show later, and is most un-Hostess-like.) Save the slivers; we'll be using them.

Using a teaspoon, carefully scoop out a nice chunk of the inside of each Bupcake, but leave plenty of bottom and sides intact — both for strength and because it makes the Bupcake taste good. This stuff is good enough, in fact, that you should save the scooped-out parts. (Put some in a bowl with milk or cream some time. Great.)

Let the scooped-out Bupcakes cool completely. If you like, you can depart from the standard Bostess Bupcake by putting a dab of raspberry jelly into each of the Bupcake cavities before filling them with whipped cream. It's not authentic, but it's delicious.

In any case, stir the confectioners' sugar and the half teaspoon of vanilla into the heavy cream and beat it until it is very stiff. With a spoon or spatula, press the cream into the cooled Bupcakes and more-or-less level off the tops.

Reposition a removed sliver of Bupcake-top back onto each Bupcake. (Without it the cream would make the frosting hard to spread.)

Put the Bupcakes into the refrigerator while you make the frosting: Melt the chocolate and butter together over very low heat. Add the hot water and salt. Sift in half the confectioners' sugar, stirring. Add the vanilla and then, while stirring, sift in as much of the rest of the confectioners' sugar as is needed to make a reasonably thick frosting.

Frost the Bupcakes rapidly, before the frosting hardens. Return them to the refrigerator while you make the decorative icing.

You can, of course, buy the icing for the decoration in little plastic tubes at the grocery store, but it's not any work to make it yourself: Stir the milk into the confectioners' sugar. Put the icing into a pastry bag with a tiny tip, or roll a narrow cornucopia with a tiny point out of a piece of good-quality (heavy) letter paper. (Pin the cornucopia together on the side.)

You can make the decoration any way you want it, of course, or you could even skip it. The Hostess Cupcake is decorated with a line of loops. I used a wavy line for my Bupcakes, just in case Hostess has a trademark on the line of loops.

Eat, sighing and groaning.

Makes 20 to 24 Bupcakes. Like Binkies, they must be kept refrigerated and are best if allowed to warm up for half an hour or so

before serving.

Now to Bing Bongs. These are really just short Bostess Bupcakes, but instead of being frosted on top they are fully covered — top, bottom and sides — with semisweet chocolate. (The Hostess versions, of course, are coated with a less costly — and less tasty — product). The finished items look like hockey pucks.

Because it takes a fair amount of expensive chocolate to encase a batch of Bing Bongs, and because the work is fairly messy and can be rather frustrating, I wouldn't advise making Bing Bongs except to serve to people who *really* love chocolate. If you're not sure, stick to Bupcakes.

Bing Bongs

1 recipe Bostess Bupcake batter (see page 54)
1 recipe filling for Bostess Bupcakes (see page 54)
12 oz. semisweet chocolate
4 tbsp. butter or margarine

Prepare the batter as for Bostess Bupcakes, but fill the muffin tins a bit less than half full (producing maybe 30 Bing Bongs). Bake and fill as for Bostess Bupcakes, being careful to flake off any easily removed crumbs on the bottom and sides. Line a baking sheet with waxed paper and put the filled Bing Bongs on it upside-down.

Making Binkies sounds hard but is easy. Coating Bing Bongs sounds easy but is hard. I'm sure that wonderful machines, closely guarded by the ITT Continental Baking Co., Rye, N.Y., have been developed for this process. I don't have one. Neither, I suspect, do you. So we'll have to do it the hard way:

Over very low heat, melt the 12 ounces of semisweet chocolate (or probably more, depending on how good you are at this), along with the butter or margarine.

When all the chocolate is fully melted, use a metal spatula or putty knife to spread some chocolate (as little as possible) evenly across the bottom of each Bing Bong; invert them on the waxed paper and coat the tops and sides. Refrigerate.

(That paragraph condenses into a few seconds' reading what can seem like a lifetime of messy agony if you're trying to do it. But if you're not compulsive about making them extra-neat, it needn't be too difficult. And they'll taste *wonderful*.)

Like Binkies and Bostess Bupcakes, Bing Bongs must be kept refrigerated, and they also benefit from being allowed to warm up for half an hour or so before they are served. Depending on the temperature of the room you're serving them in, though, the chocolate might get sticky.

I had planned to describe here how to make Bo Bos, miniature cake rolls consisting of chocolate cake and whipped cream, covered, like Bing Bongs, with semisweet chocolate. I must instead report total failure.

I tried four separate times, using three different recipes, to make a chocolate cake roll that could be thin enough, and rolled tightly enough, to make a roll an inch or so in diameter. Every single one broke. Some broke many times. It made me appreciate Hostess all the more.

A last note: Since I began to work on the Binkies, etc., the "freshness never tasted so good" advertising campaign seems to have disappeared. In its stead is one that begins with a guy in a hard

hat biting into a Hostess Fruit Pie and saying something like, "Mmmmm. Real apples!" That one made me wonder, too. Where has this guy been getting desserts made with un-real apples? Then I figured it out. Somebody had been stuffing his pie with Ritz crackers.

Little Mystery #2: Bread

When I was a lad, advertisements for Wonder Bread said that it helped build strong bodies eight ways. The last time I noticed, those advertisement were saying that Wonder Bread helped build strong bodies twelve ways. What were the eight ways, what are the twelve, and how were the four new ones discovered?

Solution: A spokesperson for ITT Continental Baking Co., Rye, N.Y., was only somewhat helpful. She said the firm "no longer uses that advertising theme, and hasn't for many years." (How time flies when you're having fun!)

As for what it used to mean, she said she was not "intimately familiar with it." That theme was used, she said, before "certain changes in advertising regulations having to do with documenting claims."

She didn't want to discuss the matter further because it might, she said, be misconstrued that the discussion was an attempt to make an undocumented health claim.

So we'll just have to guess. (Is one way that Wonder Bread helps build strong bodies that if you put it in your shoes it makes you taller?)

Classified Ads for Recipes

MONEY-SAVING OFFER: Send me $10 for the amazing secret of those classified ads for recipes that appear in the backs of magazines.

You've probably wondered about them — you know which I mean. They offer things like "My Fantastic Chili" for only $2.

I've wondered, too.

When I first noticed them, several years ago, I dismissed them out of hand. Who needs to buy recipes blind like that, I thought, when you can examine cookbooks and buy what appeals to you? This phenomenon was bound to disappear soon. A flash, in other words, in the pan.

But they're still going strong, and I decided recently that it was time to look into them.

SEND ME $5 and you'll learn what happened.

There are really two basic questions: How good are these recipes — that is, do you get your money's worth if you send for them? And could you make a killing selling the family recipe for cod-liver soup?

My survey was not exhaustive. I picked up a copy of the Atlantic Monthly and selected five recipe ads from the 25 that appeared there. They were for "Danish Dumplings — rave-producing-melt-in-your-mouth;" "Prize-winning Italian dessert;" "First time offered. Three outstanding award winning cakes;" "Sauerkraut Fudge Cake — bewilderingly delicious. No description suffices," and "Icy Tea-Based Refresher perfect for summer."

Not a balanced list, perhaps, but I like dessert. And some of the others didn't exactly sweep me off my feet: "Easy, 4 noodle puddings;" "Kosher Stuffed Peppers;" "Family secrets revealed. Fast, easy, economical recipes," and "Artichoke heart spread/Cranberry Sunset. Hors d'oeuvre and drink — let's [sic] time stand still."

Actually, these ads are kind of fun to read. One in a recent Harper's magazine offered five chicken soup recipes. It began "Surprise ailing friends with exotic home remedy." And in a Saturday Review I came across "Elegant brownie recipe, entertaining or family." Kind of hard to picture that one.

HOW ABOUT sending me $3.50 and I'll throw in the recipes?

I sent off the total of $10 that the five ads in the Atlantic required. All the addresses were either post-office boxes or street addresses without names, so I had to send checks without names filled in. That's a very peculiar sensation: It felt as if I was begging to be ripped off.

Actually, because I had to put 18 cents postage each on both my requests and the self-addressed, stamped envelopes that all the ads required, the total outlay for the five recipes was $11.80.

If that doesn't already sound outrageous, consider that at that rate a copy of The Joy of Cooking would cost you more than $6,000. And it would come in lots and lots of little pieces.

SO SURELY knowing how this all came out is worth a measly $2.50 to you.

Well, OK, I'll tell you a little more for free.

The first recipe to arrive was Danish dumplings. The sender had written "Danish Dumplings" in the return-address spot on the stamped envelope I'd sent, and I'm sure that the mailman figured it was pornography.

Anyway, what I got for my $2.36 was a badly cut quarter of a sheet of paper, crudely duplicated, containing a recipe for dumplings. The paper cutting was clearly an effort on the part of the sender to reduce costs — from maybe 10 cents to maybe 2½ cents. I resented it. The recipe produced dumplings that were, well, dumplings. Maybe a little fluffier than most. On the other hand, maybe not.

Then came Icy Tea-Based Refresher. This recipe was mimeographed, on a third of a sheet of paper (more cost-cutting).

As written it produced seven quarts. "That's a lot of Icy Tea-Based Refresher," I said to myself, and I cut it in half. I'm glad I did. Three guests and I drank one glass each. Nobody wanted seconds. The consensus was that if there were a tea-flavor Kool-Aid, it would probably taste lots better than Icy Tea-Based Refresher, which was watery, sweet and flat. I poured the other 2½ quarts down the sink. To keep it sweet-smelling.

The next recipe to arrive was the only one worth the trouble of sending away for, although I'm still not sure that any recipe is worth $2.36. This was the recipe for Sauerkraut Fudge Cake. It was nicely typed on a full sheet of paper, cleanly duplicated, and was accompanied by a bonus recipe, on another sheet — this one for Prune-Spice Cake. There was also a note suggesting that I might want to send for some additional cake recipes, and the note was signed (albeit illegibly). It felt like I was doing business with somebody instead of throwing money away.

And the recipe was pretty good. It contained much more chocolate (both cocoa and semisweet chocolate pieces) than the standard sauerkraut chocolate cake, and it also contained a half-pint of sour cream that isn't in the more traditional recipe. And the frosting went with it very well. The folks who ate it liked it a lot.

Then came "Prize-Winning Italian Dessert." Any feelings I had about being ripped off by the first two recipes were nothing compared with this one. It was photocopied directly from a cookbook! So much for copyright laws. Besides that, it's a fairly standard recipe, that must appear in darn-near half of the general-purpose cookbooks on the shelves.

It's for Sabayon (or Zabaglione or Zabaione or three or four other spellings) — a French or Italian dessert that might have won a prize in the 19th century but has hardly been unusual enough to do so since. (Is the hot dog a prize-winning American delicacy?)

Anyway, I made it and it tasted more or less like it was supposed to. Actually, it was kind of heavy on the wine.

The last thing I ordered (the three outstanding, award-winning cakes for $3) hasn't arrived yet, and it's been a month. Somehow, although I'm pretty sure I've been stung on that one, I don't mind it as much as the photocopied page out of the cookbook.

FOR $1.25, I'll tell you the end of the story. No? Frankly, I'm puzzled. Here I am, willing to part with more than $8.44 worth of recipes and a whole lot more insightful stuff for a mere $1.25 (licensed drivers only, please; you must be over 18 to enter; offer void where prohibited) and you're not interested. What do I have to do?

Well, let me tell you just a little more, then.

How about if I give you the recipes I got?

I might have felt bad about giving away other people's recipes like that (except, of course, for the Sabayon). But I don't, because of what I learned later. I won't tell you *that* for nothing.

Sabayon (or Zabaglione)

6 egg yolks
⅔ c. sugar
Grated rind of half an orange
1 c. (or less) white wine or marsala
1 tbsp. rum or kirsch (optional)

Put cold water in the bottom of a double boiler. Put egg yolks and sugar in the top of the double boiler but do not place over the heat.

Whip the yolks and sugar. Add the orange rind and the wine and beat constantly.

Put the pan on the heat and beat constantly until the sauce is thick and creamy. Remove from heat. Add the rum or kirsch if you like. (Or you might like to cut the wine in half.)

Serve hot. (Serves six as a hot pudding or drink.)

That saved you **$2.36.**

Danish Dumplings

1 c. water
½ c. butter
1 c. flour
¼ tsp. salt
2 tsp. baking powder
4 eggs
3 tbsp. chopped parsley
1 (10¾-oz.) can condensed chicken broth (or stew or other accompaniment to dumplings)

Bring water and butter to a boil. Add flour, salt and baking powder. Mix and cook one minute until mixture holds together in a solid mass. Remove from heat. Cool slightly and beat in eggs one at a time, mixing thoroughly after each addition.

If using chicken broth, dilute according to instructions and bring to simmer.

Add parsley to dumpling batter, then drop by tablespoons into simmering broth or stew. Cover and simmer for 20 minutes.

(The dumplings puff up while simmering and fall after they are uncovered.)

That saved you another **$2.36.** Total saving so far, **$4.72.**

Icy Tea-Based Refresher

(Makes 7 quarts)
(But none of them is any good)
3 tea bags
1 c. grape juice
1 c. orange juice or 2 heaping tbsp. powdered orange drink mix
½ c. lemon juice
1½ c. sugar

Bring a tea kettle full of water to boiling. In a very large pot, pour the boiling water over the tea bags. Let it steep until it is strong. While it is still warm, add remaining ingredients and enough water and ice to total seven quarts. Stir.

Serve thoroughly chilled. Taste is different when not cold.

(That last is the recipe seller's own note. We found that the taste when cold was nonexistent.)

That saved you **$1.36,** or more if you take my advice and don't make it. Total savings so far, at least **$6.08.**

Sauerkraut Fudge Cake

(Recipe requires 10-inch tube pan)
(You can make it in a Bundt pan, but it might stick)
⅔ c. sauerkraut
2¼ c. flour
1 tsp. baking powder
1 tsp. soda
¼ tsp. salt
½ c. unsweetened cocoa powder
⅔ c. butter or margarine
1½ c. sugar
2 eggs
8 oz. sour cream
1 tsp. vanilla
1 c. water
1 c. semisweet chocolate chips
<u>Penuche glaze:</u>
¼ c. butter
½ c. brown sugar
2 tbsp. hot milk
¾ c. sifted confectioners' sugar

Thoroughly grease a 10-inch tube pan. Cut a ring of brown paper to fit the bottom of the pan and grease that, too.

Drain and rinse the sauerkraut and snip it into very small pieces.

Sift together the flour, baking powder, soda, salt and cocoa. Set aside.

Cream butter and sugar until fluffy, and add eggs one at a time, beating well after each. Beat in the sour cream and vanilla.

Alternately add dry ingredients and water, stirring after each addition and beginning and ending with the dry ingredients. Fold in sauerkraut and chocolate chips.

Turn into prepared pan and bake at 350 degrees 55 minutes to an hour, or until cake is springy. (Toothpick test won't work.)

Remove from oven, cool 10 minutes, loosen cake from sides of pan with knife and invert on serving plate. Peel paper from top.

Prepare glaze: Melt butter and brown sugar together. Boil one minute or until slightly thickened. Cool 10 minutes, then beat in hot milk. Add sifted confectioners' sugar, stirring, until of glaze consistency. Drizzle over slightly warm cake.

That saved you **$2.36.** Grand total savings, at least **$8.44.** How can you pass this up?

OK, YOU DRIVE a hard bargain. For 50 cents, I'll tell you how well this recipe business is succeeding for the people who place the ads.

I must admit I was tempted several years ago to try it out myself. What deterred me from doing that was a full-page advertisement that I saw in the Saturday Review. The ad was for a $9.95 book on how to make a lot of money by selling brochures and recipes in classified ads. It went on and on with examples of people who had money pouring out of post-office boxes at them, and in a little box in the middle of the page was a test you could do to verify that it really works.

Long ago, on some early trip to a state fair, my father pointed out to me that when a pitchman says "You don't have to take my word for it," he wants you to take his word for it. And that the more he explains how you can verify what he's saying, the more people will take his word for it.

(I think my father's life study has been pitchmen. He loves them. Whenever we'd go to the fair, we'd spend most of our time watching guys selling pen-and-pencil sets and blenders. And every time he goes, my father buys some pitchman's cabbage slicer, with which he eventually cuts his thumb.)

The test in the advertisement for the book suggested that you examine a couple of issues of one of these magazines at the library and compare the classified ads. The issues should be 10 or 12 months apart, and what you'll find, the book ad said, is that many of the same classified ads appear in both issues. Nobody keeps an ad running if it doesn't make money, the book ad claimed, so they must work.

I went to the library last week and performed the test. I compared the July 1980 Atlantic (24 recipe ads) with the May 1981 Atlantic (31 recipe ads); there were no duplications. Nor were there any duplications between the May 1980 Saturday Review recipe ads and those appearing in March 1981.

Thanks for the lesson, Dad.

LOOK, YOU'VE hung on here this long, it's GOT to be worth 25 cents to you to know how it all comes out.

By sending second letters to the same addresses and begging the folks who had placed the ads to call me collect, I got one response (from Cynthia Habegger, in Bloomington, Ind., the woman with the businesslike approach and the Sauerkraut Fudge Cake).

Preliminaries out of the way, I asked her how she had decided to place one of these ads. Had she bought the $9.95 book? No, she said, she just saw the ads and thought it looked like a good way to make some money.

How long had the ad been running? Just one month, she said.

And how was it doing?

WE'RE DOWN to the wire here. I won't beg. If you're prepared to take $8.44 worth of recipes and aren't willing to give me even the time of day for the Ultimate Secret of the ads in the backs of magazines, I'm not going to try to drag another penny out of you.

So here it is, free, gratis and for nothing:

How many responses did Cynthia Habegger's ad get?

Counting mine, three.

Three? At $2 each, Habegger pulled in $6, minus her duplicating costs — and the cost of the ad. At $1.50 a word, her 16-word ad cost $24. So her net loss was more than $18. At least she hadn't bought the $9.95 book, too.

If that ad pulled in all of three responses from the entire United States, I don't feel too bad about subtracting you folks from the remaining likely buyers of the recipes reproduced here.

Well, actually, Habegger said, there were more than three responses. She got some chain letters. You send your recipe to a bunch of other people, and soon you'll be getting thousands of recipes in the mail. Habegger didn't sound like she believes in chain letters.

Neither does my father.

Where Snack Foods Come From

When I was a kid in Milwaukee, my cub-scout troop went through the factory where Mrs. Howe's potato chips were made.

I have only the vaguest memories of what the factory was like. All I recall with certainty is lots of very big machines (I was very little), the last of which spewed potato chips into boxes, and that we got some potato chips to eat.

But that tour established quite firmly in my mind what many other people know too — even people who never heard of Mrs. Howe: Potato chips come from factories.

As I grew up and encountered other crunchy things that came in boxes or bags, my powerful mind established these related conclusions: Corn chips come from factories; pretzels come from factories; cheese curls come from factories, and, more recently, sesame chips come from factories.

In the past few years, however, I have prepared in my kitchen a fair number of things that ordinarily come from factories (including marshmallows, English muffins and rather excellent home-brewed versions of Grape-Nuts and Twinkies), and it occurred to me recently that I might do the same thing with crunchy snack foods.

This attempt ought not to be quite so hard to understand as was the adventure of the marshmallows, for example. Although already-popped popcorn has long been available in bags, most people prefer to pop their own. Why not, then, home-made potato chips, corn chips, pretzels, cheese curls and sesame chips?

Some of you are probably huffing indignantly that you've been making your own potato chips for years. Some, but not many.

It's true that lots of cookbooks indicate that potato chips are still within our grasp. It was a lot harder to find recipes for the other items.

In some cases I made up my own.

In some cases I failed miserably.

This, then, is a story of triumph and tragedy, of victory and defeat, and a long day's journey into deep fat.

First, potato chips, the most obvious and the least difficult of today's exercises.

I must say that I was quite surprised at how good home-made potato chips turned out to be. They are very good indeed.

Potato Chips

1 or 2 large baking potatoes
Oil and/or shortening for frying
Salt

One large potato makes a medium bowlful of potato chips. Two would make a very large batch. (Really. A big potato weighs eight or nine ounces; a box of potato chips, including a bit of oil, weighs about the same.)

The trick in making good potato chips is obtaining nice, thin uniform slices. A food processor, unless yours is very different from mine, produces slices that are uniform but much too thick. You might be able to do it with a very sharp knife, but it would be dicey (or maybe, in this case, slicey) and awfully tedious.

Happily, a simple solution exists: Use a vegetable peeler.

Wash and peel the potatoes and use the peeler to cut them into paper-thin slices. (It's best to cut in one direction only — widthwise or lengthwise, so that all the slices are about the same size.) Put the slices in a bowl, fill it with cold water and swish things around gently to get rid of surface starch. Dry the slices on paper towels.

In a deep pot, heat the oil (some folks recommend using half oil and half vegetable shortening) to 375 degrees. When the oil is hot, put in a handful of the slices (about a third of a potato) — too many at once would cool the oil and make the chips greasy. Stir the oil to separate any slices that cling together, and fry until they look like potato chips — light golden and crisp — between three and four minutes.

Drain the chips on paper towels, salt them and repeat with the remaining slices.

Next come corn chips. Obviously you don't make them by deep-frying sliced corn. Neither, I established in several frustrating hours, do you make them by deep-frying any kind of rolled-out corn-meal batter. Most of the chips dissolve in the oil, and the corn-meal grains in the survivors are large and gritty. Not right at all. Phooey.

Then in a sudden, blinding flash, it became clear. What you need to do is to make tortillas, cut them into chip size and deep-fry them.

If that makes them tortilla chips instead of corn chips, so be it. They fried beautifully, and the first one, tried hesitantly — tremblingly — tasted just like a corn chip to me.

What a breakthrough that was! I felt like stout Cortez when, as you may re-call, with eagle eyes he stared at the Pacific and all his men looked at each other with a wild surmise, silent upon a peak in Darien. I was silent, too, having hit my peak in Minneapolis.

Where is Keats when you need him?

To make these, you'll need fine corn flour, which is available in many supermarkets under its Spanish name — masa harina.

Corn Chips

2 c. masa harina
1⅛ c. warm water
Oil and/or shortening for frying
Salt

Stir the water into the masa harina in a bowl. It should make a firm mass, a bit moist but not at all wet.

Now we're going to flatten it out. Expert tortilla makers use their hands; some folks own tortilla presses; Frito-Lay certainly uses machines. We'll adopt a sensible compromise and roll them out between sheets of plastic wrap.

Heat a deep pot of oil to 375 degrees.

Divide the dough into 10 or 12 roughly equal pieces. Place one on a sheet of plastic wrap and cover it with a second sheet. Using a rolling pin, roll the dough out into a rough square about 5½ inches or so on a side. (A 6-inch circle will do, too; you'll just have more scraps to add to the next batch of dough.) Make sure the dough is quite flat; thick spots will make thick, tough chips.

Carefully peel back the top sheet of wrap. (If a little dough sticks to it, don't worry about it; there's plenty left.) Flip the dough down onto a clean countertop and carefully peel off the other sheet. Now cut the dough into rectangles about ½ inch by 1 inch. Ease them onto a spatula and drop them into the hot oil.

(That business with all the plastic wrap sounds a bit complicated, but it's not really. And if you roll the tortillas out directly on the counter they'll stick like glue.)

Fry the chips for three to four minutes, until they are light golden brown. (Meanwhile you can be rolling out the next rectangle, incorporating any odd scraps from the last one.) Drain on paper towels and salt very well. Repeat with the remaining dough.

Some chips develop a sort of double layer, with a bubble between — I think those are from slightly thicker areas of dough. These may be a bit tough at first, but if you let them air-dry a day or so they'll be fine.

Buoyed by that experience (and by my ability to spell buoyed), I moved immediately to what I knew would be my biggest challenge: cheese curls. I was unable to find even a scrap of information about cheese curls in any cookbook, so I decided to try the direct approach: Read the ingredients off a commercial label, mix up lots of batches in different proportions and hope. It's not sure-fire, but it often works.

The ingredients varied a bit from brand to brand, but basically they were corn, oil and cheese. Early experience proved that, all other problems aside, if the cheese went into the batter before the batter was fried, it boiled out into the oil and became very unpleasant. Carefully licking the outside of some commercial cheese curls and then eating them verified my conclusion: These are corn curls, dipped in powdered cheese.

So the problem became how one makes corn curls. I'll spare you hours (in fact, days) of agony. Nothing I tried

worked. They either fell apart in the oil or were chewy and tough. Clearly they needed to have lots of air whipped into them to make them light and crunchy, but there was nothing like egg white involved to sustain the air.

(I even tried putting egg white in some of them. They were light, chewy and tough.)

Finally, suspecting the worst — that some sort of special machine is intrinsic to their manufacture — I decided to ask somebody in the business. There are a lot of outfits making cheese curls, so I knew that the process is no industrial secret, but I suspected that I wouldn't make much headway if I tried to ask somebody at a giant concern like Frito-Lay. So I called Pate Foods in Hopkins, who turn out a fine cheese curl, among other things.

Tom Vucicevic, with whom I spoke, was very pleasant about it, although he acknowledged that he wasn't on very close terms with the process. The clear upshot, however, was what I feared: A pressurized machine poots the curls of aerated batter out into the hot oil.

Unless somebody out there knows something else, so much for home-made cheese curls.

Some things really *do* come from factories.

Pretzels don't, though. They come from your oven — or so I thought.

Shape aside, there are two basic kinds of pretzels. Big, soft ones, sold warm from carts, and the little crunchy ones that come in bags.

First the big, soft ones, a recipe adapted from a nice book called Make Your Own Groceries, by Daphne Hartwig.

Big, Soft Pretzels

1 (¼-oz.) env. active dry yeast
1 c. warm water
¼ c. sugar
1 tsp. salt
2 tbsp. softened shortening
1 egg, separated
1 tbsp. water
3½ c. flour, approximately
Coarse salt

Soften the yeast in the warm water in a large mixing bowl. After a few minutes, stir in the sugar, salt and shortening.

Put half of the egg yolk (approximately; it's no big deal) and the tablespoon of water in a cup, mix and set aside, tightly covered, in the refrigerator.

Add the rest of the egg yolk and the egg white to the yeast mixture and beat in two cups of flour until the dough is smooth.

Beat in more flour until the dough is stiff. Cover the bowl tightly and refrigerate overnight.

Lightly flour a countertop and cut the dough into 32 equal pieces. Roll each piece into a rope about 12 to 14 inches long, and shape into a pretzel:

Form a U. Fold the left arm of the U down across the bottom of the right arm. Fold the right arm down across the bottom of where the left arm used to start. Twist the ends of the arms together half a turn. Press the ends firmly into what was the bottom of the U (work the dough in until it won't separate — "gluing" it in place with water doesn't work all that well).

The dough can be made into 16 pretzels instead of 32, but they are so fat they are hard to shape.

Put the pretzels on lightly greased cookie sheets, brush with the yolk-water mixture and sprinkle lightly with coarse salt. (Careful: If you overdo the salt, the pretzels will look wonderful and be almost inedible.)

Cover the pretzels loosely with waxed paper and let them rise in a warm place for about 30 minutes, until they have doubled in bulk. Preheat the oven to 400 degrees.

Bake for about 15 minutes, until they are dark — pretzel-colored, in fact. Serve warm.

Recipes for little, crunchy pretzels were not so easy to find, but I finally unearthed two, and they were very similar. They read rather surprisingly like the recipes for bagels — after the dough is shaped, the pretzels are dropped into boiling liquid until they float, then they're brushed with beaten egg and salt and baked.

Both recipes called for the boiling liquid to contain both baking soda and carbonate of ammonia, which I picked up at a pharmacy as ammonium carbonate. It smelled very strongly of ammonia, but I checked it out and established that, dreadful as it smells, it is indeed a leavening agent, that it decomposes on heating and that it's the principal ingredient in "smelling salts" (when was the last time you heard of *them?*), so I guessed that a bit of it in a lot of water wasn't necessarily harmful. (It's also used in some Christmas cookies.) Nonetheless I tried the recipes in two pots — one with and one without the ammonium carbonate.

Both recipes also called for ground caraway seeds to be mixed with the flour and for ground cumin to be sprinkled on the finished pretzels before baking. Intrigued, I tried one batch of dough with white flour and another with rye flour. I wanted to see if you could taste the cumin through the rye.

If you'll stop groaning, I'll wrap this

up: None of the pretzels worked. With ammonium carbonate or without; with white flour or rye. They all *looked* fine, they even tasted right, although the rye ones had a bit of a health-food flavor. But they were all tough and chewy. When I baked them longer, they were tooth-breakingly hard. And rolling and shaping lots of small pretzels was an impractical amount of work, too, even had they been good.

I remain convinced, though, that they can be made successfully (if tediously) at home. Having just said that they're too much work, I'm bound to hear from someone who has made them once a week for the last 50 years. When I do, I'll pass long his or her recipe.

Let's finish on a positive note. Sesame chips worked wonderfully well. Here, too, I had nothing to go on but the ingredients listed on labels, and I had to improvise on those (I don't have any soy protein isolate), but they were delicious.

Sesame Chips

1¼ c. flour
1½ tsp. soy sauce
½ c. water
3½ tbsp. sesame seeds
1 tsp. salt
Oil and/or shortening for frying

Combine all ingredients except oil. The dough should be firm and moist, not wet (add flour or water as needed).

Roll the dough out *very* thin on an unfloured surface. Heat the oil to 375 degrees. Cut the dough into rectangles ½ inch by 1 inch. Ease 20 or so onto a spatula, drop them into the oil and fry three to four minutes until they are dark golden brown. Drain on paper towels and salt if desired. Eat while frying the rest. They're GOOD!

After all this deep frying, the writer has considered having his circulatory system purged with 409.

Follow-Up

After the preceding failure to achieve corn curls appeared in the newspaper, I got a call from Al Heigl, of Eagan, who told me that his father, Cyrus Heigl, helped develop the corn curl and the cheese curl in the late '30s and early '40s for an outfit in Beloit, Wis., called Adams Corp. (later acquired by Beatrice Foods).

The younger Heigl describes his father's job in ensuing years as "bringing corn curls to the benighted of the world." Should you be, for example, in Iran and want a corn curl, there are machines there to make them.

I called the corn-curl Heigl in Beloit, and he described both the manufacturing process and the discovery. It's interesting, but it's not as important as the transistor, so let's keep it short.

Corn or corn meal is heated by friction. Steam produced from the moisture in the corn is trapped, and as the mash is extruded, the steam sprongs it out — sort of like puffed wheat.

Then the pieces are fried, salted and cheesed.

Now to the important question. Can you make them in your kitchen?

Well, the elder Heigl chuckled, not really. Running a corn-curl machine with two six-inch disks requires about 40 horsepower. "And you'd only get a couple hundred pounds an hour."

Two by Two

Have you ever noticed that many expressive terms in our language that should by all logic be one word are instead pairs of words?

That wasn't very clear, I'm sure, so let's go to the videotape.

Here we see a collection of what might be called junk or debris. Whatever it is, it isn't two things. But listen now as somebody calls it "flotsam and jetsam."

(Don't be a jerk and ask that person which is the flotsam and which is the jetsam. The combination, once two words with distinct meanings, is just part and parcel of the language — woven inextricably into the very warp and woof of our speech.)

Our next clip shows a person who is remarkably active for his advanced age. He is described as having plenty of "vim and vigor." I'd settle for some of either one.

There's a whole kit and caboodle of such paired terms floating around, giving form and substance to our thoughts.

Don't raise a hue and cry — this is a nuts-and-bolts food article, and we are getting to the food.

See, there are lots of food pairs, too — alliances so natural that we don't even think about them. (I have to get to the food eventually — I can bob and weave only so long.)

When peanut butter was invented, for example, it is probable that the inventor's very next words (after "tastes more like fresh-roasted peanuts") were "Does anybody have some jelly?"

And whichever came first, once somebody got one of the eggs away from one of the chickens he probably served it with ham — or maybe with bacon.

I could huff and puff and produce a list of such natural food pairs, but it would be quite long indeed.

And it is constantly growing, as one year's new-and-different combination becomes next year's tried-and-true standby. That happened to peanut butter and bananas in my lifetime.

There are also, of course, food combinations that *don't* catch on. It didn't happen, for example, to cottage cheese and ketchup, said to be a lunchtime favorite of Richard Nixon. The fans of that combination are few and far between.

(Each will now write an indignant letter, so in a few weeks I will be able to tell you exactly how many there are.)

I was musing about food the other day, on and off, now and again, when I thought of a potentially interesting combination. As I jotted it down I realized that there were several other combination ideas echoing through the canyons of my mind, just waiting for me to give them a try.

As long as they were coming fast and furious, I decided to put my heart and soul into it and have a whole dinner of things that might go together (or might not).

Enough of this and that. If we don't cook soon, you'll be skin and bones instead of fat and sassy.

Come and get it.

The appetizer for this dinner of possibly great combinations is hardly a combination at all — and I'm cheating a bit by presenting it here as something that just occurred to me. I have fairly often used up leftover hollandaise sauce by dipping crackers in it, but I did it only in the privacy of my own kitchen.

It only occurred to me to *serve* the sauce that way when I got a letter from a reader suggesting it. It's very rich but surprisingly good.

I have since misplaced the letter, or I would supply all 579,847 of you with the reader's name. (Who was that masked reader? I wanted to thank him.)

If I still had the name, those of you who prefer bulgur or tofu to hollandaise sauce as chip dip could have written directly to the source of the problem. As it is, I will bear the slings and arrows. But that's OK, because I'm all wool and a yard wide.

Hollandaise and Crackers

4 egg yolks
Juice of 1 large lemon
2 tsp. water
½ lb. (2 sticks) salted butter, each
     stick divided into 8 pieces
Pinch of pepper
Salt
Crackers, chips, etc.

In the top of an unheated double boiler or in a light saucepan, beat together the egg yolks, lemon juice and water. Turn on the heat (very low if using a saucepan) and add two pieces (about two tablespoons) of the butter, stirring constantly with a wooden spoon until the butter is absorbed and the mixture is the consistency of a paste.

(Normally, hollandaise sauce should be made with unsalted butter, for a creamier taste, but as a dip it benefits from some salt.)

Incorporate the remainder of the butter, two pieces at a time, in the same fashion, adding butter just as the last of the previous pieces have almost disappeared. If the mixture starts to separate at all, remove from the heat immediately and stir like crazy until the melted butter is reincorporated.

You may have to take the pan on and off the heat several times.

Stir in the pepper, pour into a dish, allow to cool a few minutes if the idea of a hot cracker dip bothers you, adjust the amount of salt (adjusting upwards is much easier than adjusting downwards), and serve.

Serves eight to ten.

Those of you who pay good money every week to read this stuff already know that I'm not overfond of salads.

In fact, I'm barely tolerant of salads. The kind of understanding I've always had with salads runs to mutual nonaggression: If I agree not to eat them, they agree not to spoil my appetite for better stuff.

But I do like salad dressings, and they seem to go best on salads — although, now that I think about it, I haven't tried them as chip dips. Anyway, for several months I've been aware that in the back of my head I have wanted to make a salad dressing with bacon, honey and mustard. Now I've done it, and I'm glad. (It's very good.)

Let there be no wailing and gnashing of teeth by salad lovers: Part of the goodness of the dressing was the spinach and lettuce it went on.

Bacon-Honey-Mustard Salad

6 slices bacon
2 tsp. Dijon mustard
Salt and pepper
6 tbsp. olive or vegetable oil
1 tbsp. honey
1½ tsp. white wine vinegar
1 (12-oz.) bag fresh spinach
½ head lettuce

Cut the bacon into 1-inch pieces and fry until crisp. Drain. Set aside.

Meanwhile, combine mustard, salt and pepper.

Stir in the oil, a little at a time, until all is absorbed. Stir in the honey and the vinegar.

Wash the spinach and remove the tough stems.

Tear the spinach and the lettuce and put in the serving bowl.

Add the drained bacon to the dressing and warm it gently, stirring. Pour over the greens and toss.

Serves six to eight.

For the main dish I decided to see whether olive oil would go well with chicken.

It would, indeed.

I substituted it for butter in a sautéed-chicken-and-sauce dish that has long been one of my favorites. It is based on a recipe in Mastering the Art of French Cooking. Not only did the sauce — a not-very-distant relative of hollandaise — pick up a little extra tang from the olive oil, but the chicken browned much more prettily.

Now I wonder whether the old economics cliché about guns and butter wouldn't work better as guns and olive oil.

Olive-Oil Chicken

⅓ c. olive oil
6 single chicken breasts (3 whole
    breasts)
1 tsp. basil
½ tsp. tarragon
Salt and pepper
4 cloves garlic, unpeeled
½ c. plus 1 tbsp. dry white wine,
    divided
2 egg yolks
1 tbsp. lemon juice

Heat the olive oil over medium heat in a large pan (an electric frypan is nice), add the chicken, skin side down, and sauté, turning several times, for five or six minutes.

Sprinkle with the basil, tarragon, salt and pepper, and drop the garlic cloves into the oil.

Cover the pan and cook about 10 minutes. Uncover, turn the chicken and baste it with the oil. Continue to cook, basting and turning, until it is done — 20 to 30 more minutes, depending on how you like your chicken. Check by piercing with a fork. Any juices should be pale.

Remove the chicken from the pan to a warm oven.

Crush the garlic cloves in the pan with the back of a wooden spoon, removing and discarding the peel.

Turn up the heat under the oil, pour in the half cup of wine and boil down the wine-oil mixture, scraping at the pan with the wooden spoon to get up all the nice little bits of chicken and garlic, until the volume is about half what it was after you added the wine.

In the top of a double boiler or in a light saucepan, beat the egg yolks and the lemon juice and the remaining tablespoon of wine.

Then beat in the cooking liquid — a

spoonful at a time at first, a little more rapidly as you near the end. When all the liquid is in, heat the sauce a few minutes over boiling water (or over very low direct heat), stirring until it thickens. Don't overdo it or it will separate.

Pour the sauce over the chicken or into a gravy dish. Serves six. (The sauce goes very well over long-grain and wild rice mix, too.)

A vegetable marriage didn't occur to me until I was just about ready to cook. I knew that onions go well with almost everything, but I couldn't think of anything that they weren't already well associated with.

Then I got it. You don't very often hear of *corn* and onions. Judging by this experiment (in which, of course, I also threw in some butter and cream), you should hear of that combination every five minutes. It was delicious. The rank and file will love it.

Onion Corn

2 (10-oz.) pkg. frozen corn
3 medium onions, coarsely chopped
5½ tbsp. butter, divided
2 to 3 tbsp. cream
½ tsp. or more salt
Pepper

Cook corn according to package directions. Drain very well (put it in a colander or sieve and let it drain, then press gently to get out a little more water).

Sauté the onions in four tablespoons of the butter slowly until they are barely golden. Stir in the corn and the cream, salt and pepper and heat through. When almost ready to serve, stir in the remaining 1½ tablespoons of butter, just until it is melted.

Serves six to eight.

If I must be honest (and why not — I'm among friends), it was the surfacing of the following chocolate combination from somewhere deep in my soul that made me come up with this entire combination-recipes theme, just so I could have some excuse for making the dessert.

It combines two of my favorite kitchen aromas, and I wanted an excuse to try it out. It sounded great to me — and it was.

But you must trust me. It might not sound good to you. Take a deep breath. Ready?

It's chocolate . . . and . . . vermouth. Dry white vermouth.

Now, now. Hold on. There are lots of recipes in which chocolate is combined with rum, with brandy, with kirsch, with Grand Marnier. So why not with dry vermouth? In fact, what happens is not that the chocolate acquires a vermouth overtone, which might be kind of odd. It seems to just enhance the winy quality of the chocolate. And it's gooood.

If you're not comfortable with that, make this same little treat without the vermouth, or substituting one of the other boozes mentioned above. It'll be fine any way at all.

It is a simple little goodie, since what I wanted to do was just try out the flavor, and I didn't feel like going to elaborate lengths.

Oh, a lie! And I had decided no more than seven paragraphs ago to be honest. OK; enough to and fro. Let's be open and above-board. *Before* I made the simple little treat, I tried making some chocolate-vermouth *truffles.* They bombed. We'll work that out another time.

Glop-Topped Cookies

1½ c. heavy cream
4 tbsp. (½ stick) unsalted butter
1 (12-oz.) pkg. semisweet chocolate
    chips
3 tbsp. sugar
3 tbsp. dry white vermouth (or, if you
    must fiddle, some other booze or
    no booze at all)
1 (7- to 12-oz.) box vanilla wafers
    (you'll have some left in any
    case)

Put the cream and butter in a medium saucepan and bring to the boil over medium heat. Remove from the heat, add the chocolate and sugar and stir until the chocolate is fully melted in. Cool and stir in the vermouth.

Cool the pan in the refrigerator (or freezer, but be much more attentive), stirring it occasionally, until it is the consistency of very thick cream or honey. If you inadvertently let it get fully hard, let it warm until you can stir it.

Whip as you would cream, until it is stiff.

Top vanilla wafers with very big blobs of it. (Blade a big peak of it on a cookie with a metal spatula or, for a prettier effect, pipe a big peak of it on with a pastry bag.)

Makes enough wonderful glop to top about three dozen cookies (or more if you hold back — unwisely — on the size of the blob on each cookie).

Had enough combinations? Then hail and farewell.

Little Mystery #3: Coffee

What is the purpose of the little door on the coffee vending machine? It's down when the paper cup drops in the wrong position, and by the time you see what has happened and lift it, all your coffee is down the drain. It also prevents you from getting a cup of coffee when you're carrying something in your other hand, and if — as sometimes happens — it is already lodged in the open position, it invariably falls on your hand when you reach in to get your cup of coffee, splashing it all over the sleeve of your nice new sweater.

Solution: According to a spokesperson for Coffeemat, a manufacturer of coffee vending machines in Kenilworth, N.J., it's called a "sanitation door" and it's there to comply with various health codes around the country.

Say you're a production firm, the vendperson said, and you work with fiberglass. Inside of every vending machine like this there's an exhaust fan to cool various components, and it's going to draw air into the machine that may be contaminated with fiberglass particles or whatever. The little door is there to prevent getting that contamination into the area where the coffee is dispensed.

Well . . . all right, but surely it would be possible to isolate that area from the exhaust fan. Is that the only reason?

No. Another — much clearer (but not very tasteful) — example of the sanitation use was provided by a fellow at Interstate United, a local vending-service firm: It keeps people from tossing gum wrappers and cigarette butts into the drain.

The Batter-Up Dinner

Those who cleave unto the words of Joe Garagiola know that baseball's exhibition season has begun.

Those who are not sports fans may not care, but it is a fact nonetheless and it must be reckoned with, along with the Super Bowl, the Stanley Cup and the Indianapolis 500.

One season following another, laden with happiness and beers.

I myself am not a sports fan. I confess, for example, that I only pay enough attention to the Olympics to know when I can get away with singing "Born to Luge."

And I have not paid much attention to baseball since the Milwaukee Braves traded Bobby Thomson about 1957. My grandmother, a pretty ardent fan, survived that one but was laid low by the similar fate of Billy Bruton.

Until those chilling events, I did follow events in the National League in some detail.

I was pretty young at the time, and I think I can be forgiven what might now seem to be shallowness of commitment.

In fact, the year I took a girl to the opening Braves game I was so young that when she said that she was cold I bought her a cup of hot chocolate.

And she didn't even like the hot chocolate.

Well, enough of my early sex life, such as it wasn't. How, you are probably muttering, can anything even remotely like this be related to food?

I thought you'd never mutter.

It is my pleasure today to bring together ever so briefly the world of the 90-foot diamond with that of the 9- by 13-inch pan; the arena of the horsehide sphere with that of the beef steak, and the field of the 36-ounce bat with that of the stainless-steel whisk.

Ladeez and gentlemen: Presenting a meal in which every dish is based on the same batter — the Batter-Up Dinner!

Now just a minute. Don't start filing out of the stadium. Give me a chance to explain!

See, the dishes that are all based on this one batter are somewhat different from each other, and many of them are very normal dishes enjoyed by millions of standard Americans.

Not *everything* I make is weird.

For today's dinner, we're going to have popovers, soup with egg-drop-like noodles, steak and Yorkshire pudding, crepes, and a puffy banana sort-of pancake with chocolate sauce.

Yes, you read that correctly. Big, puffy popovers and ever-so-flat crepes can be made from the same batter. Just one of the wonders of modern science.

But enough infield chatter. Time to put one over the plate.

After a short stop:

All of these recipes really use absolutely identical batter. So if you're going to make more than one, just make one bigger batch of batter.

If you're going to make them all, you might want to divide the resulting very large batch in two.

We want Batter-Up, not Batter All Over.

OK. Right off the bat, let's make popovers. I know we've already made them in a previous incarnation, but there is a rounded, Aristotelian wholeness to this article that the artist in me feels would be destroyed were I to omit the popover recipe. Besides, it's already been typed. So we're going to do it all again.

After painful exchanges with readers who followed this recipe the last time and had it produce little fat rocks instead of light, airy popovers, I won't say this time that you can't make popovers fail. You can make them fail if you want to.

I will say that it isn't easy to make them fail.

Popovers

1 c. sifted flour
3 eggs
1 c. milk
2 tbsp. melted butter

Put the sifted flour in a large bowl. In a smaller bowl, beat the eggs lightly. Add the milk to the eggs and mix well. Add the liquid gradually to the flour, beating with a mixer or a wire whisk. Beat in the melted butter, just long enough to smooth out the batter (30 seconds or so).

I don't know how to continue with these directions without making the same mistake I made the last time: I really found that almost any method produced popovers. And I tried it lots of ways. I even slammed the oven door on them. But I *won't* say that you can't make them fail.

Maybe it will be better if I don't give you any choices.

Preheat the oven to 400 degrees.

Heavily grease 9 to 12 (I'll give you *that* much choice, anyway) custard cups or a muffin tin with 9 to 12 cups. Grease all across the top of the tin, too. Pour the bat-

ter into the cups (and put a little water in any unused cups in the muffin tin).

Bake for 40 to 45 minutes if you're making 12 popovers, or 50 to 55 minutes if the same amount of batter is used to make nine popovers, which will be somewhat larger and need longer to bake.

Since the popovers are the appetizer for the Batter-Up Dinner, I offer here a nice dip to spread on them should you want (for some unfathomable reason) not to follow the dictates of common sense by eating them with large amounts of butter.

Dill Dip for Popovers

(or for anything else, for that matter)
¾ c. mayonnaise
¾ c. dairy sour cream
1 to 1½ tbsp. dill weed
½ tsp. seasoned salt
2 or 3 drops Tabasco sauce
½ tsp. Worcestershire sauce
1½ tbsp. finely chopped onion

Combine mayonnaise, sour cream, dill weed, salt, Tabasco sauce, Worcestershire sauce and onion.

That's it.

Not everything I make is complicated, either.

Oh, yes. If you're making this dip in the summer, you ought to keep it covered — just in case of infield flies.

To demonstrate the incredible versatility of this batter, let's take an intentional walk over to the soup pot and make some little drop dumplings.

And since we're going to have to drop them into something, let's make this very nice and *very* easy soup.

Chicken-Beef Consommé with Little Drop Dumplings

Soup:
1 (10¾oz.) can chicken broth
1 (10¾oz.) can beef consommé
1½ soup cans water
1 tbsp. tomato paste
¼ c. dry white vermouth
3 tbsp. dry sherry
Tiny drop dumplings:
⅓ c. sifted flour
1 egg
⅓ c. milk
2 tsp. melted butter

Prepare the soup:

In a Dutch oven, combine the broth, consommé, water, tomato paste, vermouth and sherry. Bring to a boil and reduce to a simmer.

Meanwhile, prepare the dumpling batter:

Put the sifted flour in a large bowl. In a smaller bowl, beat the egg lightly. Add the milk to the egg and mix well. Add the liquid gradually to the flour, beating with a mixer or a wire whisk. Beat in the melted butter, just long enough to smooth out the batter (30 seconds or so).

Those of you who have been paying close attention will have noticed that the dumpling recipe is just one-third of the popover recipe. Goodness, you're sharp!

Drop the batter, a part of a teaspoonful at a time, into the lightly boiling soup and continue to cook for three to four minutes. The batter forms blobs that are sort of like irregular pieces of egg noodle.

Serves four to six.

For the main course of the Batter-

Up Dinner, I suppose fowl might have been appropriate, but I decided to strike out on my own and make steaks to serve over Yorkshire pudding.

Steak and Yorkshire Pudding

Pudding:
1 c. sifted flour
3 eggs
1 c. milk
2 tbsp. melted butter
Sauce:
4 tbsp. butter, divided
2 tbsp. finely chopped onion
2 tbsp. finely chopped shallots
1 c. dry white vermouth
1 (10¾-oz.) can chicken broth
Salt, pepper
1 tbsp. tomato paste
1 tsp. Worcestershire sauce
2 tbsp. flour
4 (6-oz.) steaks
1 tsp. chopped parsley

Prepare the Yorkshire pudding batter. By this time you must know how:

Put the sifted flour in a large bowl. In a smaller bowl, beat the eggs lightly. Add the milk to the eggs and mix well. Add the liquid gradually to the flour, beating with a mixer or a wire whisk. Beat in the melted butter, just long enough to smooth out the batter (30 seconds or so).

Preheat the oven to 375 degrees.

Heavily grease a 9- by 9-inch pan. Pour in the batter and bake about 35 to 40 minutes, until it is puffy and golden brown.

Meanwhile, prepare the sauce for the steaks:

Melt two tablespoons of the butter in a saucepan. Add the onions and shallots and cook over low heat until they are wilted. Add vermouth and chicken broth, salt and pepper to taste and the tomato paste and

Worcestershire sauce. Cook about five minutes.

While the liquid cooks, work the flour into the remaining two tablespoons of butter. Drop this handled butter into the liquid bit by bit, stirring constantly. When all the flour and butter have been added and the mixture is smooth, let it simmer over low heat for 15 minutes.

Prepare the steaks as you normally would (broil or pan-fry).

Stir the parsley into the sauce. Serve each steak with a section of the pudding and pour sauce over all. Serves four.

Time for a seventh-inning starch. And a vegetable. Let's try something rolled up in that early French invasion, the crepe.

For reasons not clear — at least not clear to me — while the quiche, a later arrival, has become as common as the hot dog (there are probably no young things around who are sweet sixteen and never been quiched), crepes have remained the least bit foreign and fancy. But they aren't hard to make.

I chose to wrap the crepes around some asparagus in lemon butter. You would do well not to make the mistake I made — I cooked the asparagus and then let it marinate several hours in the lemon butter. It tasted fine, but it was pretty soggy.

Asparagus Crepes

1 c. sifted flour
3 eggs
1 c. milk
2 tbsp. melted butter
Asparagus:
2 (10-oz.) pkg. frozen asparagus
    spears

6 tbsp. butter
2 tbsp. lemon juice
Salt, pepper
Sauce:
2½ tbsp. butter
2½ tbsp. flour
1⅔ c. milk
2½ tbsp. lemon juice
Salt
½ tsp. pepper

Guess how to make the crepe batter. That's right:

Put the sifted flour in a large bowl. In a smaller bowl, beat the eggs lightly. Add the milk to the eggs and mix well. Add the liquid gradually to the flour, beating with a mixer or a wire whisk. Beat in the melted butter, just long enough to smooth out the batter (30 seconds or so).

To make the batter into crepes, heat a small skillet over low-medium heat and butter it lightly. Add about two tablespoons of the batter, tilting the pan rapidly to cover it with the batter. Cook each crepe for about a minute, until the bottom is lightly browned. (If it takes more than a minute, raise the heat slightly for the remaining crepes or they will be dry. If the pan is too hot, on the other hand, the crepe will start to bake before you can get the batter to cover the bottom of the pan.)

Cook the other side of the crepe briefly. Cool the crepes, overlapping them slightly, on waxed paper. You'll have about 12 to 15.

Cook the asparagus according to package directions.

Melt the six tablespoons of butter, add the two tablespoons of lemon juice and salt and pepper to taste. Pour into a shallow bowl or pan, and add the asparagus spears. Allow to rest while you prepare the sauce:

In a small saucepan, melt the 2½ tablespoons of butter and stir in the flour. Cook over low heat, stirring, about one minute.

Very slowly stir in the milk, then the lemon juice, salt and pepper.

Preheat the oven to 350 degrees. Wrap three or four spears of asparagus in each crepe and put the rolled up crepes in a 9- by 13-inch pan. Pour the sauce over all and bake about 15 minutes, until heated through.

Makes 12 to 15 crepes.

Almost time to head for the showers. But first, dessert. And for that most pleasant of all courses, let's have a puffy banana pancake with chocolate sauce, and let's name it after one of the most famous and most self-effacing baseball players of all time. After all, dessert has been very, very good to me.

Bananas Esquela

1 c. sifted flour
3 eggs
1 c. milk
2 tbsp. melted butter
2 bananas
Chocolate sauce:
4 (1-oz.) squares semisweet chocolate
6 tbsp. water
¼ c. sugar
2 tbsp. butter
1 egg yolk
1 tbsp. kirsch (optional)
1 c. heavy cream, whipped

Come on. If you haven't got the batter part down by now, go sit in the dugout. Oh, all right:

Put the sifted flour in a large bowl. In a smaller bowl, beat the eggs lightly. Add the milk to the eggs and mix well. Add the liquid gradually to the flour, beating with a mixer or a wire whisk. Beat in the melted butter, just long enough to smooth out the batter (30 seconds or so).

Preheat the oven to 375 degrees. Heavily grease a 1½-quart baking dish. Slice one of the bananas onto the bottom of the dish, pour in half the batter, then slice in the other banana and pour on the rest of the batter.

Bake for 40 to 50 minutes. It puffs up nicely and turns prettily golden, and the banana slices distribute themselves all over.

While the whatsit is baking, prepare the chocolate sauce:

(This sauce has appeared here before. But it's worth repeating. It's good.) Put the chocolate and water in a saucepan over very low heat and stir until the chocolate is melted and the mixture is smooth. Add the sugar, stirring until it is dissolved, then boil gently, stirring, for four minutes.

Remove the sauce from the heat and stir in the butter until it is melted. Cool a minute or two. Lightly beat the egg yolk, then stir in a spoonful of the hot chocolate mixture. Return the diluted egg to the hot chocolate mixture, stirring immediately. Stir in the kirsch.

Serve the hot chocolate sauce over the banana whatsit and top with whipped cream. (If you're staying with the baseball theme, serve the sauce in a pitcher.) Serves six to eight.

The writer is terribly sorry, but he didn't feel like making Ty Cobb Salad.

Rhyming Recipes

Some months ago, I received in the mail a book of recipes that rhymed.

They were truly terrible rhymes, with a lot of the backwards phrasing that characterizes very, very bad poetry. (Things like "When this salad you fix, the celery with the carrots please mix.")

That's not a real example. I made it up because I have lost the book, but that's about as good as the rhythm was, too.

I wrote a little item about the book for the Tidbits column of the newspaper and proceeded to forget about it.

But far back in the vast reaches of my subconscious — in there with a lot of stuff about the breakup of AT&T and how you say "two" in Mandarin Chinese ("ell") — my mind was churning on the subject of rhyming recipes.

Then one fateful Monday morning, when I was supposed to have a food idea to present to my boss, I opened my mouth and nothing came out. Some folks might consider that that was a perfect solution to the problem of the strange things that have appeared in the Food section, but I knew I had had an idea when I went in.

After a moment's hesitation, while the room swam in front of me, I blurted out that I wanted to try making recipes rhyme. I still don't know what I had intended to suggest, but I'm now stuck making rhyming recipes. (I should explain that I am not known for my appreciation of poetry. My favorite poet is Edna St. Vincent De Paul.)

I'm looking at this article as a challenge.

Some of you might look at it as a reason to turn to the classified ads.

But those who persevere will be rewarded with recipes that taste good — and that *sound* good, too. Don't expect prize-winning stuff, though. I'll be happy if they're good enough to be handed out with free samples of cologne by people who sell cosmetics door to door.

I'd like to be sort of the Bard of Avon Lady.

I decided that, to make things fair, I should not allow myself much choice in the selection of recipes, or I would probably wind up seeking out recipes that seemed like they had high rhyming potential.

So what I did was select the first recipe each in the stacks of appetizer, soup, main dish and dessert suggestions that have arrived over the years from food companies. I think they all turned out pretty well as things to eat. As I write this I am still looking forward to the prospect of making poetry out of them.

If you think my job is easy,
If you want to waste some time,
If your stomach isn't queasy,
Try to make some foodstuff rhyme.

The appetizer recipe, a cold dill-flavored shrimp mold, had probably been in the file for some time because it calls for a whole lot of shrimp — which makes it pretty expensive. But it was also very good.

For this recipe only, I decided to include a little rhyme in the title, and to make the ingredients list rhyme as well. That resulted in a few of the quantities winding up as footnotes, so I guess it wasn't a great idea. But I wanted to try it once. (To make up for not doing that for all the other recipes, I decided to use a different rhyme scheme for each one.)

Chiller Diller

2 packets unflavored gelatin
Tomato juice to dissolve it in*
2 tablespoons of lemon juice
¼ cup of chili suice [Oh, OK. Chili
    sauce]
¼ teaspoon Tabasco sauce
1 tablespoon dried dill, of coss
A teaspoonful of Worcestershire
Some sour cream, I'm pretty sure†
To top it off (and don't you skimp)
¾ pound of cooked, shelled shrimp

*1½ c. tomato juice
†2 c. sour cream
Assorted crackers

Sprinkle the gelatin over the juice
(in a pan, you silly goose).

Set it to cook on medium heat,
stirring constantly (that's no mean feat

if your nose develops itches
or you have to hike your britches).

When two-three minutes have gone by
or you are about to cry

of boredom, stop; it's had enough.
Time to put in other stuff.

Take it off so it won't burn
and continue to give the spoon a turn

while adding the lemon juice, the chili,
the Worcestershire sauce and the dilly.

Did we forget Tabasco sauce?
That wouldn't be a total loss.

But since it makes the flavor steamy,
add it with the sour creamy.

Stir the mixture 'til you're limp,
then set aside four pretty shrimp.

Chop the rest up — not too finely —
and stir them in; they'll taste divinely!

Put mixture in a five-cup mold
and place it somewhere very cold

until it looks and feels quite firm.
Unmold it on . . . a pachyderm.

No! That was just my little joke
and I would almost sooner croak

than have you think I really meant it!
You could honestly resent it

if I didn't clearly state:
Please unmold it on a plate!

Put the four whole shrimp atop,
then watch your guests as they all hop

to spread it on assorted crackers.
This will feed two dozen snackers.

Now to the soup. The question of rhyming aside, I have to say that I thought this was a nice soup, but not an outstanding one. Several guests thought it was *very* good, but I have to be honest and say only that as far as I am concerned it could have been verse, but that's about it.

Cream of Celery Soup

1½ c. sliced celery (that's about 2 or 3
    ribs)
1 small onion, chopped
1 tsp. salt
¼ tsp. nutmeg
Pinch pepper
Pinch ground thyme
1 (10¾-oz.) can chicken broth
3 tbsp. flour
1 c. water, divided
1 c. half and half

If you want not to give folks the croup,
make sure that your saucepan is clean.
Now put in the celery and soup
and the other stuff listed between.

(Yes, yes, for those who find fault —
who'd call such a half-list a crime —
I mean the chopped onions and salt,
and the nutmeg and pepper and thyme.)

Now bring the whole pot to a boil
then lower the heat 'til it simmers.
Cover with pot lid (or foil)
and cook it about 15 minners.

Within that brief fourth of an hour
the celery should become tender.
But soon you must deal with the flour,
so don't you go off on a bender.

Put flour in a small bowl or cup,
and slowly stir in half the water.
Keep stirring until it smooths up
(and, friend, let me tell you, it oughtter).

Stir the paste into the soup pot,
and cook not much more than a minute,
'til a-bit-thicker soup is what you've got.
In a moment or two we will thin it.

Now stir in the last of the water,
along with the nice half and half.
Warm up for your son or your daughter
and you and your spouse and giraffe.

I did it again there, I'm sorry!
I promise to transgress no more.
Don't haul me away in a lorry.
I meant that this soup will serve four.

For the main course, as luck would
have it, a bunch of nice, warm enchila-
das to ward off the wintry chill. I liked
these a lot.

I'm glad I decided to stop rhyming
the titles, though. Not much rhymes
with enchilada except Erik Estrada.

And Torquemada. (But nobody expects the Spanish Inquisition.)

Bean Enchiladas

1 clove garlic, minced
½ c. chopped onion
1 tbsp. oil
¾ lb. spicy bulk pork sausage
1 (16-oz.) can drained pinto or kidney
    beans
Salt and pepper to taste
½ tsp. oregano
6 corn tortillas
1 (11-oz.) can enchilada sauce,
    divided (take your choice of how
    spicy)
1 (8-oz.) can tomato sauce
½ c. shredded Cheddar cheese
1 c. sour cream

Mince the garlic as fine as you can.
Chop onion, on a much coarser plan.
Heat the oil in a nice large, deep pan
and put in the spicy pork sausage.

Fry the meat 'til it's crumbly and brown.
Add beans, S & P (or hold the salt
* down).*
Stir in oregano, but don't go to town
on the stirring — we don't want much
* tossage.*

Preheat the oven to 350 degrees.
Foil-wrap tortillas as tight as you please.
Heat them 10 mins, 'til they're soft as a
*   breeze.*
(That way, they'll be easy to roll.)

Back to the beans, which will soon be
*   our sup:*
Add enchilada sauce — just a fourth of a
*   cup.*
Heat thoroughly and mash the beans up.
Put the two sauces into a big bowl.

With an 8-inch-square pan by your side,
give one tortilla a deep red-sauce ride.
Then lay it flat (as though it had died)
in the 8-inch square pan you had ready.

Put on it one-third cup of beans,
then roll (and watch out for your jeans;
the sauce dribbles, but probably cleans).
Now put it, seam down, in its beddy.

By that last line what I mean to say
is "put the first rolled tortilla away
at one end of the pan where it lay."
Dip, fill, roll and place all the rest.

Pour the leftover sauce on the top;
add what bean stuff is left — it's good
*   glop —*
then the cheese (use it all up; don't
*   stop).*
Oven's still on, right? (This wasn't a
*   test.)*

Set the pan in the oven to heat
while you count 20 mins (hand and feet).
There! It's done! Let's get ready to eat.
Set the sour cream out as a topping.

Well, I'm finished. That's all. There's no
*   more.*
But there's two lines still left. What a
*   bore!*
Oh yeah! This will serve three or four —
or just one, if your appetite's whopping.

For dessert, we're having a simple but rather elegant Bavarian Cream mold.

Did you want something else? See me after class.

You could call it a Jell-O mold with whipped cream in it, but I can't. I have to call it a gelatin mold with whipped cream in it, because there are lots of other brands of gelatin.

Anyway, this is quite attractive — and it tastes pretty good, too.

Cherry-Crested Bavarian

2 (3-oz.) pkg. cherry-flavored gelatin
2 tbsp. sugar
⅛ tsp. salt
3 c. water, divided
3 tbsp. kirsch (optional, but quite
**   nice)**
2 c. heavy cream (a 3rd cup is
**   optional, for garnish)**
1 (21-oz.) can cherry pie filling,
**   chilled**

Put the gelatin in a big bowl.
Stir in sugar and salt. Hi, there, Joel.
*   (He's the editor, folks,*
*   and if he likes these jokes*
that takes care of three-fourths of my
*   goal.)*

Bring two cups of the water to boil.
Stir it in for two minutes. That's toil;
*   but it's worth it, you bet,*
*   'cause if not, it won't set —*
I don't care if it's Jell-O or Royal.

Now stir in the remaining one cup
(the water you had not heated up).
*   Add the kirsch if you like*
*   (for a mild little spike),*
and chill while you read "Arms of
*   Krupp."*

(Not much rhymes with up.) Read a spell,
'til the gelatin's started to jell.
   Don't panic or chicken;
   it takes time to thicken.
These things just don't happen pall-mall.

When an hour or so has gone by,
it should have body enough, so let's fly:
   Beat it up 'til it's cloudy.
   (Are you still with me? Howdy!)
Whip two cups cream (for the hip and the thigh).

Now ready a two-quart ring mold.
Here's what to do next: Gently fold
   the cream into the red stuff,
   then transfer that said stuff
to the ring, and put it where it's cold.

Take at least four more hours to chill it,
then unmold, taking care not to spill it.
   Top with cherry pie filling
   and — if the spirit is willing —
use the third cup of cream, whipped, to fill it.

And once more there's more poem than one needs.
All that's lacking's how many it feeds.
   Let's just say 8 to 10.
   (And let's say it again —
and we'll see how far anyone reads.)

Recipes were tried out by the writer. The writer's not such a bad blighter. When he finished this rhyme, he was on overtime and he . . . No! Whew! That's better. It's habit-forming. Next week, the writer enters the Prose Bowl.

Little Mystery #4: Avocados

There seem to be at least two kinds of avocados sold in supermarkets, at different seasons. One is bright green and rather smooth; the other is dark green and very pebbly. Signs in stores indicate that the latter, the Hass variety, is ripe when it's just about black. When does each variety appear and how do you tell when the other — non-Hass — kind is ripe?

Solution: A booklet from the California Avocado Commission indicates that the two principal varieties available here are Fuerte, the smooth-skinned, bright-colored fruit, which appears in the winter, and the pebbly Hass, which is available in the summer.

The booklet goes on to point out that the French word for avocado is avocat, which is also the French word for lawyer, and that the Spanish word for avocado is abogado, which is also the Spanish word for lawyer. (The booklet is quite wrong; the Spanish word for avocado is aguacate, which isn't even close. Abogado *is* the Spanish word for lawyer; you would probably get into some difficulty in a Spanish restaurant asking for an abogado and cruet of oil.)

So, at long last, how do you tell when they're ripe? The booklet says "To test for the proper degree of softness, cradle an avocado gently in your hand. Ready-to-eat fruit will yield to gentle pressure." That's awfully vague. How yielding? How gentle? So I asked a spokesperson for the United Fresh Fruit and Vegetable Association in New York.

Well, she said, "you hold it in the palm of your hand and when you sort of press on it, it gives a little, so to speak, quote-unquote."

Not much better, is it?

A Rainbow Dinner

Well, the moving finger writes, as the fellow said. (Nor all your tears, nor many beers, can cancel half a line.)

So, ready or not, we find ourselves once more contemplating the annual rebirth of the planet and, for those who truly abhor winter, the spirit.

It is the season of Easter and Passover, with their messages of renewal and deliverance. It is the season of the reemergence of growing things. And it is the season of puddles.

(At least it is nominally the season of puddles. I didn't stay up late last night writing this while newspaper delivery trucks honked impatiently, so I don't actually know what it's like today. It is entirely possible that we're knee-deep in snow or suffering through a 90-degree drought.)

But if there's anything left in this world that you can depend on, and you can still believe Buddy DeSylva and Al Jolson, not only do April showers come our way but they bring the flowers that bloom in May. So the rain isn't so bad.

And if you can still believe Paul Williams and Kermit T. Frog, there's a rainbow connection in there somewhere, too.

Thank goodness for that, because, as you can tell by the headline, I have to get to rainbows somehow, and all the bluebirds and daffodils in "April Showers" aren't going to do me a bit of good.

Rainbows, as any reasonably aware child can tell you, are the result of the combined diffraction and reflection of sunlight in water droplets. That doesn't make much sense to most adults, but neither do Michael Jackson and punk haircuts. On the other hand,

we have Frank Sinatra and Grecian Formula 16. And then there's Leon Redbone, whom *nobody* understands.

But I digress.

On the other hand, if I didn't digress, all you'd have to read between the headline and the recipes would be "Here are some recipes," and you'd have to start reading about the presidential primaries that much sooner. And you don't want that to happen, do you?

OK then. Stop shaking your head and muttering about my irrelevant blathering or *I'll* start writing about presidential primaries. How would you like *that*? A whole section of fancy recipes from people who have left Ceylon, Minn., titled "Puttin' on the Fritz."

A rainbow dinner, the subject of this morning's discourse, is not a dinner in which each course resembles a rainbow. (That dinner would be too difficult.) Nor is it a dinner in which each dish is made from rainbow trout. (That dinner would be too weird, even for me.) No, it is a dinner in which each course represents a different color of the rainbow, in order. (That dinner was just right, so Goldilocks ate the whole . . . .)

Sorry. Wrong story.

Where was I? Yes. Rainbow dinner.

Before we get too deeply into rainbow-colored food, I thought it might be nice to start with a dish that is a color not found in the spectrum.

You're imagining exotic colors like sky-blue pink or come-and-get-me copper, or colors not possible even to imagine, aren't you, you romantic? I must point out that tan is a color not in the spectrum. Sorry.

Granted that this appetizer is not an exciting color, it is, I think, rather tasty.

Chicken Spread

1 whole (double) chicken breast
3 to 4 tbsp. additional chicken fat or
**   butter**
2 tsp. crumbled basil
2 tsp. crumbled tarragon
Salt to taste
3 cloves garlic
¼ c. dry white vermouth
Crackers

Remove the chicken skin and any fat, and cut the skin into pieces about an inch on a side.

Heat skin and fat in a frying pan until the fat is rendered and the chicken skin is golden brown. Leaving the fat in the pan, drain the skin pieces on paper toweling.

Add the extra chicken fat or butter and the chicken breast. Sprinkle them with basil, tarragon and salt and put the garlic, unpeeled, in the pan, too. Sauté the chicken as you normally would, turning occasionally, until it is done (about 20 to 30 minutes).

Remove the chicken and allow it to cool a bit. Mash the cooked garlic (still in the pan) with a wooden spoon, which will push the soft insides out of the peel. Discard the peel. Increase the heat under the pan, add the vermouth and cook down for a minute, scraping the pan with a wooden spoon to break up the garlic and to free up any crispy bits of chicken that stuck to the pan.

Tear the cooled chicken into small pieces and put them and the seasoned cooking liquid into a food processor and whomp until the mixture is reasonably smooth. Season to taste.

Just before serving, add the bits of crisp chicken skin. (If you add them early, they'll just get soggy.)

Serve with crackers. Serves six.

Now the rainbow begins, with red. A tomato salad is the obvious choice, even if, like me, you don't care for salad.

You could do something with red lettuce if you must, but since that really isn't very red, I stuck to just a few nicely arranged slices of tomato and a few rings of red onion, topped with a pinkish vinaigrette. Watchers of television commercials know what kind of oil to use if they want to make sure that the tomato sinks all the way through the vinaigrette. Not all of us care.

Pink Vinaigrette for Red Salad

1 tsp. Dijon mustard
1 large clove garlic, crushed
Salt, pepper to taste
6 tbsp. oil
2 tbsp. red wine vinegar

Combine the mustard, garlic, salt and pepper and slowly stir in the oil. Stir in the vinegar. Shake in covered container. Enough for light dressing on six salads.

The main course, which is the orange course, of course, could have been duck à l'orange.

But how too predictable that would have been!

Instead we'll have turkey breast filets à l'orange. (And awfully good ones, too.)

Orange You Glad We Have Turkey?

Approx. 2 lb. uncooked turkey breast
1 orange
½ c. butter
¾ c. orange juice
4 tbsp. orange marmalade
½ c. flour
Salt, pepper
½ c. white wine

Skin and debone the turkey breast. Slice the meat into 12 pieces of roughly similar size. One at a time, put the slices between sheets of plastic wrap or waxed paper and roll out lightly with a rolling pin. (Enlarge the slices slightly and easily. Don't push so hard that you tear the meat.) Set aside in the refrigerator.

Peel and section the orange. If you like, for a garnish, remove the white pith from a large piece of the peel and cut that peel into 10 or 12 long, thin strips. Tie a knot in the center of each. Set aside orange sections and peel decorations.

In a large frying pan, melt the butter, add the orange juice and marmalade and cook about five minutes over medium heat.

Combine flour, salt and pepper. Dredge the turkey scallops in the mixture. Stir the wine into the orange-butter mixture and add the turkey.

Cook the turkey scallops about 1½ minutes per side.

Just before serving, add the orange sections and stir gently a minute or so to heat them through.

Transfer turkey and sauce to serving platter. Decorate here and there with orange knots.

Serves six to eight.

Sure, you've got your squashes and your wax beans, but when it comes to downright yellowness, there's really no vegetable that can hold a candle to corn.

This version is so tasty it inspires great warmth of emotion.

Yellow Fervor

4 slices bacon
2 (10-oz.) pkg. frozen corn
3 tbsp. butter
1½ tbsp. flour
⅔ c. milk or half and half
Salt, pepper

Fry and crumble the bacon.

Prepare the corn according to package directions. Drain.

In a small saucepan, melt the butter, stir in the flour and cook, stirring, one minute. Slowly stir in the milk or half and half. Season to taste.

Stir sauce and crumbled bacon into corn. Serves four to six.

It might not be very easy to *be* green (Kermit T. Frog again), but *cooking* green is another matter. The choice of green vegetables is . . . ZZZzzzz.

No, really. There are lots of green vegetables. Too many, in fact. So I made a dish with *two* green things, just to get rid of an extra one.

If peas and lettuce strikes you as a weird combination, it might ease your mind to know that they are often combined in French cooking. If it does not strike you as a weird combination, how about baked beans and cottage cheese?

This version of peas and lettuce is based on a recipe in Make It Easy in Your Kitchen, by Laurie Burrows Grad.

Green, Green French-Style Peas

2 tbsp. dry white vermouth
1½ c. shredded lettuce
1 (16-oz.) can tiny peas, drained
¼ c. chopped green onions (just the
    green part)
1 tsp. sugar
Salt, pepper
2 tbsp. butter

Put the vermouth in the bottom of a small saucepan. Add half the lettuce. Without stirring, add the peas and onions. Sprinkle on the sugar, salt and pepper.

Dot with bits of the butter and top with the remaining lettuce.

Cover and cook over medium heat for about five minutes. Stir gently and serve.

Serves four.

Since all the trendy restaurants serve water (or fizz water) with a slice of lime, I thought I'd go them one or two better for the rainbow dinner, and serve slices of orange, lemon and lime in each glass.

I thought it was rather a nice touch. But then, what do I know?

In the blue portion of the spectrum, things are a little thin.

There are blueberries, but we're not ready for dessert yet.

There is the blue plate special (this week it's a hot beef sandwich, mashed potatoes and gravy and canned green beans — beverage and dessert extra), but that's a bit heavy for so late in the meal.

That leaves blue cheese, and a tiny wedge of it for each diner turned out to go quite nicely at this juncture.

Those who learned that the colors of the rainbow have first letters that spell out Roy G. Biv are now waiting for indigo. They can forget it. As far as I'm concerned, we move from blue to purple. If you must, a glass of milk with bluish-purplish food coloring could be served here, and it could be alleged that it came from a cow that mooed indigo.

NOW it's dessert time, and there is an obvious choice. Grape something, right? Here's a recipe straight from Welch's, the grape folks, that produces the purplest, and possibly soupiest, apple dessert you ever saw. But it tasted pretty good. I renamed it, of course.

Grape Caesar's Ghost Cobbler

4 medium apples (Rome Beauty, if
    you care to preserve the pun)
1 (6-oz.) can frozen grape drink
    concentrate
2 tbsp. quick-cooking tapioca
1½ c. unsifted flour
2 tsp. baking powder
½ tsp. salt
½ c. sugar
1 egg, well beaten
½ c. milk
½ c. (1 stick) butter, melted
Vanilla ice cream

Peel, core and slice the apples and put them in a buttered 9-inch-square pan.

Combine the grape concentrate and the tapioca and pour over the apple slices.

Preheat the oven to 425 degrees.

Sift together the flour, baking powder and salt. Add the sugar. Combine the egg, milk and melted butter and stir gently into the flour mixture. Spread over the apples. Bake for 30 minutes.

Serve with ice cream. Serves eight.

I had intended to wind things up by serving a really peculiar liqueur called Parfait Amour, which is bright purple and rather florid. It turns out that Bols, the Kentucky liqueur folks who used to make it, haven't done so for at least a year, and I couldn't find any of the imported versions either, so my guests were spared that experience.

As I recall, though, it was kind of expensive, so maybe it's just as well I couldn't find it. I didn't want to spend a whole pot of gold just to end the rainbow meal.

I don't normally discuss anything that takes place at dinner except the eating, but I cannot end this article in honesty without describing what happened after dessert and coffee.

Maybe it had something to do with the springtime feeling imparted by the meal. I don't know. Anyway, while my guests sat around the table talking, I went down to the basement to look for my collection of amusing typographical errors. (When I have a party, boy, it gets wild!) When I returned, I found that the entire group of guests — five regular attendees and two perfect strangers (oh, nobody's perfect; two very nice strangers) — had left the table and were hiding in my bathroom.

I was never offered an explanation. It couldn't have been my company.

All I can think of is that they were looking for the April shower.

Little Mystery #5: Cheese

Have you noticed that if you open your mouth lately somebody is stuffing Monterey Jack cheese into it? Why are we suddenly eating so much of a cheese that nobody ever heard of ten years ago? Where did it come from, anyhow?

Solution: According to the National Cheese Institute in Chicago, Monterey Jack cheese has been around a long time.

They say it was invented by some fellow named Jack in Monterey County, Calif., and that it was made a great deal on farms in that county starting in about 1892.

The cheeseperson said that in many locales the name Monterey Jack has been replaced by just-plain Monterey.

As to why it appeared so suddenly on the sandwiches of every fern restaurant in town, the Cheese Institute was not particularly helpful. (A little mystery remains.)

Things That Go Bump in the Oven

Did you ever wonder, when you were eating a piece of bread, how in the world anybody figured out that yeast would do what it does in there?

Or have you wondered what caveman reasoned that smashing a chicken egg into some other stuff would be anything but peculiar? (Or how many times he did it before it occurred to him to remove the shell?)

Probably nobody figured these things out, wise persons answer whenever I wonder them out loud; these were serendipitous discoveries — long-ago accidents that worked out so well that they were repeated. The transistor was born in such circumstances, these wise persons point out; why not the soufflé?

OK. Fair enough. But in these modern times, when we know darn well how cake is made and nobody thinks it's made any other way, what explains the development of recipes that behave in ways that no reasonably knowledgeable person would expect?

What was in the mind of the person who first made Tunnel of Fudge cake, for example? Was he or she intent on making a cake with a chocolate-brownie center? Or did a kid track mud across the floor at a critical moment, causing a momentary loss of attention that resulted in tossing the frosting mix into the cake batter?

Surely Pillsbury, which has trademarked the name of the cake and makes both the frosting mix called for in the recipe and the complete-in-one-box Tunnel of Fudge cake mix, had something to do with it.

Similarly one suspects that General Mills, which produces Bisquick, had a hand in the development of various "Impossible" pies — pie fillings that contain Bisquick and that produce their own crust, sort of, while they bake.

But even if there was an economic interest in the production of these peculiar recipes, what would that mean? Are there people at Pillsbury and General Mills who are paid to sit around dropping iron filings into cake batter in hopes of producing a cake that bakes its own pan?

Or do they add miscellaneous things like aftershave lotion, chicken wings and bubble gum, just to see whether anything good happens?

There are enough of these shall-we-say "odd" recipes around that it seemed worthwhile to find out a little about them.

I called Pillsbury, and consumer relations manager Catherine Hanley told me that the company didn't invent the Tunnel of Fudge cake — it was a $5,000 winner in the 1966 Pillsbury Bake-Off.

OK, Pillsbury didn't dream it up. What possessed the woman who did?

Hanley said she was interested in that question herself a few years ago and called Ella Helfrich in Houston, Texas, and asked her. Helfrich told Hanley that she added the frosting mix on purpose, because it was one of the products emphasized in that year's bake-off. She was hoping to get a very moist, brownie-like pound cake. The first time she made it, she said, she took it out fairly early, and the middle was so runny it had to be eaten with a spoon. But she knew she was on to something, and she kept trying until it worked.

"I still don't know," Hanley said, "whether she's a great cook or hasn't the vaguest idea how you put a cake together."

I decided to call Helfrich and find out. "I do this kind of thing all the time," said Helfrich, who clearly knows darn well how to bake a cake. "I always try all the contests," she explained, and, since the idea in so many recipe contests is to use a specific ingredient, Helfrich said she has developed lots of very peculiar recipes.

"I got a small prize from Kraft for some rolls with Marshmallow Creme in them, and I've made a macaroni cake, and a Coca-Cola cake (that was before the one that got so popular) and I've put mashed potato flakes in different things."

Well, that's as good an explanation as anyone is likely to get: You throw lipstick into a cake in the hope of winning money from Max Factor.

But even if Pillsbury didn't actually invent Tunnel of Fudge cake, aren't there any people over there trying to outdo the Ella Helfriches of our land?

Sure there are, Hanley said. For example, they've developed new recipes to make a high-quality loaf of bread in less time. "They'll take an idea like that," Hanley said, "and keep at it until it works or is abandoned." But that apparently isn't anyone's regular job. "On the whole," she said, "they're doing specific projects that aren't as creative." Like more-normal recipes for the backs of packages.

So hang in there, Ella, we need you!

Meanwhile, here's the Tunnel of Fudge cake recipe, as it appears on the backs of some Pillsbury frosting mix packages. Hanley noted that even now, although the recipe has been adapted to make it as "tolerant" (of errors and mismeasurement) as possible, it is still a very tricky cake because it's nearly impossible to tell when it is done enough to come out of the oven.

My own experience is that you just have to have faith and let it stay in as long as the recipe says it is supposed to, ignoring the rather done-looking brownie crust that develops earlier. After all, if you can't trust Pillsbury, who can you trust?

Tunnel of Fudge Cake

(A Pillsbury recipe)
1½ c. margarine or butter, softened
6 eggs
1½ c. sugar
1 (13.9-oz.) pkg. Rich 'n Easy Fudge
    or Double Dutch frosting mix*
2 c. flour
2 c. chopped walnuts or pecans*
2 tsp. water

Preheat oven to 350 degrees. Using solid shortening, generously grease a 12-cup fluted tube pan or 10-inch angel-food tube pan.

In a large bowl, cream the margarine. Add the eggs, one at a time, beating well after each addition. Gradually add the sugar, creaming the mixture until it is light and fluffy.

Reserve half a cup of the frosting mix. By hand (use a spoon), stir in the remaining frosting mix, the flour and the nuts. Stir until well blended. Pour batter into prepared pan and bake at 350 degrees for 60 to 65 minutes. (You can't test this cake with a knife or a toothpick because it's *supposed* to be gooey inside. Let it go the full 60 to 65 minutes; it should develop a shiny, brownie-like crust well before then.)

Cool the cake one hour (*not* inverted), then remove it from the pan. Cool completely before glazing.

Prepare the glaze by blending the reserved frosting mix with the two teaspoons of water. Spoon over the cooled cake.

Store tightly covered. Makes 16 servings.

*According to the recipe, both this particular frosting mix and the nuts are essential for the success of the cake. I took their word for it and used the Pillsbury frosting mix. It worked fine. Then I made it again, using a Red Owl frosting mix. It worked fine, too. Despite my deep and abiding faith in Pillsbury, I guess I wasn't too surprised.

If you just hate the idea of making cake from scratch (even if it includes frosting mix), Pillsbury makes a complete Tunnel of Fudge mix. But it's not the same. You prepare the cake batter and the batter for the gooey part from packets. Then you pour the cake batter into a Bundt pan and add the gooey part on top, being careful to keep it away from the sides of the pan. Apparently it sinks further into the cake during baking. There isn't very much magic in that.

Let's move on, then, to the "Impossible" pies, which rely on the addition of Bisquick to provide something between a self-forming crust and a filling thick enough to eliminate the need for a crust.

There have been a number of such pies over the years, starting with Impossible Coconut Pie, and including recently Impossible Chicken Pie (which won $10,000 in the National Chicken Cooking Contest), Impossible Garden Pie and, for a Halloween theme, Impossible Pumpkin Pie.

In the never-ending battle for truth, justice and peculiar food articles, I called General Mills, the maker of Bisquick, and tried to get to the bottom, as it were, of the crustless pie.

Marcia Copeland, director of Betty Crocker food services, was as helpful as she could be, which wasn't very.

General Mills, it seems, didn't invent the Impossible Pie any more than Pillsbury did the Tunnel of Fudge Cake. And in this case, the real inventor is unknown so we can't ask what drove him or her to the extreme of dumping Bisquick into a pie filling. At least it wasn't a Bisquick contest.

"We can't pin down exactly how it started," Copeland said. "American Home magazine ran an article about it four or five years ago, and it began circulating as a grass-roots thing." Newspaper food sections around the country would reproduce the Impossible Coconut Pie recipe now and then, but "in the beginning we didn't see much potential in it," she said, "because it doesn't use much [Bisquick]."

But as the number of variations grew (and it become apparent that the Impossible was within their grasp), the General Mills folks began working up their own Impossible recipes. "We've done both dessert and main-course variations," Copeland said, "including an Impossible Cheeseburger and an Impossible Fudge Pie."

Although the Impossible pie wasn't their own idea, General Mills, too, has people trying to develop original recipes. "We continually look for the new idea, the new breakthrough," Copeland said. "And we constantly look for the new idea that would be a new product or a new way to use an older product."

I wonder whether they've tried iron filings yet.

Impossible Pumpkin Pie

(A General Mills recipe)
¾ c. sugar
½ c. Bisquick baking mix
2 tbsp. margarine or butter, softened
1 (13-oz.) can evaporated milk
2 eggs
1 (15- or 16-oz.) can pumpkin
2½ tsp. pumpkin pie spice
2 tsp. vanilla

Preheat the oven to 350 degrees. Grease a 9- or 10-inch pie plate. Beat all the ingredients together until the mixture is smooth. Pour it into the pie plate (but do not fill quite to the rim — the pie rises during baking). Bake 50 to 55 minutes, until a knife inserted in the center comes out clean.

If you're expecting that an actual pie crust will somehow form under the pumpkin, you're expecting a bit much even from something called Impossible Pie. It is, nonetheless, a pumpkin pie, and it manages to hold itself together as though it had a crust. Close enough.

There are three other items that I thought of when my mind, such as it is, turned to recipes that don't behave normally. All of them have been showing up in church cookbooks for years, and even attempting to find the person truly responsible for one of them is a task I decided not to attempt.

The first is sometimes called Fudge Upside-Down Cake, or other names to that effect, but it is most often referred to as Pudding Cake. It's a batter that's put into a pan and topped with dry ingredients and boiling water. The result, after all of this undergoes half an hour in the oven, is a cake on the top and chocolate sauce underneath. It's pretty good, too.

Chocolate Pudding Cake

1¼ c. sugar, divided
1 tbsp. butter
½ c. milk
1 c. flour
1 tsp. baking powder
¼ tsp. salt
5½ tbsp. cocoa, divided
½ c. chopped walnuts
½ c. brown sugar
1¼ c. boiling water

Preheat the oven to 350 degrees. Cream together three-fourths cup of the sugar and the butter. Add the milk, mixing well. Combine the flour, baking powder, salt and 1½ tablespoons of the cocoa, and add to the butter mixture, mixing well. Pour into a buttered 9-inch-square pan.

Sprinkle the batter with the walnuts. Combine the remaining half cup of sugar, the half cup of brown sugar and the remaining one-fourth cup of cocoa. Spread over the top of the batter. Pour the boiling water over all.

Bake at 350 degrees for 30 minutes. If you're doubtful that it's done, don't plunge the toothpick or knife all the way in, because the bottom is gooey even when the cake is finished.

Next comes Crazy Cake (or, more often, Krazy Kake). This one is in a class by itself. Tunnel of Fudge and Pudding Cake produce a gooey portion along with the cake. Impossible pies eliminate the need for buying or making a crust. Krazy Kake has absolutely nothing to recommend it; it simply is put together weirdly.

If that turns you on, you ought to see my car.

Krazy Kake

3 c. flour
2 c. sugar
6 tbsp. cocoa
2 tsp. salt
2 tsp. soda
1 tsp. vanilla
1½ tbsp. vinegar
10 tbsp. vegetable oil
2 c. water

Preheat the oven to 350 degrees. Pour all the dry ingredients into an ungreased 9- by 13-inch pan and mix with a fork. Pour the liquids into the dry ingredients and mix with a fork. Bake for 25 to 30 minutes.

That's it, but I should note that if you don't mix the dry ingredients enough, some of your guests may complain that the cake is salty, others may notice a pronounced baking-soda flavor, and so on. You might also find that parts of the cake have risen much better than other parts. That's probably OK; what point would there be in making a cake this way and having it turn out perfectly normal?

On the other hand, you might well ask, what point is there in making a cake this way at all?

Last and possibly least, if for no other reason than the elegance of its name, is a thing called Dump Cake.

I assume that the name derives from the cake's untraditional method of assembly — you more-or-less just dump the ingredients into a pan. I find the result pretty sweet but not bad, and it went over very well at the office. Those who don't care for it may feel that the name has more to do with what should happen to the cake *after* it is baked. That is certainly the interpretation that I would put on one version of this recipe that I heard on an Iowa radio station in 1967: Chocolate Blueberry Dump Cake. We'll skip that one.

Actually, I suppose Dump Cake doesn't really belong in this discussion at all. Although its preparation is indeed peculiar — you pour cherry pie filling into a pan, top it with crushed pineapple, then with dry cake mix and then with melted butter, nuts and coconut — nothing much happens to those ingredients while they bake. The finished product is cherry-pie-pineapple stuff on the bottom and what tastes like a thick layer of streusel on the top.

Pineapple-Cherry Dump Cake

1 (21-oz.) can cherry pie filling
1 (20-oz.) can crushed pineapple (do not drain)
1 (18½-oz.) pkg. yellow cake mix
10 tbsp. (1¼ sticks) butter, melted
1 c. flaked coconut
1 c. chopped nuts

Preheat oven to 350 degrees. Spread the cherry pie filling evenly on the bottom of a greased 9- by 13-inch pan. Layer the undrained pineapple on top of the cherries. (You needn't be too careful here. Some versions of the recipe have the pineapple on the bottom and the cherry on top, so any way that it all gets into the pan is probably fine.)

Sprinkle the cake mix over the pineapple. Cover with melted butter. Top with coconut and nuts.

Bake at 350 degrees for about one hour. Top, if you like, with whipped cream or ice cream.

Little Mystery #6: Bananas

How come all of a sudden it's OK to put bananas in the refrigerator?

If even the question is a mystery to you, you must be under 30. Ask an Old One to sing you the Chiquita Banana Song. Chiquita Banana wasn't always just a stylized cartoon character on a little blue label. She used to be a *person*, and she had all sorts of banana hints. And her biggest hint was always that you must *never* put bananas in the refrigerator.

More recent banana commercials haven't included that warning, and occasionally one hears suggestions that bananas can be refrigerated if they're ripe but you're not ready to use them.

One such suggestion is contained in a publication of the banana industry's public-information outfit, The Banana Bunch, headquartered in New York. I called The Banana Bunch to straighten this matter out, but I had a little difficulty. After explaining who I was, running through the history of Chiquita and asking my question, I was told that I was talking to a dental office. It appeared that, having said in black-and-white that it's OK to refrigerate bananas, The Banana Bunch went into hiding.

Thanks to a little help from Mary Hart, who remembered the name of the public-relations firm that handled the banana account (Mary remembers everything) I finally got in touch with The Banana Bunch. It seems that some time after issuing the press release with the refrigeration note, they moved.

In any case, I have an answer. I'm not at all sure I believe it, but here it is, straight from the banana's mouth:

Solution: When the Chiquita Banana jingle was written, they needed a word to rhyme with equator, so they threw in a line about the refrigerator.

That's the whole explanation.

So for all those years we let our bananas rot just for the sake of a jingle?

Well, not really, said the bananaperson. "All fruit is better if you don't refrigerate it. But you can refrigerate bananas if they're beginning to get too ripe. However, the peel will get black, and that isn't very attractive."

OK, now that we've heard that, whether or not we believe it, why not a little nostalgia trip for the Old Ones present? Here are the complete lyrics to the original Chiquita Banana song:

"I'm Chiquita Banana and I'm here to say
Bananas must be ripened in a certain way.
When they are flecked with brown and have a golden hue,
Bananas taste the best and are the best for you.

You can put them in salad, you can put them in a pie-yi!
Any way you want to eat them,
It's impossible to beat them.

But bananas like the climate of the very, very tropical equator,
So you should never put bananas
In your refrigerator.
Oh, no, no, no!"

The SPAM Dinner

Thirty-eight years ago today, Allied forces landed on the Normandy coast of German-occupied France.

Of the military struggle of those times much has been written, and it is fitting that we remember it today. It was a time of great national and personal sacrifice, the like of which we have not seen since.

It is also fitting, however, that we recognize that those soldiers were bringing to the yearning millions of Western Europe not only the breath of freedom but also, incidentally, American chocolate bars, chewing gum and, perhaps least consciously, SPAM.

SPAM, that much-maligned but much-eaten canned-meat product of the Geo. A. Hormel Co., Austin, Minn., was an inseparable element of the Allied advance. Where there were GIs, there was SPAM.

Not that all of them were thrilled about it, you understand.

If it were subjected to a rational evaluation, SPAM would surely have done quite well. It's nutritious, it's really quite tasty and it keeps almost indefinitely, which makes it an immensely practical food in wartime situations — and in many others.

But familiarity breeds contempt, and by the time of the invasion of Europe, our boys were mighty familiar with SPAM and the other government-supplied culinary staples. Whatever they thought about SPAM by then, it was not that it was fantastic.

There is a second side, however, to the matter of the desirability of sitting down to some SPAM.

Of the two men I know who served in France around the end of the war, both have told me much the same anecdote. On the basis of that small sample, I assume that it happened to others, too.

A bunch of Yanks were going somewhere or other and stopped at a French farmhouse or inn. The French folks could provide shelter but could offer little in the way of food because their larders were almost empty. The Americans said all they had was @%*# canned rations. The French took the SPAM and whatever and transformed it into the best food the Americans had ever eaten.

Well, friends, that's a challenge if ever I've heard one, even almost 40 years after the fact.

Could I equal the French artistry with SPAM? Could *I* turn it into a truly memorable dish? I decided to give it a try, despite giggles from colleagues.

It might be true that you can't make a silk purse out of a sow's ear, but canned pork shoulder, it seemed to me, was another thing altogether.

(To be perfectly accurate, SPAM consists of "chopped pork shoulder meat with ham meat added and salt, water, sugar, sodium nitrite," but you can't turn very many clever phrases with a list like that.)

The Hormel folks, incidentally, insist that SPAM is spelled in capitals. And I have to go along, because it is *their* name for *their* product (and it is not to be used for just any luncheon meat).

A word about those giggles: Without help from me or the creative cooks of France, SPAM continues to sell quite nicely (one source, not Hormel, estimates sales at 90 million pounds a year).

But I think it's safe to say that it isn't being consciously merchandised as a potential ingredient in gourmet cooking.

Although the folks in Austin, bless 'em, put recipes on the SPAM cans, they tend to be for things like "SPAM Picadilly," a sandwich spread consisting of SPAM, cream cheese and pickle relish.

It may be that fancier recipes just wouldn't fit on the cans, but I suspect that we don't find them there largely because the SPAM folks don't have the audacity to suggest them.

Well, if they don't, I do.

In my usual burst of excess, I have produced an excellent garlic-laden SPAM-and-avocado appetizer, a creamy and delicate (and beautiful) SPAM mousse, an incredibly tasty SPAM-and-spinach gratin, a very mellow sauce for thin slices of SPAM, and a glazed dessert bar in which SPAM contributes to a sort of mincemeat mixture.

You could, it is true, make any of these recipes with ham (some of them were ham recipes before I got to them). But not only is SPAM rather good, and not only does it have almost no waste (a can of it contains no bones, no fat — nothing, other than the tiniest amount of gelatin, but SPAM), it also costs about half as much as canned ham.

You could also, it is true, make any of these recipes with some other brand of canned luncheon meat. I can't stop you.

But if you want the authentic experience, complete with knowing chuckles from ex-servicemen, genuine SPAM is what you need.

This first recipe is uncomplicated enough that it could easily fit on a SPAM can.

And containing as it does one of nature's two most perfect foods, garlic (the other is chocolate), it is a sure winner.

Avocat au SPAM

(Avocado with SPAM)
2 avocados
1 small clove garlic
½ c. mayonnaise
About ½ (12-oz.) can SPAM, or 1 (7-oz.) can

Halve but do not peel the avocados, and remove the pits. Crush or very finely mince the garlic into the mayonnaise.

Cut the SPAM into small dice (⅛ inch to ¼ inch on a side).

Thoroughly combine the SPAM and the mayonnaise, coating the SPAM cubes well, and put a mound of the mixture into each avocado half. Serves four as an appetizer.

The next dish uses a lot of pretty fancy ingredients almost certainly not found in the almost-bare French pantries of World War II. So what? It's delicious.

The recipe is adapted from one (which did not contain SPAM) in The Gourmet Cooking School Cookbook, by Dione Lucas.

It wouldn't fit on a can of SPAM (unless they make it in 50-pound cans), but take my word; it's very, very good.

Cold SPAM Mousse

2 (12-oz.) cans SPAM
½ c. water
2 tbsp. oil
4½ tbsp. flour
1½ (¼-oz.) env. unflavored gelatin
Dash of salt
Dash of cayenne pepper
1¼ c. milk
2 sticks (½ lb.) unsalted butter
1 tsp. tomato paste
3 tbsp. sherry
2 egg whites
1 c. heavy cream
Aspic (optional):
1 (¼-oz.) env. unflavored gelatin
1 (10¾-oz.) can chicken broth
1 tbsp. tomato paste
¼ c. sherry
Optional decorations with aspic (see
    text)

Put the SPAM through a grinder or food processor until it's finely ground (or finely chopped).

Put the water and oil in a small saucepan. In a small bowl, mix the flour, the 1½ envelopes of gelatin (it's an approximate measure; don't worry about being exact — something like a rounded tablespoon), the salt and cayenne. Stir this dry mixture into the water until the mixture is smooth. Slowly stir in the milk and heat the mixture on a medium-high burner, stirring constantly, until it just boils.

Pour it onto a large dinner plate or serving platter, cover it with plastic wrap and chill until it is cold and set. (This mixture serves to bind the other ingredients in the mousse. You can prepare it in advance.)

Cream the butter (don't substitute salted butter; with this much of it you'll really make the final product salty instead of creamy). Add the chilled gelatin mixture a little at a time, continuing to beat. Stir in the ground SPAM.

In a small cup, dissolve the tomato paste in the sherry and stir it into the mixture.

Beat the egg whites until they are stiff but not dry. Whip the cream. Fold the beaten egg whites into the cream and the whole thing into the SPAM mixture. Taste it (ain't that good?), and adjust seasonings if necessary.

This has been a fair amount of effort, and it tastes wonderful, but so far it doesn't look like much. Splashy presentation is a big help for something that can be described like that.

Affix a collar to a 1½-quart soufflé dish, or another round dish of similar capacity: Tear a sheet of waxed paper long enough to go around the dish and overlap a bit. Fold it in half along its length. Brush one side of the paper with oil, and wrap it, oiled side in, around the dish; the paper should extend at least two inches above the top of the dish. Tie the collar tightly around the dish with string or rubber bands.

Pour the mousse into the dish, smooth the top against the collar and chill at least two hours. (Take the collar off the dish before serving.) For an even-more glamorous appearance, top with a little pale aspic (maybe with a few decorations):

Soften the gelatin in half a cup of the chicken broth. Combine the remaining broth with the tomato paste and sherry, and heat. Stir in the softened gelatin and cook over medium heat, stirring, until the gelatin is fully dissolved.

We're leaving out all the messy straining with egg whites, so strain instead by pouring the mixture through a funnel or strainer lined with a tea towel. Refrigerate or freeze until the gelatin is syrupy. (If you waited too long, heat it again, very briefly.)

Put the soufflé dish on a plate to catch any aspic that leaks past the collar. Pour the aspic over the top of the mousse and spread it evenly. If you want to throw in a few decorations (slices of hard-cooked eggs or olives, maybe, turned into flowers with stems of green onion or dill), pour on less than half the aspic, let set briefly in the refrigerator, place the decorations and pour on the remaining aspic. Chill at least another hour. Now it's delicious and gorgeous, too.

Serves 10 to 12 (it's very rich).

Next the SPAM-and-spinach gratin, adapted, rather freely, from Mastering the Art of French Cooking. This recipe too, take a little time. But even without the SPAM it's excellent, and the SPAM improves it.

Gratin d'Epinards au Fromage et SPAM

(Spinach gratinéed with cheese and you-know-what)
2 (10-oz.) pkg. frozen chopped spinach
4 tbsp. butter
Salt and pepper
Pinch of nutmeg
3 tbsp. flour
1 (10½-oz.) can consommé
½ (12-oz.) can or 1 (7-oz.) can SPAM, diced into ¼-inch cubes
1 (6-oz.) pkg. grated Swiss cheese (1½ c.), divided
4 tbsp. dry bread crumbs
3 tbsp. melted butter

Prepare the spinach according to package directions. Drain well.

Heat the four tablespoons of butter in a five-quart Dutch oven over moderately high heat. When the butter is bubbling, stir in the spinach. Continue stirring five to ten minutes until all the moisture from the spinach has evaporated. The spinach will start to stick to the pan. Add a little salt, pepper and nutmeg.

Lower the heat to medium, sprinkle on the flour and stir for two minutes.

Stir in the consommé, bring to the simmer and cook over medium heat, stirring occasionally, for 15 minutes. Stir in the diced SPAM. Cook five to ten more minutes, stirring occasionally, until the mixture has some body and is no longer liquid.

Stir three-fourths cup of the cheese into the spinach, and pour the mixture into a well-buttered two-quart baking dish. Mix the rest of the cheese with the bread crumbs and sprinkle it over the top. If you're preparing ahead, stop at this point.

When ready to go, preheat the oven to 375 degrees. Sprinkle the melted butter over the cheese and crumbs.

Bake 30 minutes in the upper third of the oven. You've probably never had better-tasting spinach. Serves six.

Now to the sauce for thin-sliced SPAM. I don't know what to say here, except "Wow!" (and apologies to Julia Child for what I did to her recipe).

Sliced SPAM, Splendid Sauce

2 (12-oz.) cans SPAM, sliced thinly
3 tbsp. butter
1 tbsp. oil
3 tbsp. flour
2 tbsp. minced shallots
1 c. (most of a 10½-oz. can) consommé
½ c. sherry
1 tbsp. tomato paste
Pepper
No salt
1½ c. heavy cream
3 tbsp. Cognac

Note: This sauce has plenty of salt on its own. Don't add any in the course of routine seasoning.

Brown the slices of SPAM lightly in the butter and oil. Cook each side only a minute or so. Set the SPAM aside.

Stir the flour into the fat in the skillet (if necessary add another tablespoon or so of butter). Then add the shallots and cook over low heat two to three minutes. Remove from heat.

Heat the consommé and the sherry in a saucepan until the mixture is simmering. Using a whisk, stir the liquid into the flour mixture until it is smooth. Add the tomato paste and pepper. Return the sauce to simmering, stirring, and then stir in the cream. Simmer four or five minutes, until the sauce coats a spoon.

Stir in the Cognac.

Add the SPAM slices (maybe cut in strips as a further disguise) and stir to cover them with sauce. Simmer slowly for a few minutes to heat the SPAM. Serves eight to ten.

And last we come, as always we must, to dessert. Yes, SPAM in dessert.

It's kind of a mincemeat bar cookie. Some of you will recall that mincemeat used to be made with meat in it, instead of coming, meatless, from jars or boxes found on supermarket shelves. Return with us, now, to those thrilling days of yesteryear. Real meat in mincemeat!

Under another name, and made with lean ground beef instead of SPAM, this recipe won first prize last year in a contest sponsored by the National Livestock and Meat Board. The meat board sent it to me, and I had my way with it.

Great Bars of SPAM!

Filling:
2 (12-oz.) cans SPAM
1 (16-oz.) can whole-berry cranberry sauce
1¼ c. brown sugar
1 c. seedless raisins
¾ c. coarsely chopped walnuts
½ c. orange marmalade
½ tsp. salt
1 orange
Dough:
4 c. flour
2 tbsp. baking powder
2 tsp. salt
1⅓ c. milk
⅔ c. oil
Glaze:
1½ c. confectioners' sugar
3 tbsp. milk
1 tbsp. rum

Prepare the filling: In a food processor or meat grinder (or with a knife, if you have some time) chop the SPAM until it is the consistency of hamburger. Put the SPAM, cranberry sauce, brown sugar, raisins, walnuts, marmalade and the half-teaspoon of salt in a Dutch oven.

Grate the peel of the orange into the mixture, then squeeze in the juice of the orange (catching any seeds in a strainer or your hand). Stir well.

Cook, stirring, over medium heat until the mixture boils. Continue cooking 20 minutes, stirring very often. Cool.

Prepare the dough: Combine the flour, baking powder and the two teaspoons of salt in a bowl. Add milk and oil, stirring until the flour is fully moistened. Knead the dough briefly on waxed paper, and divide in half.

Roll half the dough between two sheets of waxed paper until it is slightly bigger than a 17- by 10-inch cookie sheet or jelly-roll pan. Peel off the top sheet of waxed paper, invert the pan over the dough and invert the pan and dough together. Peel off the other sheet of waxed paper. Press the dough so it covers the bottom and goes up the sides of the pan.

Spoon the filling evenly over the dough.

Preheat the oven to 425 degrees.

Roll the second half of the dough between two sheets of waxed paper to the same dimensions — slightly larger than the pan. Remove the top sheet and quickly flip the dough onto the filling. (He who hesitates is in trouble here. Once it starts falling off of the waxed paper, there's no reasonable way to catch the dough.)

Remove the backing sheet and press the top and bottom layers of dough together. Don't worry if the top layer doesn't quite make it to the edge; it'll be fine. Make four long diagonal slashes through the top layer to minimize shrinkage.

Bake 25 to 30 minutes, until the crust is golden brown.

Remove from oven and prepare the glaze: Combine confectioners' sugar, milk and rum. Mix until smooth.

When the bars have cooled slightly, drizzle the glaze over them and spread evenly with a knife or spatula.

Allow to cool, and cut into bars.

Little Mystery #7: Bananas

Not long ago we looked into the Chiquita Banana jingle that for years advised people:

*"Bananas like the climate of the very,
  very tropical equator,
So you should never put bananas in
  the refrigerator!
Oh, no, no, no!"*

To review, that question was taken up because banana advertising had more recently been suggesting that refrigerating bananas was just fine.

Why, then, were we told for years never to refrigerate bananas? Because, a spokesperson for a public-relations outfit called The Banana Bunch said, when the Chiquita jingle was written they needed a rhyme for "equator."

I could barely believe that — that for years, all over this great land of ours, people were letting bananas rot for lack of refrigeration, just because some jingle-writer didn't think of "elevator," "dictator" or "percolator" as rhymes for "equator."

To demonstrate that those, too, would have been useful rhymes, and would not have wasted so many bananas, I have constructed these alternate last verses for the Chiquita Banana Song:

*"Bananas like the climate of the very,
  very tropical equator,
And you should never take bananas
  into an elevator!"*

Or:

*"Bananas like the climate of the very,
  very tropical equator,
But you should never give bananas to
  a right-wing dictator!"*

Or:

*"Bananas like the climate of the very,
  very tropical equator,
But you should never boil bananas
  inside your percolator!"*

A Burger and a Cherry Coke

A lot of American life seems to consist of stumbling across things you didn't know you needed until you saw them. Suddenly, inexplicably, there's another thing you've got to have.

Lots of folks have this problem at stores; I have it at flea markets.

I don't have the vaguest idea why my hidden needs seem to center on old things instead of new ones. I don't think I'm trying to get my childhood back — my adulthood is pretty nice. Lots of the stuff I find myself craving isn't even something I had when I was a kid. It is, though, always something that invokes those more carefree times.

That's the way it was when I read an article in the paper a couple of years ago about a fellow in Edina who had assembled an entire soda fountain and counter in his basement. I really don't want to have a soda fountain in my basement (if you think I'm fibbing you haven't seen my basement), but suddenly I longed to recapture the experience of going into Pete's Drugstore in Milwaukee on a summer afternoon and having a chocolate phosphate while I pondered whatever one ponders at age eight or nine. (Maybe it was which of Pete's many candy bars I might buy if only I had another nickel.)

Today's kids probably wouldn't be able to understand what was so appealing about the drugstores of my youth. Why, they didn't even have Pac-Man or Donkey Kong. But there *was* an appeal. Armed with only a nickel you could while away most of an afternoon at Pete's (if you didn't bother the other customers by slurping forever at the last bubbles of phosphate or idly kicking the counter).

Pete didn't have a grill, but there was a Walgreen's nearby that did, and when I got a little older and began to have real pocket money some of us would occasionally go to Walgreen's for a hamburger. They weren't great hamburgers, but they were great *drugstore* hamburgers, a special class of burgers that, along with chocolate phosphates, cherry Cokes and not-particularly-thick malts made with honest-to-Pete (or honest-to-Walgreen) ice cream, constitute a kind of endangered species: drugstore food.

In the spirit of 1950, and with no apology to those who prefer a Big Mac and a "thick shake" (made with who-knows-what) it seemed appropriate to try to recreate just a few drugstore favorites.

No, there will not be included any of the elaborate sundaes whose appalling names ("Idiot's Delight," "Fat Man's Misery") decorated the wall above the inevitable Bastian-Blessing fountain. They're easy enough to make up yourself, though; just assemble umpteen scoops of various flavors of ice cream, a banana, lots of whipped cream, a little caramel sauce, hot fudge, some nuts and a maraschino cherry in a dish that can't possibly hold it all once the ice cream starts to melt.

Maybe I continued to like drugstores when I was a teen-ager because I wanted to be a soda jerk. If you weren't muscular enough to make the football team, you could still aspire to being a soda jerk, and, wearing your natty paper hat and expertly manipulating the gleaming silver tools of your trade, you could dream of winning the affection of the nubile head cheerleader by favoring her with an extra-large swirl of whipped cream atop the Fat Man's Misery you made for her.

To what can today's scrawny but oversexed teen-agers aspire? No self-respecting head cheerleader can be won over with an extra pickle slice on a Quarter Pounder.

(Yes, yes. We'll get to the recipes eventually, but I have a little more I have to get off my chest.)

Whenever I attempted to discuss drugstore food with the folks at work, the conversation did not stay long with hamburgers and ice cream but always shifted rapidly to candy. Unlike the selection available at even the largest drugstore candy counter these days, drugstores used to have lots of inexpensive candy in addition to the standard candy bars. Although some of these candies are still around — especially, for some reason, in theaters — most have bitten the dust. Whatever, they seem to hold a special place in lots of hearts, even though the coating on some of them tasted like soap and others would stick in your teeth for half an afternoon. Who could forget:

Snaps and Nibs, as well as licorice whips; Jujubes, Dots, Black Crows and the little hard dots on paper strips; thin, striped coconutty strips that looked like watermelon slices or rainbows; little molded candies that for some unfathomable reason were made to look like babies, and especially the variously shaped wax items containing a few drops of flavored liquid. My favorite of that sort was what appeared to be five tiny bottles of pop, each a different flavor. The whole thing cost five cents and was called Nik-L-Nip. If

it's still around somewhere, which I doubt, it's probably called Dol-R-Nip.

You were supposed to be able to chew the wax from which these things were made, but it seldom congealed — it just hung around in your mouth in several flaky lumps. But everybody said it worked, so I always tried.

I recently visited the last place I knew about that had large amounts of this kind of stuff, and the space has been taken over by imported chocolate bars at $1.75 a whack.

Folks also remembered regional candy bars that they miss, including: Giant (a Milwaukee alternative to Mr. Goodbar, in case you're looking), Look and Big Hunk (West Coast goodies), Sugar Daddy (a Slo-Poke), Slo-Poke (a Sugar Daddy) and Snirkles, a large, rectangular spiral of white and brown caramel (CAHR-mul, or as they say on television, CARE-a-mell, or, as they say in a town in California, cahr-MELL).

OK, I'm done reminiscing. On to the recipes.

Drugstore hamburgers are not at all like fast-food hamburgers. They are also not at all like the half-pound cutely named theme-burgers with avocados or sprouts or Monterey Jack and mushrooms that are served at restaurants decorated with packing-crate strips and ferns growing out of light fixtures removed from British trains. (These restaurants invariably have been converted from warehouses or automobile dealerships or mine shafts, a history that is supposed to add a certain *je ne sais quoi*. I certainly don't know *what*.)

The true drugstore hamburger is a

flat, slightly crisp slab of well-done ground beef, served on an inexpensive but nicely grilled bun, with the option of cheese (Velveeta or the equivalent, not Monterey Jack) and maybe fried onions. That's it. Catsup, mustard and pickles are not recommended, but they can be added by the diner if absolutely necessary.

The difficulty in preparing drugstore hamburgers at home is only that you need several large frying pans to take the place of the grill. Don't eliminate grilling the bun — it's a must.

Drugstore Hamburgers

4 tbsp. butter or margarine, divided
1 medium onion
1 lb. ground beef
5 or 6 inexpensive hamburger buns
5 or 6 slices pasteurized process
    cheese (optional)

In a small saucepan, melt 1½ tablespoons of the butter over low heat.

Chop the onion coarsely and stir it into the butter. Let the onion just cook away on the back burner, turning translucent and maybe a little brown. Add a little more butter if necessary. If it gets really brown, turn off the heat.

Set aside a large pan for frying the hamburgers.

Spread the cut surfaces of the buns with the remaining butter and set them in a very large pan, over low to medium-low heat. Check on them often, to make sure that they're grilling but not burning. (We're starting this early because you'll have to do it in shifts unless you have a huge pan. When the first buns are done, plop in the next ones. You could use the broiler in a pinch, but it tends to dry out the buns.)

Now the burgers. Heat the large frying pan, ungreased, over low-medium heat for a couple of minutes. While it's heating, divide the ground beef into five or six equal portions. Shape them by flattening each on a countertop and pressing it out until it is about 6 inches across. Really. They should be THIN. (If you like, you can do this ahead of time; if so, stack the patties, separated by waxed paper or plastic wrap, in the refrigerator.)

When the pan is hot, arrange the patties in it, turn the heat up to medium and let them fry for a couple of minutes, pressing down on them occasionally with a spatula. (They're not supposed to be thick and juicy; they're supposed to be thin and almost crunchy.)

When the bottoms of the burgers are fully browned (not just gray), flip them with a spatula. Press down again and fry the other side. (Drain off any very large accumulation of grease; a small amount should be left for authenticity.) When the second side is almost done, put a slice of cheese on any burgers that are supposed to have it, add a heap of the nice, slightly greasy onions to burgers that are supposed to have them (in a real drugstore every hamburger got onions unless you practically screamed your refusal), and in any case cover each burger with the top of a bun. A burger with neither cheese nor onion should probably get a tiny bit of butter before the bun goes down, just for grease.

When the bottom of the burger is done (and the cheese, if any, is melted), slide a spatula under the whole thing and plop it onto a grilled bun bottom. As they never said in any drugstore I attended, "Voilà!"

To go with the drugstore hamburger, we have to make French fries, which isn't too easy to do well at home. There is no alternative side dish. Certainly not yogurt or a salad. And let's not even mention the "fries" that you get by baking some potatoes on a cookie sheet.

It's not that there's anything really difficult about the process of making French fries; it's just that there's a temperature-control problem. Your usual cooking pot doesn't hold very much oil — nothing like what a commercial deep-fryer holds. The result is that when your pot of oil gets to the right temperature for frying and you dump in a bunch of potatoes, it cools off nastily and the potatoes get greasy instead of nicely fried.

Well, you don't want to buy a commercial deep-fryer, and the prospect of minimizing the cooling effect by cooking one serving of fries at a time while the gang is at the table is more than a little off-putting. Happily, there is an approach that isn't too bad. The process isn't absolutely authentic, and it takes a little extra time, but the result is a whole lot better than anything you're going to get by baking potatoes in the oven. (Yucch.)

Double-Cooked French Fries

4 to 5 medium potatoes
Cooking oil
Salt

Peel the potatoes if you like. (Washed but unpeeled is fine, too.) Cut them into ¼-inch slices, stack the slices and cut them into ¼-inch strips. These thin fast-food-style fries are easier to make decently at home than the larger, more-authentic drugstore model because they cook through more quickly, so if you're in doubt, slice thinner, not thicker.

Soak the potato strips in water — not cold and not in the refrigerator — for about an hour. Drain the strips and pat them dry with toweling.

Meanwhile, pour the oil into a large, deep pot. Don't fill it to closer than a couple inches from the top, because the oil will foam up. Heat it to 390 degrees. (If you don't have a deep-fat thermometer, you're in a little trouble here. You can use 1-inch squares of bread to measure temperatures approximately — at 390 degrees, it takes a bread square about 40 seconds to brown.)

Lower about half the potatoes into the oil (on slotted spoons or a strainer or in a basket if you have one). This overload of potato will cause the temperature of the oil to drop to about 350 degrees, which is what we want to maintain. (Adjust heat to maintain that temperature if you have a thermometer.) Cook the potatoes for about four to six minutes, moving them around occasionally, until they are softened but not brown. Remove them to drain on paper towels, reheat the oil to 390 degrees and cook the second batch the same way.

When both batches have been cooked, raise the oil temperature to 390 degrees again and fry the potatoes a second time in smaller batches (about one serving at a time). This time the oil temperature should be maintained at 390 degrees. (This won't be too hard, as the load of potatoes is smaller and they should still be warm.) Fry each small batch for two or three minutes until the potatoes are light golden colored. Drain, salt and, if necessary, keep warm in a low oven until the other batches are done.

And to go with burgers and fries you must have a chocolate malt. Or at the very least a cherry Coke.

First the malt. This method makes a malt that fills about two standard drinking glasses. It's not very thick, but you could make it thicker by cutting down the amount of milk or increasing the amount of ice cream. A blender is the ideal tool (short of a malt mixer) for making a malt. A food processor tends to liquefy the ice cream. An electric mixer is a little sloppy because of the open bowl, but it works adequately if you cut the ice cream into small pieces.

Chocolate Malt

1 c. milk (or ½ c., for thicker malt)
¼ c. chocolate syrup
2 tbsp. malt powder
3 to 4 scoops vanilla ice cream

If you're working with a blender, put in the milk, syrup and malt powder, then add the ice cream in half-scoop chunks and blend only until smooth.

If you're using an electric mixer, put in a quarter of the milk, and add the syrup and malt powder. Then, with the mixer at low speed, add the ice cream in small chunks (start with several) and add more milk only when necessary until all the ice cream is in. (Too much milk too early will splatter badly.)

The cherry Coke is very easy or a little difficult, depending. Do you have (or can you get) cherry syrup? Then it's easy. If you have to make the syrup, it's a little harder (see below). Don't be tempted just to add unsweetened cherry flavoring to the Coke. The real thing is made with syrup, which makes the Coke a whole lot sweeter. (Incidentally, isn't it odd that no matter how successful all the other brands of cola have been at making inroads on Coke, one never hears of a cherry Pep-

si, for instance, or a cherry RC?)

Once you have the syrup, pour a couple of tablespoons of it (more or less, to taste) into the bottom of a glass. Pour a little Coke into the syrup and stir until it's thinned and bubbly. Authenticity would require a needle-spray of Coke at this point. If you want to make a stab at it, one of those plant-spraying bottles with the adjustable nozzle isn't bad. Either spray or pour in the remaining glassful of Coke, and stir once more.

If you can't get cherry syrup ready-made, making syrups really isn't all that hard. The trick is to avoid having them crystallize when they cool. To that end, follow the rather peculiar directions below more carefully than you might otherwise.

Once you've made the syrup, of course, nothing requires you to confine yourself to adding it to Coke.

One thinks immediately of cherry malts and of cherry (or other flavor) phosphates.

Make the latter like cherry Coke, by stirring a glug of club soda or fizzy mineral water into the syrup, filling the glass with poured or needle-sprayed fizz water and stirring again.

And, if you have something that crushes ice, pour some syrup over a hunk of it and you've got one of those flavored ice things that drips all over small children at fairs and carnivals. If, as seems likely, you don't have any conical paper cups, make it in a regular cup or a glass.

(I must admit that the conical paper water cup is one of the things I dearly loved about drugstores. It held an endless fascination for me. I really don't know why that might have been; it was certainly no more remarkable a feat of engineering than television, radar or Dynaflow — or, for that matter, the flat-bottom paper cup, which didn't leak, either.)

Back to phosphates. The needle spray is kind of pointless with a cherry Coke or cherry phosphate, but it's swell with a chocolate phosphate, made with regular canned chocolate syrup and club soda or fizzy water, because the spray really makes those big bubbles pop up. (When I wrote about making your own pop recently, several readers took me to task for not mentioning the availability of soda siphons — gadgets that turn water into carbonated water with the aid of a CO_2 cartridge. Well, I'll mention them now. They didn't stop making them when the Marx brothers quit making movies, and they work just fine.)

Cherry Syrup

2½ c. sugar
2 c. water
3 to 4 tbsp. cherry flavoring
Food coloring

Combine the sugar and water in a saucepan over low heat, stirring only until the sugar is fully dissolved. Wet a paper towel and wipe the sides of the pan above the surface of the liquid to remove any grains of the sugar. Then cover the pan and bring to a gentle boil. Boil five minutes.

Allow to cool. When the syrup is not much more than lukewarm, stir in the flavoring and coloring. Use plenty of coloring (maybe half a teaspoonful — at least enough to make the syrup quite dark) in case you wind up using the syrup in something besides Coke. A pale phosphate is not appetizing.

Pour into a jar that has been carefully washed, and store in the refrigerator. Makes enough for maybe 18 cherry Cokes.

You can make other flavors of syrup, of course, and you can use real fruit ingredients instead of artificial flavors if you like. For lemon, lime or orange syrups, for example, put three tablespoons of lemon, lime or orange rind in the sugar and water and boil together. Some juice will help, too, but it isn't as potent as the rind. (Additional boiling time will help the flavor but runs an increased risk of crystallized syrup.)

You'll have to strain the bits of rind out of the syrup before you put it in the jar — well, you won't *have* to, but to leave them in would be tacky. Add the coloring after the syrup has been strained and cooled.

Another reason not to stint on the coloring is that it seems to have as much to do with the experience as the flavoring itself. When I made my first attempt at syrup, I used orange rind for flavoring, but all I had was green food coloring. I used it, and I could have sworn that the result tasted not like orange but like Green River, the lime-flavored pop once sold widely from machines in theater lobbies.

You can, if you like, add booze-based flavoring ingredients to the syrup after it cools. Kirsch, for example, makes a heck of a cherry Coke or a cherry malt.

If your recollections include lime rickey (the drugstore fountain item, not the collins or sour mixed drink), you can make one, knowledgeable sources indicate, with shots of lime and cherry syrup in fizzy water. My own favorite phosphate (other than, of course, chocolate) was made with vanilla syrup and orange syrup, a combination that tasted like circus peanuts. Alas, when I tried to duplicate it recently it tasted more like circus-tent sweepings.

No invocation of drugstore food

would be complete without a hot fudge sundae. The aroma of a real drugstore counter around the afternoon snack hour is a complex blend of coffee and hot fudge with a little tang of hamburger grease, and it must not be allowed to disappear from our lives.

You know how to make a hot fudge sundae, of course, but let's depart from authenticity in the direction of deliciousness by making a hot fudge sauce that's heavier on the chocolate and butter than any you'll find ready-made.

Hot Fudge Sauce

1 (6-oz.) pkg. chocolate chips
4 tbsp. (½ stick) butter
2 c. confectioners' sugar
1 c. heavy cream
1 tsp. vanilla

Melt the chocolate and butter over very low heat. Stir in the sugar and cream and bring to boiling, stirring constantly. Boil about five minutes — the sauce should be dark, smooth and thick. If you boil it too long the butter will begin to separate out (it will still be delicious but a bit greasy). Stir in the vanilla. Consume as Nature intended.

Little Mystery #8: Artichokes

How do we get artichoke hearts? Are there artichoke-heart-recycling programs in artichoke-packing country in which you eat the artichoke leaves and put the hearts on the porch for somebody to pick up?

Solution: A spokesperson for the California Artichoke Advisory Board, Castroville, Calif., (no, they advise *about* artichokes), said the term artichoke heart is a misnomer. The marinated and frozen "artichoke hearts" are really baby artichokes that are trimmed of their outer leaves and tops.

That doesn't sound like it makes much economic sense, given what you can get for a full-grown artichoke. Why sell them when they're little?

No, said the chokesperson. See, the artichoke plant puts out all different sizes of artichokes. The biggest one is at the top, then there are what are called "secondaries," which are somewhat smaller, and baby artichokes — which grow further down and in the joints of the plant. The baby artichokes just don't get any bigger.

They *can* be cooked fresh, of course, the artichoke lady said, and lots of trendy Californians do just that — sautéing them and tossing them into everything imaginable (she mentioned spaghetti sauce) — but there is very little demand for fresh baby artichokes elsewhere, so most of them are sold as "hearts."

Artichoke bottoms, which she noted are also called "crowns," are, she said, the bottoms of large artichokes, completely trimmed of leaves.

So *that's* where the artichoke-recycling program is used — people eat the leaves and return the *bottoms?*

No again. The artichokes that are used for bottoms are culls — maybe they have some cosmetic damage, or an insect hole in a leaf or whatever, so they can't be sold as artichokes, but the bottoms are still good.

That makes sense, but I've never heard them referred to as anything but bottoms. Who calls them crowns?

"Snobby people call them crowns," she said. "After all, a bottom is a bottom." Words to live by.

Torte and Retorte

Some time ago, my colleague Kate Parry suggested to me that, as the office pastry lover, I might want to prepare some Viennese pastries for an article in the Food section. I refused. I was probably downright unpleasant about it. I didn't like Viennese pastries, I said, and I didn't want to have to eat them, much less make them, much less write about them.

Parry took that as a challenge. She had developed a fondness for Viennese food during the four months she had worked on a farm near Vienna as an exchange student.

She suggested that she prepare three Viennese pastries and that, based on my nine months in Paris (as a newspaper copy editor and nonstop pastry eater), I prepare three French pastries. We could sample the results, she suggested, and settle the burning issue of French versus Viennese pastry once and for all.

Here is the taste-off discussion that resulted.

Kate: I think we ought to start by talking about when this love you have for French pastries turned into an obsession.

Al: When I was in France I ate pastry several times a day. I had pastry for breakfast and pastry for lunch. And I don't mean *with* breakfast and lunch. Several people told me, "If you like the pastry here, you really ought to go to Vienna — especially for the Sachertorte." So I did. And I was never so disappointed in my life. I ate Sachertorte in a cafe, and I ate Sachertorte at the Hotel Sacher. It was equally bad both places. It was hard, heavy, dry and flavorless. The principal virtue of Sachertorte is that it is *durable*.

Kate: We can decide that when we take a bite of it. But what you say points out a basic difference between Viennese and French pastries. There's a certain durability to those Viennese tortes on the table over there, compared to the light, creamy French concoctions.

Al: Well, who wants a hearty pastry?

Kate: An Austrian. When I lived on the farm in Austria we didn't eat many pastries. I doubt French farmers get into nouvelle cuisine much. But we did make one pastry that was a localized version of the Linzertorte. Gitterkuchen was made with a walnut crust instead of almond and filled with a mean little berry called riebisal instead of raspberries.

Al: My disappointment in Vienna wasn't limited to Sachertorte. I bought a whole bunch of wonderful-looking stuff in different little pastry shops I'd pass. I ate some, and I found them amazingly underflavored. I lugged the others around all day in a shopping bag. Cameras and books got thrown in on top, and the pastries remained absolutely undamaged. I'd never seen such sturdy desserts. You can't walk across the *street* with a wonderfully delicate French pastry without risking severe damage to it. In France they believe, correctly, that pastry is a branch of architecture.

Kate: If you've ever seen an Austrian home, you may understand why they make their tortes this way. The house we lived in was built in 1473. It wasn't crumbling.

Al: I think you should make it real clear that you like Austria, and Austrian food.

Kate: Yes, yes, I like Austria. I like their tortes and pastries. There's no denying that they aren't as light as their French counterparts, but as far as I'm concerned that's not a flaw. They use lots of ground nuts to give them distinctiveness. In some batters no flour is used at all — it's simply ground nuts plus some bread crumbs and egg whites. It give the tortes a texture you don't get elsewhere. In many ways they use the agricultural products available around Vienna.

Al: I will have to allow that, in addition to effort, what characterizes the desserts I have brought for your consideration today is rather incredible cost. The French don't stint at all on ingredients. If something costly is what will make it taste good, that's what goes in.

Of course, ground nuts aren't particularly cheap here, either.

Kate: True, the marzipan for the two layers in the Schokoladetorte cost about $6. If I was living in Austria we would have ground our own almonds into paste. The result would have been better, cheaper and three hours of extra work. Still, we seem to have a basic difference of opinion on what a delicacy is.

Al: Yeah. A delicacy is delicate. That doesn't mean it's necessarily light. That Feuille d'Automne over there weighs in at quite a bit. It's got more than a pound of chocolate in it. Nonetheless, it's still airy and fragile.

Kate: It's also the flavors you grew up on and love. I must admit, two of the pastries I chose to make for today are chocolate, simply to test what I believe is your inability to find fault with anything made with chocolate.

Al: Yes, and I went way out of my way to bring in only one chocolate thing, elimi-nating several favorites of mine, because I know how little you like chocolate. This is sort of the Tribune version of "The Gift of the Magi."

Kate: I think when you look at the flavors in the tortes I prefer, they reflect the tastes of Eastern Europe — they're filled with apricot and marzipan, raspberry and hazelnuts. Those are the flavors I grew up on. You don't find those flavors very often in the wispy little sniveling pastries you prefer.

Al: We haven't tried these things yet, so I don't know, but I'd bet that the other difference is not so much lightness but that the French pastries tend to creaminess rather than to textures like ground nuts.

Kate: Yes. My guess is that when we bite into the French pastries, we'll get a sensation of airiness and smoothness on our tongues. With the Viennese, you're gonna get texture.

I think it's important for us to determine why vulnerable pastries appeal to you.

Al: I think the problem is that real flavor doesn't appeal to you. We should mention right off the bat that you're only comfortable with a chocolate dessert when it's the color of Wheaties.

Kate: I think the frivolous nature of French pastries says something about the character of those who prefer them.

Al: As opposed to the hard-working, low-heeled shoes of Viennese pastries. The whole idea of a sensible pastry is offensive.

Kate: If you'd just hiked down a mountain to get the pastry, you'd be in a fairly sensible frame of mind, wouldn't you?

Al: I am much impressed, actually, with the appearance of the three items you

brought in. I think you've fallen short of sensible, to your credit. To whatever degree one aspires to sensible pastry, one is NUTS!

Kate: But philosophically, what is dessert? What place should it have in our lives?

Al: AAAUUUUGGH!

Kate: If a cake falls in the woods, will it make a sound?

Al: An Austrian cake certainly would.

Kate: In some instances, these pastries aren't meant to be desserts, but the wonderful mid-morning and mid-afternoon meals planned into the Austrian day. They could stand on their own.

Al: Let me ask you something. On that awful trip, I bought a whole lot of things that looked great but turned out lousy. Is the iron crust an imitation of something else?

Kate: Tourism is the major industry of Austria. There is a fallacy that the country is built on whipped cream and Julie Andrews. A sizable number of pastries have to be cranked out each day to satisfy the tourists. It's possible you got substandard pastry.

Al: I mean do they prefer a cream puff that won't crush or is it an inability to make a decent cream puff? It was my suspicion that if an Austrian set out to make a cream puff, he'd make one that couldn't be destroyed.

Kate: When you're wedged in the middle of Eastern Europe with shifting borders, you grab for durability and stability anywhere you can find it — including food.

Al: The French haven't exactly been without geopolitical difficulty. But they continue to make desserts that would be destroyed by the passage of a bird.

Kate: You have to wonder about that. Something tells me that when we touch one of yours with a knife, it's going to phhhhuuttt. When you bite into one of those pastries, just what is it that you want?

Al: I want real, intense flavor; light, creamy smoothness, and sometimes flaky texture. I want visual pleasure, too. I want evidence of craftsmanship. I must say that what you brought in looks nice. But then, so did the stuff I bought in Vienna.

Kate: What *I* would look for is the appearance that makes me want to find out what's in it. A Viennese pastry hints at what's inside. It lets you bite into it and get a surprise.

Al: If we bite into these Viennese pastries and they're good, *that* will be a surprise to me.

Sachertorte

Al: I should note as you cut the Sachertorte that it looks like it takes about 50 pounds of pressure to do it.

Kate: The knife is a little dull.

Al: Come on. The cake came up with the knife as you tried to lift it. Describe the inside color.

Kate: The inside color is a medium chocolate.

Al: Ohhh. That's a light chocolate. It's the color of mailing paper.

Kate: No, this isn't light. When we cut into the Schokoladetorte over there you'll see light.

Al: I can hardly wait. I must say that when that beautiful dark outside is cut to reveal this deathly pale interior, that's the kind of surprise nobody needs. And look at this! [Picks torte up and drops it about a foot with no visible effect.]

See the damage being caused? This is a cake that endures! There's a store — part of the Hotel Sacher, from which you can *mail* a Sachertorte anywhere in the world.

Surface mail. And it arrives in the same condition it left.

Kate: Well, it is holding up quite well, but we've discussed the durability . . .

Al: I can't get the fork through it . . . . And now I can't get the fork out . . . . Yup, that's Sachertorte. I feel better about how good it looked. It's tasteless.

Kate: That's not tasteless. I can taste strong chocolate . . . .

Al: What *is* in it?

Kate: It's a cocoa torte with apricot filling and a hard chocolate glaze.

Al: Right. This torte doesn't taste chocolate at all. It tastes cocoa; and not very cocoa at that. Chocolate is not cocoa. Cocoa is not chocolate. The outside chocolate glaze is very nice. The cake without it is absolutely flavorless.

Kate: Oh, I don't think it's flavorless. It's real dense.

Al: I bet this would make wonderful insulation.

This is authentic, and congratulations. You've beat the Hotel Sacher on its own torte; you can't get a fork through this.

Kate: I got *my* fork through it.

Feuille d'Automne

Kate: When you cut into this one, it drove home what I mean about the structure of French pastry. I have on my plate what amounts to a chocolate meringue hash.

Al: You got the first piece, and you wanted it thin.

Kate: It is an incredibly light texture. But the flavor is so overwhelmingly chocolate that I can hardly stand it.

Al: You don't like chocolate.

Kate: I like chocolate.

Al: Anybody who thinks that Sachertorte is flavorful and who calls cocoa

chocolate can't say she likes chocolate.

Kate: I think there's a limit to the intensity of chocolate the average person can stand.

You have to admit that you're the curve-wrecker on chocolate charts. This is like eating pure fudge. The meringue gives it a nice variation in texture.

Al: It's three layers of crisp meringue, and chocolate mousse made with butter is spread between them and on top of them and all around them, and the whole thing is enrobed with semisweet chocolate. It's light, it's airy, it's crunchy.

And it *tastes* like something. Something delicious.

Kate: It doesn't look that way.

Unlike with the Viennese tortes, I'm not curious about what's inside. I'm worried.

Al: That's merely my faulty execution. What I tried to do — making fans of wrinkled chocolate for the top — is very difficult, and I didn't succeed.

Linzertorte

Kate: If there's a sporty torte on the table, it's the Linzertorte.

Al: It looked kind of pretty, but again, watching you, I was surprised at how difficult it was to cut. It's hard.

Hmm. It is kind of good, but it's not what I expected looking at it.

Kate: What did you expect, puff pastry?

Al: It's a nutty cake batter.

Kate: It's a dense almond crust. Technically, that's the basis for a classic torte. We've redefined torte in this country until for most people it's simply a cake with lots of layers.

Al: It's good, but it's not light.

Kate: I never said it would be. For me a little piece of Linzertorte is incredibly satisfying. I get all the textures and flavors.

Al: It's good, but it reminds me of something my Milwaukee neighbors used to make, called Mandelbrodt.

Kate: Mandelbrodt being another pastry of East European origin.

Al: A drier, less interesting piece of stuff than that I never had in my life. It's the kind of thing little old ladies give a kid and say "Here, have a treat." And the kid takes a bite and goes "Eeeuughh!"

Bagatelle aux Fraises

Kate: If you set out to make a torte to break my spirit of debate, it would combine marzipan and strawberries.

Al: This really got dry. My apologies. The edges are exposed; I should have wrapped it while it was in the refrigerator overnight.

Kate: Now, this is very good.... This I like a lot.

Al: I can't say I care much for it, I just threw it in for you. Although the buttercream between the strawberries is very good. The cake is rich, too, and it's brushed with kirsch. The top is a layer of almond paste.

Kate: I like the fresh fruit in it, which you probably abhor.

Al: That's the one aspect of the French psyche I cannot understand — the constant eating of useless fresh fruit on wonderful things like pastry cream. I do forgive them it. The juice that the fruit leaves behind when you pick it off is real nice.

Kate: Unless that third one knocks my socks off, this is the best of the French pastries.

Al: You won't like the third one. Too much falderal.

Kate: This is nice.

Al: Interesting. It's past its prime for me — the cake is dry and the buttercream

is stiff — and you like it.

Kate: Maybe the staleness gave it texture.

Al: We've really touched something here. Something that's important for our relationship if we intend to keep this up.

Schokoladetorte

Al: As you cut this it didn't lift up with the knife, but you cut yourself a very thin sliver and when you picked it up you flipped it over and it still didn't break. It bent like cloth! Another indestructible product.

Kate: It's moist and laced with kirsch in layers of marzipan and apricot.

Al: This is very good. I can't taste the cake itself, though.

Kate: The cake is a hazelnut base with semisweet chocolate shavings in it.

Al: It doesn't have much flavor on its own, but in combination... Still, I'd have used a darker chocolate frosting.

Kate: This combines several of my favorite flavors.

Al: In this case, if it's durable and flexible I don't care. It tastes good, too. What is this little ball of glop here?

Kate: That's marzipan rolled in chocolate shavings with a hazelnut on top.

Al: Where's the pickle? This is good. Oh, am I going to be sick this afternoon from eating all this.

Kate: Yeah.

Anyway, while we must admit that, in general, French pastries are arrogantly insubstantial....

Al: We've admitted nothing of the kind. We've admitted that Viennese pastries could be used to construct office buildings.

Kate: Nevertheless there are exceptions that cross borders.

Al: We're almost done, aren't we?

Kate: Just one more.

St. Honoré Chiboust

Kate: First of all, when Al cut this thing and put it on my plate it shook like a piece of lutefisk.

Al: It didn't fall apart.

Kate: No, but it quivered in a most unseemly way.

And talk about lack of taste — this is like pie crust with egg whites on it. The caramel flavor is on one part; the rest is froth.

Al: I never had this before, and I think you're right. I should have made something I love.

Kate: And talk about durability. It's a perfect example of a French pastry that looks out of this world. My expectations are high. When I bite into it, it's hard.

Al: Where do you get off? That's every criticism I have of *Viennese* pastries.

Kate: At least they don't deceive you with appearances.

Al: Yes they do. That's exactly what's the matter with that beautiful Sachertorte. And I keep hearing about how wonderful Sachertorte is, whereas I'm never going to make this thing again.

Al: Well, OK. What have we learned?

Kate: There was a realization that there is a difference in our own food preferences that may help decide whether or not we like a particular nationality of food.

Al: And there was the moment with the Bagatelle aux Fraises, which was getting too dry and firm for me and that you enjoyed for those same qualities.

Kate: Yes. What's an asset for me is a drawback for you.

Al: And never the twain shall meet. Maybe this is the underlying reason for all those European wars. People getting sick of eating desserts that are too hard or too fluffy for their tastes.

Kate: Yes. It's politics on a plate.

Al: Very nice. If we could only make a firm but intensely flavored eclair maybe, that could be shipped back and forth across the borders...

Kate: Well, you could ship Sachertortes.

Al: Yes, but nobody in France would want them. They would use them for wheel blocks to trap cars that had parked at expired meters.

Kate: Of course if you tried to carry a French pastry across the border by *hand* you'd end up with an empty plate.

Al: So we need to develop a middle ground of tasty but durable desserts.

Kate: Maybe there's some country in between.

Al: Alsace-Lorraine. We need to sample the Alsace-Lorraine pastries.

Kate: That might be the way to go.

Al: Except that the pastries probably change every time there's a troop movement near the border.

These are the recipes for two of the three French desserts. (I have decided that the third one wasn't worth the effort.) Both are lots of work. Both are based on recipes in Lenôtre's Desserts and Pastries.

▶

Feuille d'Automne

(Autumn Leaf Cake)
Meringue:
½ c. and 1 tbsp. granulated sugar, divided
1 scant c. confectioners' sugar
5 egg whites
Mousse:
11 oz. good-quality semisweet chocolate
¾ c. (1½ sticks) unsalted butter
5 egg yolks
8 egg whites
3½ tbsp. granulated sugar
Enrobing:
6 oz. good-quality semisweet chocolate

Prepare the meringue circles: Preheat the oven to 275 degrees. Place sheets or three circles of parchment paper (available at gourmet shops) onto two baking sheets. (You can try waxed paper, but I don't recommend it.) Fit a pastry bag with a large (½- to ¾-inch) tip. Sift together the half cup of granulated sugar and the confectioners' sugar.

Beat the egg whites until they are very stiff; halfway through add the tablespoon of granulated sugar. When the whites are fully beaten, fold in the sifted sugars. Working quickly, fill the pastry bag with meringue and pipe it, working in spirals, into three circles about 7 inches in diameter. (You can do this without a pastry bag, too: Using a wide spatula, spread three mounds of meringue into rough circles about 7 inches in diameter on parchment paper. Make the top quite flat and the edges as high as the rest, or they will burn or break off.)

Bake all the meringues at the same time, for 1 hour and 15 minutes. They should be very light brown and completely dry top to bottom. If they brown too quickly, turn the oven down.

Prepare the mousse: Melt the chocolate in a double boiler or over very low heat. Remove from the heat and add the butter, broken into small pieces, and stir until the butter is fully dissolved. Allow the mixture to cool completely, then stir in the egg yolks one at a time.

Beat the egg whites until they are very stiff; halfway through add the sugar. Fold the chocolate mixture into the egg whites. The mixture will acquire a grainy, speckled appearance; go no further.

Assembly: Evenly spread about a fourth of the mousse on one of the meringue circles, going all the way to the edges. Top with another meringue circle, another fourth of the mousse, and the last meringue circle. Spread the top meringue more thinly with mousse.

Coat the sides of the assembled cake thickly, using most of the remaining mousse, working it in between the layers as needed. Use any remaining mousse on top.

Prepare the enrobing: Melt the six ounces of chocolate in a double boiler or over very low heat. Using a wide spatula or putty knife, spread the chocolate evenly to cover a standard (10½- by 15-inch or so) baking sheet. Cool the sheet in the refrigerator 10 minutes, then allow it to rewarm for a few minutes on a countertop.

Score a lengthwise line into the chocolate so as to make a strip about the height of the finished cake. Holding the putty knife almost horizontal, slowly scrape up that wide strip of chocolate. Go very slowly at first — if the chocolate cracks it's too cold. Let it warm a few minutes more and try again. When you have the strip scraped up, cool your hands (rinse them in cold water and dry them thoroughly) to avoid melting fingerprints into the chocolate. Or wear dishwashing gloves. Pick up the chocolate and pat onto the side of the cake. It'll probably go about halfway around. Repeat.

Make narrower strips of the remaining chocolate, flex them so they bend into ruffled circular ribbons, and drape them in concentric rings of ruffles on the top of the cake.

(The real thing calls for wide, fan-shaped ruffled ribbons, which I've been unable to do.)

Cool the cake several hours in the refrigerator.

Bagatelle aux Fraises

(Strawberry bagatelle)
Genoise cake:
⅓ c. plus 1½ tbsp. sugar
3 large eggs
2 tbsp. butter
½ c. plus 2 tbsp. flour
1 tsp. vanilla sugar (or substitute 1
    tsp. sugar and ¼ tsp. vanilla)
Kirsch syrup:
⅓ c. sugar
6 tbsp. water
2 tbsp. kirsch
Buttercream:
2½ sticks unsalted butter
6 egg yolks, or 1 egg and 5 egg yolks
⅔ c. plus 3 tbsp. sugar
3 tbsp. plus 2 tsp. water
1½ tbsp. vanilla extract
2 tbsp. softened unsalted butter, if
    needed
1½ pt. fresh small strawberries
Almond paste:
1 (7-oz.) pkg. almond paste
1 drop green food coloring
¼ to ½ c. confectioners' sugar

Prepare the cake: Preheat the oven to 350 degrees. Grease and flour an 8- by 8-inch pan. Put the sugar and eggs in a mixing bowl over, but not in, boiling water. Beat at low speed for one minute. Remove

from the heat and beat at high speed for five minutes and again at low speed for ten minutes more, or until the batter is very pale and forms a ribbon when it falls from the beater.

Barely melt the butter in a small saucepan. Sift the flour and vanilla sugar and fold into the egg-sugar mixture. Fold in the warm butter but leave the milky residue from the butter in the pan. Pour the batter into the prepared cake pan and bake for 30 minutes, or until it tests done. Let cool 10 minutes, turn out onto a rack and cool.

Prepare the kirsch syrup: Put sugar and water in a saucepan and bring to boil, stirring until the sugar is dissolved. Remove from heat. When cool, stir in the kirsch.

Prepare the buttercream: Cream the butter until it is light and fluffy. Put the egg yolks in another mixer bowl and beat briefly. Bring a small saucepan of water not quite to the simmer. Meanwhile, in another saucepan, boil the sugar and the water until it reaches 236 degrees (the soft-ball stage). Immediately beat that syrup into the eggs by pouring it in a fine stream as the mixer bowl turns. (Keep the stream away from beaters and sides of the bowl.)

Set the bowl onto the saucepan of almost-simmering water and beat at moderate speed for several minutes, until the mixture is light, foamy and hot to the touch. Set the bowl in cold water and beat for several minutes until it has cooled to tepid and forms a ribbon when it falls from the beater. Beat this mixture by spoonfuls into the bowl of creamed butter. Then beat in the vanilla. If the mixture looks as if it is separating, beat in a little softened butter.

Carefully cut the cooled cake into two layers, and trim off hard crusts. Put the bottom layer of cake on a plate and soak it with the syrup, using a pastry brush.

Clean and de-green the strawberries. Dry them very thoroughly. Select about 20 nicely shaped berries — all of similar size — cut them in half vertically and set them aside. Spread a thin (⅛-inch) layer of buttercream on the cake, and cover it to within ¾ inch of the edge with upside-down whole strawberries. Try to use berries that are roughly the same height.

Spoon most of the buttercream over the strawberries and spread it so that it fills in the spaces between them. Using a spatula, put a wall of the buttercream around those strawberries, to within ½ inch of the edge of the cake. Save a bit of the buttercream. Press the strawberries halves (upside down) into outsides of the square of pastry cream. Top with the other layer of cake, and brush that with kirsch syrup. Spread remaining buttercream atop the cake.

Prepare the almond paste: Put the purchased paste in a bowl and add the smallest possible amount of green food coloring. You want a very light green. Knead the color into the paste. Sprinkle the counter with confectioners' sugar, put the almond paste down on it, and sprinkle it and a rolling pin with confectioners' sugar. Roll the almond paste out until it is a bit bigger than the cake. Dust off any confectioners' sugar. Drape the almond paste lightly over the roller and unroll it on top of the cake. Refrigerate 15 minutes.

Using a very sharp knife, trim the almond paste and cake layers even with the cut strawberries. You might slice a bit off of the berries, too, to make the edge even.

Here are Kate's recipes for the Viennese tortes. Some require a major time commitment:

Linzertorte

¾ c. plus 2 tbsp. soft butter
¾ c. plus 2 tbsp. sugar
3 eggs
Ground cloves
½ tsp. ground cinnamon
Peel of ½ lemon, grated
1 c. butter-cookie crumbs
1¼ c. ground almonds
2 c. flour
1 c. raspberry jam
1 egg yolk, beaten
<u>Garnish:</u>
Mint leaves
Fresh raspberries (or whole frozen, thawed)

Cream the butter and sugar. Add the three eggs one at a time, alternating with a pinch of cloves, the cinnamon and lemon peel. Mix in cookie crumbs and almonds. Using hands, fold in flour. Pat into a ball and wrap with plastic wrap or waxed paper. Chill for two hours.

Heat oven to 375 degrees. Grease a 10-inch springform pan. If you don't have one of these, this can be made in a layer-cake pan. Cut a circle of wax paper to put in the bottom of the pan and grease the sides. (From that point, follow directions for a springform pan until removing from the oven. Then let the torte cool completely in the layer cake pan. Invert cooled torte onto a plate and carefully turn right side up.)

Whichever pan you are using, press two-thirds of the dough into the bottom of the pan to form a crust about ½ inch deep. Mold ½-inch-wide edges up about ¼ inch higher than the rest of the crust. Spread the jam over the dough.

On a floured board, roll out the rest of the dough to about ⅛-inch thickness. Using a sharp knife or a pastry cutter, slice the dough into ½-inch strips. Carefully take half the strips and lay them diagonally across the crust about ½ inch apart. Press the ends of the strips into the edge of the crust. Now lay remaining strips across the first strips at right angles to the others and press into edge of crust. Trim any ragged edges. The effect should be to form a lattice pattern on top of the jam.

Brush the torte with beaten egg yolk. Bake 35 minutes or until light brown. For a springform pan, let torte cool in pan half an hour, then remove and cool on a rack.

To garnish, place three mint leaves in the center of the torte and top with four berries in a little pile. Repeat this at four points along the sides of the torte. Do not refrigerate, or the crust will get soggy and soft. To serve, cut like a pie.

Variation: Replace almonds with ground walnuts. Almost any tart jam can be used to fill. Currant and apricot work well.

Sachertorte

Bread crumbs
7 eggs, separated
¾ c. plus 2 tbsp. sugar, divided
8 tbsp. butter
½ c. unsweetened cocoa powder
1 c. flour
¾ c. butter-cookie crumbs
Topping:
¾ c. apricot jam
8 oz. semisweet chocolate
Chocolate sprinkles
Garnish:
Orange slice

Grease two 9-inch layer cake pans and dust with bread crumbs. Heat oven to 400 degrees.

Cream egg yolks and half a cup of sugar in a large bowl, beating eight minutes with an electric mixer. Melt the butter and cool to lukewarm. Combine cocoa and flour. Fold into egg mixture along with butter.

Beat the egg whites until foamy. Add the remaining sugar and beat until stiff. Fold egg whites and cookie crumbs into yolk mixture. Do this gently but thoroughly. The egg whites are the leavening for the cake. If you stir them out of the batter, the cake will be flat.

Spoon the batter into the pans. Bake for half an hour. Reduce oven temperature to 350 degrees and bake until done, about 15 minutes longer (test with a toothpick). While the cake is baking, avoid working in the kitchen. Cakes made in this way fall easily. Don't open the oven door at all for the first half hour. Cool the cake in the oven for 15 minutes with the door ajar. Then turn onto a rack to cool completely.

When the cakes are cool, warm up the jam. Remove any large pieces of the fruit. Spread about one-third on one layer and top with second layer. Spread the rest of the jam over the top and sides of cake.

In a double boiler, melt the chocolate. Pour it quickly over the cake and smooth down the sides. (Make sure the cake is on the plate that will be used for serving.) Work quickly, because the chocolate cools and hardens fast. The outside of the torte should be a smooth, glossy shell of chocolate. Press chocolate sprinkles into the chocolate shell along the bottom layer of the torte. When the chocolate is cool and hard, slit the orange slice halfway through and twist. Place in center of torte.

To cut the torte, use a very sharp, thin knife. Run it under hot water and wipe dry before starting, to avoid cracking the chocolate shell.

▶

Wiener Schokoladetorte

6 eggs, separated
1 tsp. vanilla
Pinch of salt
⅔ c. sugar
3½ oz. semisweet chocolate, grated
1½ c. butter-cookie crumbs
¾ c. ground hazelnuts
Filling:
¼ c. kirsch
1 c. apricot jam
2 (7-oz.) tubes almond paste
Frosting:
4 oz. semisweet chocolate
4 tbsp. butter
1 egg, beaten
1⅔ c. confectioners' sugar
Garnish:
1 oz. semisweet chocolate, grated
12 whole hazelnuts

Grease the inside bottom of a 10-inch springform cake pan. Heat oven to 350 degrees. Beat egg yolks, vanilla, salt and sugar until creamy, about eight minutes with an electric mixer. Stir in grated chocolate. Beat egg whites until stiff. Carefully fold into chocolate mixture. Do not beat. The egg whites are the leavening, and if you beat the air out of them the cake will not rise.

Fold the cookie crumbs and hazelnuts into the batter. Pour the batter into the pan and smooth out surface. Bake for an hour or until a toothpick comes out clean. Do not open the oven door while this cake is baking; it will fall easily. Cool in springform pan for 10 minutes. Then remove to rack to cool for about one hour. Wrap in plastic wrap and freeze cake overnight (this makes it easier to cut the thin layers).

Next day, slice the cake into three layers, using a large, very sharp knife. Sprinkle the bottom layer with half of the kirsch.

Spread with half the apricot jam. Take one roll of almond paste and cut off about one fourth of it. Set that aside. Roll the rest out on a board covered with confectioners' sugar into a circle the size of the cake.

Carefully fold the almond paste into quarters and lay on top of the apricot jam. Unfold and adjust to cover the cake. Trim edges flush with cake. Top with second layer. Sprinkle with remaining kirsch. Spread with remaining apricot jam. Repeat process with second tube of almond paste. Top with final layer. Place your hand on top of the cake and apply light but firm pressure for a few seconds to "set" the torte.

Wrap the remaining almond paste to prevent drying. Melt the frosting chocolate in a double boiler. Cool to warm. Melt butter. Stir beaten egg and confectioners' sugar into chocolate. Add the butter. Beat with electric mixer until frosting is creamy. Quickly spread over the top and sides of cake. This frosting hardens somewhat as it cools, so it's important to work fast.

Take the remaining almond paste and form into 12 1-inch balls. Roll the balls in the grated chocolate. Press a hazelnut into each ball to flatten slightly. Place one ball in the middle of the torte and the rest in a circle along the top edge. Cover and refrigerate cake to store.

Wrong Way Corrigan Dinner

We're well into the tornado and mosquito seasons, which means we're also well into the picnic season. I haven't been to a sponsored picnic in some time, but I do recall the picnics that my father's Masonic lodge had when I was a kid in Milwaukee.

I remember those picnics for two reasons: First, whoever was responsible for the soft drinks every year managed to get them in a very wide assortment. There would be flavors of pop (we called it soda water, but you know what I mean) that you never saw anywhere else: pineapple, banana, grapefruit — and chocolate.

The chocolate pop was actually rather unpleasant, but it was so much fun to look at that I usually didn't decide I didn't like it until late in the day.

The other memorable thing about those picnics — and all organized picnics — is the games for kids. When you go on a regular picnic, you might bring along a thing or two to keep kids occupied, but chances are you don't set up several hours of activities for them. Such things are standard, though, at sponsored picnics, and I remember the looks of weary bewilderment on younger kids' faces when, after an hour or so of frenzied activity, they began to fall apart.

Invariably in some sack race or spoon race or whatever, some kid would get turned around and head for the starting line, bringing whoops and cheers from the spectators and a hesitant smile to the kid's face — probably hesitant because he couldn't believe he was winning.

One of the things that people always shouted at that juncture was "Wrong Way Corrigan!" This, of course, only puzzled the poor kid, who had never heard of Wrong Way Corrigan. I only figured out later what that was supposed to mean. (Yes, dear reader, I was often that poor kid.)

I haven't heard anybody shout "Wrong Way Corrigan" in a long time. How soon they forget.

Corrigan came to mind recently when I was puzzling over how to enhance an already weird dinner idea.

I got a suggestion in the mail (of course I've misplaced it since, so I can't tell you who it was from) that I put together a meal of foods like tomato-soup cake — foods in which there is an ingredient that doesn't seem to belong there. The letter writer (who *was* that masked reader? — I wanted to thank her) noted that most such recipes seem to be desserts (sauerkraut cake, pork-sausage cake, etc.) but she was sure I could think of enough non-dessert items to put together a whole meal of recipes each of which had an odd ingredient.

It became clear after a bit of recipe pondering that the field was too wide. I needed some second constraint on my fevered brain. That's when I thought of Douglas Corrigan.

Corrigan, you may or may not remember, was a flier who, in 1938, was refused clearance to fly alone in his dilapidated monoplane from New York to Europe in an attempt to duplicate the Charles Lindbergh flight. So he said he was going to go back to California. The next thing anybody knew was when he landed in Dublin, Ireland, almost 24 hours later and asked the astonished officials, "Is this Los Angeles?" He claimed that his compass (his only instrument) got stuck.

He earned instant fame, including a ticker-tape parade down Broadway and a starring role in a movie about his life; and the sobriquet Wrong Way Corrigan passed into the language — at least for a while — as something to holler at drivers who ignored one-way signs, and at hapless children at picnics.

(Corrigan continued to maintain that he really was trying to get to California. Interviewed on the 20th anniversary of his flight, he said, "That's my story. I've been telling it so long I'm beginning to believe it.")

Back to food. (You thought I'd lost my way, didn't you? Never. My compass was just stuck briefly.) What occurred to me was that as long as I was going to put an unlikely ingredient in each recipe, maybe I could put some coffee in the appetizer, a dessert ingredient in the salad, and so on — have the weird ingredients running the wrong way through the dinner.

It worked out rather well, I think. So well that if you are strange enough to want to duplicate this entire menu (rather than an individual item or two), you wouldn't necessarily have to explain anything to the guests. It's all nice food. If you want to drop a hint, though, you might consider serving Tums at the beginning of the meal.

For the appetizer, as I said, I wanted to use some coffee. So I made a coffee-flavored spread. With a little bacon on top, the whole thing was kind of like breakfast.

As with any other appetizer involving cream cheese spread onto crackers, don't assemble these far in advance. Moisture migrates from the cream cheese into the crackers, drying the cream cheese and making the crackers soggy. Nice folks won't ask me how I know this.

Java Sunrise Appetizers

About ½ lb. sliced bacon
2½ tsp. instant coffee
2 tsp. hot water
2 tsp. sugar
¼ tsp. salt
¼ tsp. pepper
1 (8-oz.) pkg. cream cheese, softened
Crackers

Cut each strip of bacon into four or five pieces and fry them until they are crisp. Drain on paper towels.

Dissolve the instant coffee in the hot water, then stir or beat the coffee mixture, sugar, salt and pepper into the softened cream cheese.

Shortly before serving, spread the cream cheese mixture onto the crackers and top each with a piece of bacon.

Makes about four dozen appetizers.

For the salad, as I said (if you expect to get anything more than a barely passing grade, you have to pay attention), I wanted to employ a dessert ingredient.

The obvious solution — obvious to those of us who hang on every word from the world's trendy-eating capitals — was one of those nouvelle-cuisine combinations now no-doubt already passé: lobster in vanilla sauce on spinach leaves.

This being the Midwest, we'll ignore whether it's passé in New York.

This not being funded by a grant from the Mobil Oil Corp., we'll switch to crab instead of lobster — and mock crab at that. (As much as my mind rebels at the idea of pollock flavored and shaped to look like crab legs, I must admit that it's very pleasant to eat.)

And this being me, and liking the flavor of sauces a whole lot, we'll mix the sauce and "crab" together instead of following the nouvelle-cuisine practice of setting unsauced food down in pretty puddles of sauce.

I must say this went over very, very well. If I had had more "crab" in vanilla sauce I could have peddled it easily.

This reinforces my life-long contention that there is no situation in which dessert is inappropriate. Next comes brownies in roast beef. (Only kidding.) (Well, maybe . . . .)

Vanilla Mock-Crab Salad

2 tbsp. finely chopped shallots
3 tbsp. butter, divided
¼ c. dry white wine
½ c. condensed chicken broth
1 c. heavy cream
5 tsp. vanilla, divided
Salt, pepper to taste
1 (8-oz.) pkg. mock crab legs (or mock crab "salad pieces"), thawed
1 (10- to 12-oz.) bag fresh spinach

Briefly cook the shallots in a saucepan over medium heat with one tablespoon of the butter. Add the wine and cook down, stirring, until almost all of the liquid has evaporated. Add the chicken broth, raise the heat to high and cook down, stirring, until the liquid is reduced to about half its original volume.

Reduce the heat to medium, stir in the cream and four teaspoons of the vanilla and cook about 15 minutes, stirring, or until the mixture has reduced to about one cup in volume.

Stir in the remaining one teaspoon of vanilla and pour the sauce through a sieve into another saucepan, removing the pieces of shallot.

Press the shallots in the sieve to get all the lovely sauce out of them, then discard them. Add salt and pepper to the sauce and bring to the boil. Remove from heat.

Cut the remaining two tablespoons of butter into three or four pieces and swirl them into the sauce one at a time until each is melted and absorbed.

Cut the mock crab legs into bite-size pieces (if using "salad pieces," you're all set), and stir them into the sauce.

Rinse the spinach leaves and remove tough stems.

Make a foundation of spinach leaves on six salad plates or in a large salad bowl.

Rewarm the "crab" and sauce over very low heat, stirring, then spoon over the spinach.

Serves six. Nummy!

If you followed the discussion of how the Wrong Way Corrigan principle would apply to this meal, you might have wondered what would happen in the middle, when the dishes going forward (appetizer, salad, main course, vegetable, dessert, coffee) met the odd ingredients going the other way (coffee, dessert, etc.).

What happened in this case, partly because I got confused as to which course which odd ingredient was to go in, was that I wound up trying to put a second meat into the meat course. That's not so odd, when you think about it. Lots of restaurants serve steak-and-lobster combinations (admittedly not rolled together, but on more-or-less the same plate). So if you can have surf 'n' turf at a nice restaurant, what's wrong with some chicken breast rolled around some hamburger at home? Nothing, so let's get into the restaurant spirit and call it:

Chuck 'n' Cluck

¾ lb. ground beef
1 small onion, chopped
Salt, pepper
2 to 3 tbsp. red wine
2 tbsp. Worcestershire sauce
1½ tbsp. cornstarch
¼ c. water
1 egg yolk, beaten
6 skinless, boneless chicken-breast
    halves (from 3 whole breasts)
6 tbsp. butter or margarine
Sauce:
¼ c. white-wine vinegar
1 tbsp. minced shallots
1 tsp. crushed dried tarragon
¼ tsp. pepper
2 egg yolks
¾ c. (1½ sticks) butter

Break up the ground beef in a frying pan and brown along with the chopped onion, salt and pepper. Drain off fat. Add the wine and Worcestershire sauce. Cook two or three minutes. Dissolve the cornstarch in the water, stir in the beaten egg yolk and add that mixture to the ground beef. Cook briefly until the liquid has thickened. Adjust seasoning and set aside. After a few minutes, pour off any fat that has separated out.

Pound or roll out the chicken breasts lightly to flatten and enlarge them. Roll each around a portion of the beef mixture

and fasten shut with toothpicks. (To allow the chicken to be fried easily, make the toothpicks run along, rather than across, the length of the chicken roll. Where that isn't possible, break off any protruding pieces of toothpick.) Salt and pepper the rolls.

Melt the six tablespoons of butter in a large skillet or electric frying pan and fry the chicken rolls, over medium heat, about five minutes on each of two opposite sides and two or three minutes each on the in-between sides. Remove the toothpicks, cover the chicken and keep it warm.

Meanwhile, prepare the sauce: In a medium saucepan, boil the vinegar, shallots, tarragon and pepper until there is only about a tablespoon of liquid remaining. Cool the liquid slightly, then beat in the egg yolks. Over very low heat or in a double boiler, stirring constantly, stir in the three-fourths cup of butter a tablespoon at a time, making sure each piece has been fully incorporated into the sauce before the next one is added.

Serve the sauce over the chicken rolls. Makes six.

If you elect to serve this whole thing on toast, you could call it Chuck 'n' Cluck on a Mukluk.

For a vegetable containing a salad ingredient, the obvious candidate is peas French-style (braised with lettuce). Except for two things: We just used that in another article, and it is too obvious.

So how about *corn* braised with lettuce?

Not a bad combination at all, it turns out, and rather delightfully springlike in color. (Like the *season*, you difficult person, not like the thing that's rusting under your car.)

Corn Française

2 (10-oz.) pkg. frozen corn
1½ to 2 c. coarsely torn lettuce
⅓ large onion, cut into rings
1½ tsp. sugar
½ tsp. salt
¼ tsp. pepper
3 tbsp. butter

Cook the corn according to package directions, but only until it is thawed. Drain.

Put half the lettuce in a large saucepan. Add the corn and the onions. Sprinkle with sugar, salt and pepper and dot with butter. Top with the other half of the lettuce, cover and cook over low-medium heat eight to ten minutes, until the lettuce on top is hot. Stir and add salt and pepper if needed.

Serves six.

What do we have for the people now, Johnny?

We've got dessert, Bob! Lots and lots of dessert! And not just *any* dessert . . . . It's dessert with an appetizer ingredient in it!

Shouldn't some nonvegetable course have had a vegetable in it by now, Johnny?

We got kind of confused, Bob. But we're pretty sure the folks will like this one anyway.

Chocolate Mousse Sandwichettes

1 (12-oz.) pkg. semisweet chocolate
    chips
¾ c. (1½ sticks) unsalted butter
8 eggs, separated
3½ tbsp. granulated sugar
1 (13-oz.) (large) box Triscuits
1 or 2 oz. semisweet chocolate
    (optional, for decoration)

Melt the chocolate chips in a double boiler or over very low heat. Cut the butter into one-tablespoon chunks. Remove the chocolate from the heat and stir in all the butter until it is fully melted. (Reheat briefly, if necessary.) Allow to cool completely, then stir in the egg yolks, one at a time.

In a large bowl, beat the egg whites until they are foamy and beginning to rise. Gradually beat in the sugar, then beat the whites until they form stiff peaks. Stir about one-fourth of the whites into the chocolate mixture to lighten it, then gently fold in the remaining whites. (The mixture probably won't get fully blended without excessive folding. Quit when it's evenly speckled, with no patches of white.)

If the mousse is not thick, allow it to chill an hour or so.

Assemble the sandwichettes: Blade a big, thick blob of mousse onto a Triscuit. Top with another Triscuit, pressing down slightly. If you're "that sort of person," you'll want to even up the sides so they look like little ice-cream sandwiches. If you're not "that sort of person," you won't. This has been a test.

If you like, melt an ounce or so of semisweet chocolate and dribble it across the tops of the sandwichettes. Refrigerate until serving time. Makes about three dozen.

Now to coffee. What could we put in coffee? Even forgetting what course the weird addition represents, what could we possibly use?

I spent some time fooling around with things that didn't work at all, and when I hit on this one, which I thought worked well enough that it wasn't repulsive, I quit. Imagine my surprise when, although I offered plain coffee too, about half the folks asked for seconds of the doctored version.

Peanut Butter Coffee

(That's right!)
6 cups brewed coffee
About 1 tbsp. peanut butter

Put the peanut butter and a cup or two of the coffee in a blender. Whomp until it's well blended, then stir back into the rest of the coffee. Serves six.

Little Mystery #9: Bananas

I couldn't believe the rhyme explanation to the mystery referred to on previous pages — that we were told for years not to put bananas in the refrigerator because the jingle-writer needed a rhyme for equator. So I've done some more digging. It doesn't get better.

Some of the digging involved cleaning off my desk, where I found a 1981 press release from Chiquita Brands, Inc., about refrigerating bananas. The release claims that the jingle "at the time was most accurate."

"At the time of Miss Chiquita's debut in 1945," the release says, "bananas arrived green at your local grocer on stalks, which he would then hang from the ceiling. When you bought these bananas, it would take a while for them to ripen. The act of putting them in the refrigerator would halt the ripening process, and hence the line forbidding refrigeration went into Miss Chiquita's song.

"Today . . . Chiquita bananas are shipped from the tropics in cushioned cartons and then taken to special warehouses to be ripened under careful temperature and humidity conditions. When you purchase bananas in your supermarket, they are most likely yellow with green tips — practically ripe. Most consumers let them sit for a day or two, until the peel has brown flecks in it. When they reach this stage (or the stage you like), feel free to put them in the vegetable compartment of your refrigerator for storage."

If that all leaves you feeling a little confused, you're in good company. Just because in 1945 bananas mightn't have been very ripe when you brought them home, why was it a bad idea to refrigerate them when they *had* ripened?

If we can understand today that we should wait until they are ripe before we refrigerate them, why was it "most accurate" to say in 1945 that they should never be refrigerated?

(And, for that matter, who says bananas in supermarkets today are generally only a day from full ripeness? I've seen piles of bananas so green they look like long limes.)

Well, phone calls and press releases have an ephemeral quality — you can say almost anything in them and hope nobody will remember. That's why my eyes lit up when I found a book, a 1974 paperback called "The Chiquita Banana Cookbook," prepared and produced by Chiquita Brands.

When they realized they were committing ink to paper that might be saved and looked at for years, what did Chiquita Brands have to say about the great turnaround on the refrigeration issue? Here is the complete text:

"Recent research now shows that the fact is that once bananas have ripened at room temperature to the point you like to eat them, they may be kept several days longer in the refrigerator."

It's difficult to imagine what the "recent research" involved. Possibly putting a banana in a refrigerator.

Stewing in My Own Au Jus

One day a few weeks ago, when my kids were in town for a visit, we were driving around near the University of Minnesota and passed the two-story McDonald's that, for some reason, exists in Dinkytown.

Dave, who is nine and perfectly normal but occasionally lapses into a second personality rather like that of Eddie Haskell on "Leave It to Beaver" ("That's a beautiful dress you're wearing, Mrs. Cleaver"), noticed the McDonald's out the window, shifted into smarmy and remarked:

"Why, what a charming restaurant. I'll bet it's lovely in there. They probably don't even have tin ash trays!"

Even for Dave, who plays a mean game of Highway Alphabet, that was an unusually insightful remark.

There *are* little touches that instantly convey something about the tone of a restaurant, and the disposable ash tray is certainly one indicator of a bargain-basement beanery.

Dave has always had a good eye for restaurant detail.

Several years ago, when he was quite small and could not yet read, the neighborhood Red Barn introduced a salad bar. There were posters and mobiles all over the walls and ceilings of the place, raving about this development. They featured photos of a jumble of salad ingredients — things like pieces of lettuce, slices of cucumber and onion, tomato wedges and globs of salad dressing.

Dave pointed to one of the posters and said, "Look, Dad! They have garbage!"

My thought exactly. Dave is a (chocolate) chip off the old block.

Anyway, after I made much of the ash-tray remark, both Dave and his older brother, Joe, who is no slouch in the observation department himself, began pointing out other indicators of restaurant class, such as the presence or absence of plastic water tumblers, whether you have to bus your own tray, and, moving up several notches, how many forks there are at a place setting.

I myself have always been put off by eating places that put lemon in your iced tea even if you don't ask for it, but that is neither here nor there.

(This whole *thing* is neither here nor there, and I recognize that, but bear with me; I'm beginning to come to the point.)

It is possible, of course, to have *wonderful* food at a restaurant that has foil ash trays, plastic glasses and the disposable spoon-and-fork combination that I've never known whether to call a spork or a foon.

And it is certainly *very* possible to have lousy food at a restaurant where the tableware is real.

So these are not indicators of the quality of the food, but of how tony the place is.

A dinner date at a two-fork restaurant is more likely to impress some sweeties (even if the food is reminiscent of college dorm cafeterias) than is a mess of really excellent ribs thrown onto a paper plate by a surly guy who needs a shave and can't seem to make change.

Another such indicator, and the focus of today's sermon, is the number and severity of misspellings and other amusements on the menu.

The "roast beef au jus with gravy" — or "roast beef served with au jus gravy" — may be terrific, but you probably will lose points if your boss, mother-in-law or other severe critic notices many entries of that sort on the menu of the restaurant you have selected.

I have long been a fan of such menu irregularities, and after a recent encounter with a particularly outrageous spelling of zucchini I decided it was time to put together some kind of salute to them.

So here, at last, it is: The Bad Menu Dinner.

The first entry is a generic, not a specific dish:

Wet Your Appetite With Our Selection of Hor Derves

True, many restaurants (to their credit) would never even attempt to spell a term like hors d'oeuvres, but there are also lots of places at which you are encouraged to "wet" your appetite with an appetizer.

Despite straining what we like to call my brain for five or ten minutes, I couldn't think of a specific appetizer that is commonly misspelled.

But it doesn't seem fair not to give you a recipe, so here's one that isn't misspelled.

This is the kind of thing often served in very large restaurants, where they seat a whole group of folks in a kind of waiting area off to the side with a basket of crackers and some kind of spread and hope you'll buy some drinks.

That is wetting your appetite.

Ham or Shrimp Butter

1 (6½-oz.) can chunk ham or 2 (4½-oz.) cans shrimp or 1 (6-oz.) bag frozen shrimp
2 shallots
¾ c. (1½ sticks) unsalted butter, divided
2 tbsp. lemon juice
1 tbsp. dry sherry
½ tsp. tarragon
Salt, pepper
Pinch of cayenne pepper
Crackers

(NOTE: This spread is best if it is refrigerated a day or two before serving.)

Thaw the shrimp if they are frozen. Mince the shallots. Melt two tablespoons of the butter, add the shallots and cook until they are soft. Put the shallots, ham or shrimp, lemon juice, sherry, tarragon, salt, pepper and cayenne in a food processor or blender.

Melt the remaining butter and pour it into the processor or blender while it's whomping the shrimp or ham around. Taste and fiddle with the seasonings if you like. Pour into an attractive (clear glass?) bowl and refrigerate.

For spreadability, take it out of the refrigerator half an hour before serving. Serve with crackers. Makes about one cup.

Next, a multiple winner:

The Soup de Jour of the Day: Clam Chowder Soup

I've always been partial to a little redundancy now and then; I've been known to repeat myself redundantly myself. And I am quite fond of the story of the widow woman who had a big St. Bernard dog and used to take him for a walk on Easter Sunday until she met a Jewish rabbi.

This particular dish is about as far as menus generally go in that direction. The added touch of the misspelling of Soup du Jour is my own — *I've* never actually seen both "Soup de Jour" and "of the day" on the same menu, but I'm sure that even as we speak somebody somewhere is staring over "our bottomless cup of coffee" at those very words.

Anyway, here's the soup. It's New England style, but not so thick that your spoon stands up in it. If you prefer your chowder to resemble pudding, throw in more potatoes or use less half and half or milk. That way you can eat it with the fork de jour of the day.

Clam Chowder

2 medium onions
2 large potatoes
2 slices bacon, cut into 8 or 10 pieces
    each
2 c. water
2 (8-oz.) bottles clam juice
3 (6½-oz.) cans minced clams, not
    drained
1 tsp. salt
¼ tsp. pepper
1½ tbsp. butter
1½ tbsp. flour
2 c. half and half
1 c. milk

Peel and chop the onions. Peel and cube the potatoes.

In a Dutch oven, fry the bacon pieces until they're almost done. Add the onions and sauté gently three or four minutes. Add the water, clam juice (or use two extra cups of water instead, if you prefer), clams, potatoes, salt and pepper.

Cover and simmer one hour.

Melt the butter in a small saucepan. Stir in the flour and cook, continuing to stir, for 30 seconds. Slowly stir in about a cup of the hot chowder and cook briefly until the mixture is smooth and thick.

Pour this white sauce slowly back into the clam chowder, stirring, and bring the chowder slowly to the boil. Stir in the half and half and the milk and simmer five minutes.

Serves eight to ten.

Next a little greenery:

Our Famous
Ho-Made Cold Slaw

There's really nothing more wrong with "Ho-Made" than there is with any other cutesyism like "Lip-Smackin' Good" (except if you live where the street usage would indicate that ho-made slaw was prepared by someone you wouldn't want your son bringing home to dinner). It is a phenomenon of life, though, that terms like this usually spread until they make no sense at all.

On a recent vacation trip, for example, I saw a sign outside a restaurant advertising "Ho-Baked Pies."

Moving right along, here's the recipe, which cheats a little because it uses bottled salad dressing, but I did an exhaustive survey of menus before I did the cooking for this article, so I was exhausted.

The recipe produces a cole slaw with a slight orange cast and a nice creamy texture.

▶

Cole Slaw

1 medium head cabbage, finely
　　shredded
1 small onion, finely chopped
½ c. French dressing
¼ c. sour cream
1½ tbsp. chopped chives

Place all the ingredients in a large bowl
and toss thoroughly. Cover and refrigerate
two to three hours. Stir before serving.

Makes four to six servings.

For a vegetable dish, there can be no
contest. It's got to be your favorite
squash and mine, in a nice combination with some Italian sausage.

Zuhccinni Medaly

Have you ever wondered what we ate
ten or more years ago, when nobody
had ever heard of zucchini?

For that matter, have you ever wondered what the Italians put on noodles
before the tomato was brought back
from the New World?

We'll have to look into that some
time.

For now, let's make some zucchini.

Zucchini Medley

1 lb. Italian sausage, sliced ½-in.
　　thick
2 tbsp. oil
½ small onion, chopped
4 small (bratwurst size) zucchini,
　　thinly sliced
½ medium head cabbage, thinly sliced
½ tsp. sugar
Salt, pepper

Brown the sausage 15 to 20 minutes, un-

til it is cooked through.

Meanwhile, in a small Dutch oven, heat
the oil. Sauté the onions for a few minutes.
Add the zucchini, cabbage, sugar, salt and
pepper and stir well.

Cover and continue to cook, stirring often, about 10 minutes, until zucchini and
cabbage are somewhat tender and the cabbage has lost its shape.

Add the cooked sausage pieces and cook,
uncovered, about 10 minutes more.

Serves four to six.

This next dish might seem an obvious candidate — right up there with
the au jus gravy — but it's not. In fact,
it doesn't belong here at all, except
that everybody thinks it does. (Consider this exposition one evidence of the
educational mission of the newspaper.)

Macaroni "n" Cheese
au Gratin

(I threw in the "n" instead of 'n' —
or even *and* — just to make it look
normal.)

The heavyweights of the cooking biz
(by which I mean those with prestige,
not those who need to go on a diet) will
tell you that au gratin does not mean
"with cheese." The French word for
cheese is fromage, not gratin. Au gratin
means that the dish in question is
topped with bread crumbs and/or grated cheese, and usually some melted
butter, and is then subjected to high
heat in the oven or broiler to produce a
crust.

So there is macaroni and cheese, like
it comes out of the box, and there is
macaroni and cheese au gratin, which
gets additional treatment to make the
top crusty.

There. Now that you have a fascinating fact with which to bore some-body at a cocktail party, let's make some macaroni and cheese au gratin.

Regular readers (both of them — Hi, Dad) know that I believe in making things from scratch, with more-or-less real ingredients, so that's what I did to make the macaroni and cheese. In the process, I acquired tremendous respect for the boxed macaroni and cheese din-ner, which costs *much* less and, I must admit, tastes at least as good as the recipe I followed.

I'm not in love with boxed M&C dinners, having subsisted on them for much of a year in my college days, but I think that this first production of M&C from scratch will also be my last.

The gratin part, on the other hand, was pretty good — after one very bad try with a recipe that had four times more bread crumbs than it needed. (I *knew* it sounded wrong. I've got to learn to trust me.)

I'd suggest trying out the gratin on some boxed M&C. But here's the en-tire recipe, for those of you who just won't take my word. I repeat: The reci-pe is fine, but the boxed product is eas-ier, much cheaper and no less tasty. If you don't think so, you can add Worcestershire sauce, dry mustard and chopped onions to *that*, too.

Macaroni and Cheese au Gratin

7 oz. (2 c.) elbow macaroni
1 tbsp. butter
1 medium onion, chopped
1 tbsp. flour
¼ c. milk
½ tsp. seasoned salt
Pepper
1½ c. (6 oz.) shredded Cheddar cheese
    or pasteurized process cheese

1 tbsp. Worcestershire sauce
½ tsp. dry mustard
Topping:
¼ c. dry bread crumbs
½ c. (2 oz.) shredded Cheddar cheese
    or pasteurized process cheese
3 tbsp. butter

Cook the macaroni according to package directions. Drain.

Melt the one tablespoon of butter in a saucepan, stir in the onions and sauté until they are transparent. Stir in the flour and cook a minute or so, stirring. Slowly add the milk, stirring constantly.

When all the milk is in and the sauce is smooth and creamy, stir in the salt, pepper, the 1½ cups of cheese, the Worcestershire and dry mustard. Reheat a bit if necessary to melt all the cheese. Stir in the cooked macaroni.

Now comes the au gratin part:

Turn the macaroni and cheese into a greased two-quart casserole. Combine the bread crumbs and the half-cup of cheese and sprinkle over the surface of the M&C.

Melt the three tablespoons of butter in a small pan and drizzle over all.

Bake at 350 degrees for 10 minutes or so (unless the mixture had gotten cold before it went into the oven, in which case make it 20 to 30 minutes), and run it under the broiler quickly at the end to brown the top. Serves six.

For dessert there are many choices, but I kind of like this one for its gener-al appeal:

**Our Own Banana Cream Pie,
Made with Fresh Banana's
and Piled High with
Real Whip Cream**

Part of the charm of this entry is its

application of the maxim apparently taught to menu writers, produce-counter clerks and sign painters: When in doubt, throw in an apostrophe.

As for the whip cream, it is from the same school of thought that gives us mash potatoes and ice tea.

This is quite a nice recipe. There's nothing wrong with straight banana cream pie, of course, but it's even better with a layer of a different flavor under the banana.

Those who cannot guess what flavor I used should consider a course in remedial eating.

Those who guessed carob should sign up immediately for "Eating as a Second Language."

Black-Bottom Banana Cream Pie

Bottom filling:
1½ (1-oz.) squares unsweetened
    chocolate
6 tbsp. milk
1 egg yolk
2 tbsp. sugar
1½ tsp. cornstarch
⅛ tsp. salt
1 baked 9-in. pie shell
Banana filling:
½ c. sugar
6 tbsp. flour
¼ tsp. salt
2½ c. milk
1 egg plus 1 egg yolk
1 tbsp. butter
½ tsp. vanilla
3 ripe banana's (or bananas)
½ c. heavy cream, whipped

Prepare the bottom filling:
Melt the chocolate in a small saucepan; set aside.
Scald the milk in a saucepan. In a mix-

ing bowl, beat together the egg yolk, sugar, cornstarch and salt. Gradually beat in the scalded milk.

Return the mixture to the saucepan in which the milk was scalded and cook over low heat, stirring constantly, until the custard is smooth and thick — don't boil it.

Stir in the melted chocolate and spread over the baked pie shell.

Prepare the banana filling:

Combine the sugar, flour and salt in the top of a double boiler over boiling water.

Gradually stir in the milk and cook, stirring constantly, until the mixture is thickened. Cover and cook 10 minutes more, stirring occasionally.

Beat the egg and egg yolk and beat in a small amount of the hot milk mixture. Lower the heat under the double boiler so that the water stops boiling.

Return the diluted egg to the pan of hot milk mixture, stirring it in rapidly. Allow the mixture to cook over the hot water for two minutes, stirring constantly.

Remove the mixture from the heat and stir in the butter and vanilla. Cool.

Slice one banana and arrange on the chocolate layer.

Immediately slice a second banana into the warm custard mixture and pour into the shell. (If you wait a long time before you cover them, the first banana slices will darken.) Chill.

Just before serving, whip the cream and pipe or spoon it over the top of the pie.

Slice the last banana and arrange the slices around the edge of the pie, inserting them into the whipped cream at a slight angle. Serve immediately. Serves six to eight.

I passed up the opportunity to make expresso, lemonaid and consumme. Another time.

National Hot Dog Month

Quick. What's tomorrow?

If you said the Fourth of July, give yourself five points. If you said Monday, give yourself one point and consider getting out more often. If you said the fourth day of National Hot Dog Month, give yourself 25 points, for having read the headline, for being fairly weird, or both.

There are many edibles whose existence is observed in national weeks or months. We have noted here in the past such distinguished festivals as National Potato Lovers Month and National Sauerkraut Week. But none really feels quite so American — or so appropriately timed — as National Hot Dog Month.

All right, so frankfurters come from Europe, not America, and the stories about how they got to be served in buns are a little suspect. The fact remains that, wherever they came from and however they got to be the way they are, they are now a very American institution. Almost as much as baseball, apple pie and the Chevrolet Motor Division of General Motors.

And the Fourth of July, even more than Memorial Day, is when the hot dog is really in flower. Except for those of us with small children (kids can be counted on to eat hot dogs when nothing else will work), many of us deal with hot dogs mostly on special occasions: Fourth of July, Labor Day, Twins games, State Fair and Resident Cook Gone to Visit Mother.

The National Hot Dog & Sausage Council (yes, there is a National Hot Dog & Sausage Council — you read it here first) is no doubt aware of this phenomenon and is quite anxious to make sure that you miss no opportunity to consume mass quantities of tube steaks. To this end, it has sent forth across this great nation any number of peculiar recipes.

I hesitated at first to involve myself in so relentlessly cylindrical a venture as testing lots of frankfurter recipes. I have a reputation to maintain, after all, and — odd as it is — it has not to this point included a dinner in which everything I made looked the same.

I realized, though, after a moment's thought, that not every wiener recipe had to involve whole wieners (I'm a little slow sometimes), so I decided to have a go at it.

An aside about nomenclature: According to the National Hot Dog & Sausage Council (let's just call it the NHD&SC, shall we?), the U.S. Department of Agriculture makes no distinction, in its regulations, between the terms "hot dog," "frank," "furter," "frankfurter" and "wiener."

I'd never even *heard* of "furter" (I think it's a sly attempt by the NHD&SC to emulate "burger"), but I had been carelessly using the other terms interchangeably, and I was glad to learn that, at least according to our federal government, I had not committed a grease misdemeanor.

In selecting the food for the Wonderful Wiener Wepast, I decided not to commit the kinds of culinary outrages that seem so possible when one's main ammunition is the frankfurter. For example, I did not prepare the Viennese veal delicacy, Wiener Schnitzel, with wieners. In fact, three of the recipes I used came straight from the NHD&SC, although I fiddled with them a bit, just to keep things honest.

I served the food with fairly little comment, but my smart-aleck guests were in absolutely revolting form. I will pass along some of their choicer remarks, but, to save these folks from being pilloried by friends and neighbors, I will not reveal their identities.

The appetizer was a dip containing ground hot dogs (my own innovation — the NHD&SC folks had suggested using hot-dog pieces as dippers.) It was nice and smoky and actually pretty darn good, but it looked a little odd.

Guest 1: "This isn't bad if you're hungry."

Guest 2: "Well, I ate two days ago, so I'm going to pass."

Hot Dog Dip

½ lb. frankfurters
1 tomato
1 sweet red pepper
½ c. drained and pitted green olives
2 (3-oz.) pkg. cream cheese, softened
2 tsp. Dijon mustard
Onion salt or onion powder to taste
1 to 1½ lb. assorted raw vegetables
    for dipping (carrot sticks,
    broccoli and cauliflower florets,
    etc.)

Finely chop the frankfurters (by hand or in a food processor). Core the tomato and the pepper. Cut both into chunks and chop them and the olives coarsely.

Cream the cream cheese and stir in the mustard and the chopped meat, tomatoes,

peppers and olives. Add onion salt to taste.

Serve with raw vegetable dippers. Serves six.

Getting folks to eat a salad containing hot dogs presented something of a challenge. But, as Guest 3 and Juwius Caesar put it, "Wienie, widi, wici."

I thought the result was very respectable, particularly after my substitution of refried beans for chili beans, but to be perfectly frank it would have been almost as good without the hot-dog component. I did slice the hot dogs thin instead of putting them in in big chunks as recommended, a move that made them not quite so obvious. The furter you got from the salad, the better it looked.

Mexican Hot Dog Salad

Dressing:
⅔ c. salsa or red taco sauce
⅓ c. mayonnaise
⅓ c. sour cream
Salad:
1 medium avocado
Lemon juice
½ head of lettuce
2 medium tomatoes
3 c. tortilla chips (about 4 oz. of chips)
1 (16-oz.) can refried beans
1 lb. hot dogs
1 (8-oz.) jar pasteurized process
    cheese spread
1 (4-oz.) can chopped green chilies,
    drained
2 tsp. chili powder

Prepare the dressing in advance: Combine salsa, mayonnaise and sour cream; cover and refrigerate until serving time.

Peel and pit the avocado, cut in slices

and dribble lemon juice over them to keep them from discoloring. Chill until serving time (or, as I did, until two days later, when I found them in the refrigerator).

Shortly before serving time, shred the lettuce and make a small mound of it on each salad plate. Chop the tomatoes and sprinkle them on the lettuce. Put about half a cup of tortilla chips in the middle of each salad. Heat the beans in a saucepan, slice the franks into the beans and simmer until heated through.

Meanwhile, in another saucepan, heat the cheese spread (Guest 4: "Mmm. What kind of cheese is this?" Host: "Whiz.") until it is just melted, then stir in chilies and chili powder. Pour one-fourth cup of the cheese mixture over the chips on each salad, and top with about half a cup of the beanie wienie. Garnish with avocado slices, if you remember, and serve with the dressing in a bowl. Serves six.

As we moved toward the main course, I brought out the special wine I had purchased for this occasion: a Binger St. Rochuskapelle Kabinett. It's a nice little wine, produced in Bingen, West Germany, which is about 30 miles from a much larger city. Given that 30 miles isn't very far as these things go (if somebody from, say, Elk River were traveling in West Germany, he might well identify himself as a Minneapolitan), I feel justified in calling this a Frankfurter wine.

Guest 3 immediately began referring to it as "wieno."

For the main course, frankfurters in their entirety (finally), each nestled in a boat crafted from a scooped-out zucchini half. I found all of the items on the menu quite respectable, but I though this one *really* cut the mustard.

These hot dogs contain cheese, prompting Guest 4 to ask, "This recipe isn't called 'Easy Cheesy something,' is it?" No. It is one of my very few rules that I do not prepare recipes called "Easy Cheesy something."

(Another is that I do not prepare recipes called "something Surprise." When I sit down to eat, I don't *want* to be surprised. Pleased, yes; surprised, no. Things called "something Surprise" remind me of a business firm in Milwaukee with a very jarring slogan: Blau's Sudden-Service Plumbing. Every time I see it, I picture plumbers bursting into the house at three in the morning, while searchlight-equipped helicopters hover outside.)

Well, now that I have *that* off my chest, let's get back to our main course. It's not "Easy Cheesy Zucchini," it's not "Zucchini Surprise," it's:

Wienie Zucchini

---

4 (8- to-10-in.) zucchini (1½ to 2 lb.)
½ c. chopped green onions
2 tbsp. chopped parsley
½ tsp. oregano
¼ tsp. tarragon
¼ tsp. basil
Dash pepper
2 tbsp. butter
2 tbsp. oil
1 c. bread crumbs
½ tsp. garlic salt
Oil for brushing
1 lb. cheese hot dogs

Preheat the oven to 350 degrees. Cut the ends off the zucchini, then cut each in half lengthwise and scoop out each long zucchini half (reserving the scoopings) to leave boats with sides about ½ inch thick.

Chop the part of the zucchini you scooped out of the boats, combine it with the green onions, parsley, oregano, tarragon, basil and pepper, and fry in the butter and oil. Stir in the bread crumbs.

Sprinkle the hollowed-out zucchini boats with garlic salt and fill each with the fried zucchini mixture. Put the filled zucchini boats in a shallow pan, and brush the tops with oil. Bake for 25 minutes, then put a cheese hot dog on each one and bake seven or eight minutes more, until the hot dog is heated through.

Makes eight, and they're quite good.

As good as these hot-dog items sounded — and as well as they turned out — I couldn't see serving a hot-dog vegetable. That, I figured, would be the wiener of our discontent. So I made my favorite spinach recipe, which you've already seen (with the SPAM recipes). You don't need to see it again, do you?

Thanks. You're a nice person.

It was when dessert approached that my guests got really restless. "What's it going to be?" inquired one uneasily. "Hog 'n' Dazs?" "No," responded another, "probably Pudding on the Dog."

They needn't have worried. Dessert, believe it or not, was not a difficult place to use up some hot dogs in a reasonable manner — it is not unheard of for meat to appear in a sweet item. Usually it's not hot dogs, but that's only a small additional stretch.

Mincemeat pie with hot dogs instead of beef was slightly smoky-tasting, but I didn't find that at all unwelcome. Maybe I was just relieved that it wasn't worse, but I don't think so. Several folks took seconds.

Hot-Dog Mincemeat Pie

½ lb. hot dogs
3 medium apples
1 c. raisins, or ½ c. raisins and ½ c. currants
½ c. fruit-cake mix (candied fruits)
4 tbsp. butter
1 c. packed brown sugar
1 c. apple cider
½ c. apple jelly
2 tbsp. molasses
1 tsp. salt
1 tsp. ground cinnamon
½ tsp. cloves
½ tsp. nutmeg
1 tbsp. lemon juice
Dough for 2-crust pie

Chop the hot dogs quite finely. Wash, peel, core and chop the apples. Chop the raisins, currants, and fruit-cake mix.

Melt the butter in a Dutch oven and add the hot dogs, apples, raisins, currants, fruit-cake mix, brown sugar, cider, jelly, molasses, salt, cinnamon, cloves and nutmeg. Cook slowly, uncovered, one hour, stirring occasionally, until most of the liquid is absorbed. Add the lemon juice.

Preheat oven to 425 degrees. Line a 9-inch pie pan with one crust, fill with mincemeat, top with second crust, crimp edges and cut a few slashes in the top.

Place pie on a cookie sheet to catch any drips, and cover the edges of the crust with strips of foil to prevent burning.

Bake 25 to 30 minutes, removing the foil strips after 15 minutes. Serves six to eight.

When dinner was over, guests helped themselves from a candy dish full of antacid tablets.

Food in a Cloud

I was watching television one Sunday when Bill Cosby interrupted rather a fine session of Wonder Woman to extol the virtues of Coca-Cola. Or was it Pepsi?

That reminded me of Jell-O Pudding Pops, whose merits Cosby had been praising not long ago, and of Pudding in a Cloud, which he'd been enthusing about before that.

Remember Pudding in a Cloud? Cosby told us how to make it. Often. Just swirl a ring of Cool Whip into a dessert dish and then fill the center with Jell-O Pudding (another General Foods product). Bring it out, grinning, and listen to the kids go "Yaaaay! Pudding in a Cloud! Ummmmm!"

Cosby has become sort of a television junk-food institution.

Sigh. Whatever happened to "I Spy?"

Anyway, Pudding in a Cloud sort of stuck in my mind, and I began to muse about it, to the point that I never did find out how Wonder Woman prevented the destruction of IRAC, the smart-aleck computer. If pudding in a cloud of Cool Whip was so great, I figured, surely there were possibilities in other food in clouds of other stuff.

After the idea had echoed around in my head for a while, I had a number of cloudy possibilities. One, chestnut mousse in a cloud of meringue, was a disaster, and I'll spare you the recipe. (You can look it up yourself if you like; make it only if you're really fond of bland.)

The rest were pretty good. The clouds added contrasts in texture, flavor, color and temperature, and in no case were difficult to supply.

Although I served a number of cloud dishes at the same meal, that probably isn't the best idea, as it tends to diminish the dramatic effect of any one of them. (I've looked at clouds from both sides now, but it's clouds' profusion I recall.)

Here are some possibilities for you to ponder. Others will certainly suggest themselves, perhaps while you're trying to fall asleep (be sure to write them down). In almost every case you can add to the fanciness of the presentation by piping the cloud material out of a pastry bag.

Appetizers:
Herring in a cloud (of blended sour cream and yogurt)
Hard-cooked eggs in a cloud (of mayonnaise)
Soup:
Chilled zucchini-dill soup in a cloud (of sour cream)
Main courses:
Moussaka in a cloud (of egg-yogurt custard)
Shepherd's pie in a cloud (of mashed potatoes)
Dessert:
Brownie in a cloud (of whipped cream, topped with hot chocolate sauce)

The first dish is the most peculiar. You can buy herring already packaged in sour cream sauce. Why would you bother to serve it this way instead? First of all, in honor of Bill Cosby. Second, because this way you get to glop up the herring with as much sour cream as you like.

I tried this with one big dish, as a sort of community dip. It doesn't work nearly so well as providing individual dishes, with individual little clouds of yogurty sour cream, each with its herring center. That way every guest gets his or her own cloud with a herring lining.

Herring in a Cloud

1 (8-oz.) carton sour cream
½ c. plain yogurt
1 (8-oz.) jar herring in wine sauce, well drained

Blend yogurt and sour cream. Swirl a small circular ridge of the mixture onto each of four small saucers.

Into the hole in the sour cream, place a small mound of drained herring, onions and whatever else came out of the jar. Serves four.

Oeufs Mayonnaise (halved hard-cooked eggs topped with mayonnaise) is a standard appetizer in France. Oeufs en Nuage (eggs in a cloud) is only the merest perversion of that classic: Instead of topping the eggs with mayonnaise, top the mayonnaise with eggs.

Oeufs en Nuage

(Eggs in a cloud)
4 lettuce leaves
1 c. mayonnaise
4 to 6 hard-cooked eggs

Arrange a lettuce leaf on each of four salad plates. Spoon or pipe mayonnaise into a small mound.

Halve the eggs and arrange two or three halves on each mound of mayonnaise.

If you have ten minutes and some oil, home-made mayonnaise is delicious and not very difficult at all:

Mayonnaise

1 egg yolk
¾ tsp. Dijon mustard
Salt and pepper
Pinch of sugar
Generous ¾ c. oil (olive oil is best, others are perfectly fine)
1 tbsp. tarragon vinegar (or other vinegar if you don't like tarragon)

Put the egg yolk in a medium-size bowl. Add the mustard, salt, pepper and sugar and stir with a whisk or wooden spoon. Add a few drops of the oil and stir until it is fully incorporated and the mixture is absolutely smooth. Add more oil, a little at a time, stirring hard after each addition, to incorporate the oil fully.

When more than half the oil is in, you can add it a bit faster, but never add oil until the last batch is fully incorporated, or you can kiss your mayonnaise good-bye.

When all the oil is in, stir in the vinegar. Makes about a cup.

You can probably do this more easily in a blender. On the other hand, you can do it still more easily by buying a jar of mayonnaise at the supermarket.

The zucchini-dill soup can be served either hot or cold, and either way the cloud of sour cream would be nice. A hint is in order, though: This is a very filling soup. It's more like a whole lunch than it is like part of dinner.

Zucchini-Dill Soup in a Cloud

4 tbsp. butter
2 medium onions, cut into rings or
    coarsely chopped
1 clove garlic, crushed
1 (10¾-oz.) can chicken broth, diluted
    with only ¾ c. water
1 lb. zucchini
2 medium potatoes
1 tsp. salt
⅛ tsp. pepper
1½ tsp. dill weed
1 c. heavy cream
2 c. sour cream

Melt the butter in a five-quart Dutch oven. Sauté the onions and garlic in the butter until the onions are translucent. Add the canned broth and the three-fourths cup of water.

Wash the zucchini and peel the potatoes. Grate or slice the zucchini and potatoes and add them to the broth, along with the salt, pepper and dill.

Simmer 15 to 20 minutes, until the vegetables are tender.

Pour, half at a time if necessary, into the food processor or blender and purée. Add cream and stir. Chill thoroughly or heat (but not to boiling).

Divide sour cream among soup bowls and swirl a ridge of it below the rim of each bowl.

Ladle the soup into the bowl, being careful not to spill any on the sour cream. Serve immediately. Serves eight to ten.

Here's a recipe that almost didn't need any fiddling to turn it into something in a cloud. The only departure from standard moussaka is that, instead of pouring all the sauce over the moussaka and letting it wind up who-knows-where, you provide a margin in the pan for the sauce to gather and form the cloud. (I can hear those kids now: "Yaaaay! Moussaka in a Cloud! Ummmmm!")

Moussaka in a Cloud

1 tbsp. oil
3 cloves garlic, crushed
2 large onions, chopped
1½ lb. ground lamb
1½ tsp. salt
Pepper
Dash paprika
Dash cinnamon
2 lb. eggplant, peeled and cut in ½-
    inch slices
Flour for breading
Oil for frying
3 eggs
1½ c. unflavored yogurt
1 c. shredded Swiss cheese
Pinch grated nutmeg

Heat the oil in a large frying pan, and sauté the garlic and onions until the onions are translucent. Add the ground lamb and salt, pepper, paprika and cinnamon. Break up the lamb and cook until the pink color is gone.

Using a slotted spoon, transfer the lamb-onion mixture to a bowl and set it aside. Heat the fat remaining in the frying pan (adding oil if necessary).

Meanwhile dredge the eggplant slices in flour. Fry them lightly on both sides, adding oil to the pan when necessary. Set fried slices aside.

Place a layer of eggplant slices in a 9- by 13-inch baking dish, leaving a 1-inch margin around the sides. (For the cloud, remember?) Top with about half the meat mixture. Place a second layer of eggplant slices on top of the meat mixture, and top

135

with the remaining meat. Finish off with a third layer of eggplant slices. The last may be only a partial layer of eggplant. That's OK; just make it look like that's what you intended.

Preheat the oven to 375 degrees.

Thoroughly beat the eggs, and slowly add the yogurt to them. Mix in the cheese and the nutmeg.

Spoon the yogurt mixture into the 1-inch border, and dribble a bit of it across the top of the moussaka as well.

Bake about 45 minutes, until the top of the yogurt is golden brown. Serves six to eight.

———

If lamb is not your cup of meat, how about Shepherd's Pie, which is made, in this version, with ground beef? The mashed-potato cloud is a standard part of this dish.

Shepherd's Pie

2 c. mashed potatoes (instant spuds
 work fine)
2 eggs, separated
Dash salt
2 tbsp. butter, divided
1 medium onion, chopped fine
1 lb. ground beef
Salt and pepper
1 tsp. Worcestershire sauce
½ c. prepared gravy (or ½ c. canned
 consommé in which 2 tbsp.
 cornstarch has been dissolved)
1 tbsp. grated cheese (optional)

Add the egg yolks to the prepared mashed potatoes. Beat the egg whites with the dash of salt and fold them into the potatoes. Spread half of the mixture in a 9-inch pie pan, building up the rim.

Heat one tablespoon of the butter and fry the onions in it until they are translucent. Add the ground beef, salt, pepper and Worcestershire sauce and cook until the meat loses its pink color. Drain off the fat. Add the gravy or the consommé-cornstarch mixture and cook until well mixed and thickened.

Preheat the oven to 400 degrees.

Fill the potato cloud with the meat mixture and top with the remaining potatoes (leaving a ring of meat peeking out, if you like). Dot the mashed potatoes with the remaining butter and/or cheese.

Bake for 35 minutes. If not nicely browned, run it under the broiler for 30 seconds or so.

Serves six. Eat with caution, because the middle stays HOT! (Leftover mashed potatoes might be the very thing we need to replace urea formaldehyde foam insulation.)

———

Dessert time. What could be a more appropriate dessert cloud than whipped cream? And what could it better surround than something chocolate?

I toyed with the idea of chocolate mousse in a whipped-cream cloud, as the grown-up-and-moved-to-a-better-neighborhood version of pudding in Cool Whip, but I decided that it would be better to go for something with the possibility of temperature variation (always nice at dessert time). So ladies and gentlemen, for our closing number this evening we proudly present Warm Brownie in Cold Whipped Cream, topped with Hot Chocolate Sauce.

This excellent brownie recipe (from *Best Loved Recipes of the American People,* by Ida Bailey Allen) calls for chocolate chips, but you could use one-ounce semisweet chocolate squares instead. Half of the chocolate gets melted; the other half gets stirred in at the end in chunks, so if you use block chocolate you'll have to break it up. (The advantage is that you can break it in fairly big pieces, which are a *real* treat when you hit them in the brownie.)

Brownie in a Cloud

Brownie:
**12 oz. semisweet chocolate (chips or
    1-oz. squares), divided**
⅓ c. butter or margarine
½ c. sugar
2 eggs
1 tsp. vanilla
½ c. flour
½ tsp. baking powder
¼ tsp. salt
½ c. chopped walnuts
Chocolate sauce:
4 (1-oz.) squares semisweet chocolate
6 tbsp. water
¼ c. sugar
2 tbsp. butter
1 egg yolk
Cloud:
1½ pt. heavy cream

Over low heat, melt one cup of the chips (or six one-ounce chocolate squares) with the butter in a saucepan. Remove from heat and pour into the bowl of a mixer. Beat in the sugar, then the eggs one at a time, beating well after each. Stir in the vanilla.

Sift together the flour, baking powder and salt and add the mixture to the chocolate; mix well. Stir in the nuts and the remaining cup of chips (or the remaining six one-ounce squares of chocolate, broken into chunks).

Preheat the oven to 375 degrees.

Oil an 8-inch-square pan, and spread the brownie batter in it evenly. Bake 25 to 30 minutes. (When testing for doneness with a toothpick, try several places; if you stick the toothpick into one of the chips or chunks of chocolate it'll come out gooey even if the brownies are done.) Cool to warm. Makes nine good-size brownies. These can be made in advance and re-warmed just before serving, or they can be served cool.

While the brownies are baking, prepare the chocolate sauce: Put the chocolate and water in a saucepan and melt over very low heat. Stir until the mixture is smooth. Add the sugar and stir until it is dissolved, then boil gently for four minutes. Remove from heat and stir in the butter, stirring until it is melted. Cool slightly.

Beat a spoonful of the chocolate into the egg, then stir the egg into the chocolate mixture.

If the brownies aren't still warm when you're ready to serve them, you might return them to a 250-degree oven for ten minutes. Meanwhile, whip the cream (unsweetened — there's enough sugar in the brownie and sauce to sink a bismarck).

If the chocolate sauce has cooled, warm it gently, stirring.

Swirl a cloud of whipped cream in each dessert dish, plop a brownie in the middle and spoon hot chocolate sauce over it. Makes nine. You'll never be tempted by Pudding in a Cloud again.

The Raw Dinner

On a recent plane trip I was paging listlessly through the in-flight magazine (I had forgotten my list, and I figured the magazine was a better choice than either the cheap thriller I had grabbed at the airport bookstore or my well-thumbed copy of How to Face Death in the Air), when what to my wandering eyes should appear but one of those city-profile articles that in-flight magazines seem to love — and it was about the city I grew up in! (And the city in which I learned not to end sentences with prepositions. And not to write sentence fragments.)

What a chance, I figured, to catch the slick magazine writer with his adjectives down! I just knew that he would attempt to paint Milwaukee as either a gloomy industrial town or the Beverly Hills of Wisconsin, bustling with goat-cheese and raspberry-vinegar parties.

There was, in fact, a hint of the latter suggestion, but I was disappointed to find that, by and large, the city described in the magazine was fairly closely related to the actual place. What fun is there, I began to grumble, in reading an article like that?

The only thing I carried off the plane (beyond my luggage, a bag of peanuts and a slight headache) was a bit of puzzlement that the author of the article had mentioned, as an interesting fact, that Milwaukeeans (that's the term of choice — not Milwaukeeites or Milwaukeeoids) like to eat raw ground beef.

Well, sure, I thought. But so do other people. Steak tartare, or variations of it, is eaten around the world. When I mentioned this peculiar magazine assertion to various folks who aren't from Milwaukee (or as natives pronounce it, Mwaukee), they allowed that, although they might have eaten steak tartare at a few fancy parties, they really didn't have it very often at all. They didn't remember, for example, ever eating raw ground beef on rye bread as an after-school snack. I didn't do that all the time, but I certainly did once in a while. It was pretty good, too.

Well, then, maybe Milwaukee consumption of what we used to call cannibal sandwiches does exceed the national average. (Or at least eastern Wisconsin consumption — the only one of my friends who had fond recollections of this snack is from Sheboygan).

That, as we like to say, set me to thinking. ("Thinking" is sort of a grand description of what it set me to doing, but it will have to suffice. We don't have a concise term for "saying 'uhhh . . . ' a lot.")

(Gee. Maybe I could tone up these articles if I used *lots* of more elegant phrasing. If I larded each opus with things like "I found the resulting tuna casserole wholly admirable" and "peanut butter has a special affinity for jelly," would I sound like Craig Claiborne? Probably not, but I don't have anything better to do.)

Anyway, spurred by the discussion of cannibal sandwiches, I decided for lack of a better idea to prepare a dinner of uncooked foods.

Sushi, the Japanese delicacy consisting largely of various kinds of absolutely raw fish, entered my mind, but I showed it right back out because, unless you have excellent assurances about your suppliers — as restaurants should — raw fish can contain parasites that you wouldn't care to read about, much less consume.

Gravlax, the Scandinavian dish consisting of salmon cured in a dill marinade, also occurred to me, but only when it was too late to marinate it. Maybe the next time we do raw food.

"What do I care what he didn't make?" you are probably asking.

"What do I even care what he *did* make?" you are possibly asking.

Just simmer down, now. If yours was the first question, we're merely clearing the decks for the goodies to come. If yours was the second question, you have clearly mistaken this for some other section of the newspaper. Might I recommend the Entertainment or Travel sections, which are very nice today. (My name is Al; I'll be your obsequious servitor. If you have any questions, I'll be happy to answer them. Is everything OK here? You can just pay me when you're ready.)

All right, then. If you're all set, let's hear it for dinner. Raw! Raw! Raw!

Regular readers will know that I am not the man to whom one should turn for ideas on the consumption of raw vegetables. I'm not so fond of cooked vegetables that I am eager to deal with them before they got to be *that* good.

But in a dinner like this one, one appetizer has got to be raw vegetables and a dip. So here goes. The dip (based on one in the Los Angeles Times California Cookbook) is very nice; you can pick your own raw vegetables to dip in it.

Mexican Cheese Dip

¼ c. (½ stick) butter or margarine, softened
8 oz. (2 c.) shredded Cheddar cheese
1 tbsp. chopped parsley
1½ tbsp. chopped canned hot peppers
½ tsp. or more Tabasco sauce (to taste)
1 tbsp. steak sauce
½ tsp. salt
Assorted raw vegetable dippers

Cream butter or margarine. Add cheese, parsley, peppers, Tabasco sauce, steak sauce and salt, and beat until smooth.

Serve with assorted vegetable dippers. Serves six to eight.

On, now, to what started all this, the cannibal snadwich. No, that's not a typographical error. Somewhere in the dim past, somebody in my family saw "snadwich" on a sign, and that became a preferred family pronunciation. So, as long as we're having this recipe from my past, that's how we're going to spell it.

Cannibal Snadwiches

¾ lb. lean steak, ground
1 egg yolk (optional)
½ c. chopped onion
Salt to taste, but be generous
Pepper
Slices of cocktail rye bread

You can certainly start with plain ground beef (that's certainly what we did), but starting with steak and having the butcher grind it assures you of less fat — and of ground beef that hasn't been exposed to air (and spoilage potential) for as long.

Work in the egg yolk (if you like — it adds some body and richness) and the onion, salt and pepper.

Spread thickly on slices of cocktail rye bread and serve open-face.

If there's one ingredient that's really necessary to successful cannibal snadwiches, it's plenty of salt. I underdid it when I served these, but that's easy enough to fix. Just have the salt shaker handy next to the plate of snadwiches.

Makes about 16 appetizer snadwiches.

I must confess to splendid ignorance about seviche, although I've eaten it several times. The first time I had it was in an Italian restaurant, and that fixed it in my mind as an Italian dish. When I couldn't find it in any Italian cookbooks, I tried French, too, figuring it might have been just southern European.

It turns out, as all of you no doubt know, that it is part of the local cuisine from Mexico to the tip of South America, and it is said to be of Polynesian origin.

Here, technically minded readers will note, we stretch the definition of raw, because although the scallops are not cooked they are marinated in a citric acid mixture which performs a similar function. (The scallops turn white and opaque in acid just as surely as they do when cooked with heat.)

Seviche

1 lb. bay scallops (or quartered sea
    scallops)
½ c. chopped onion
1 clove garlic, crushed
1 medium tomato, chopped
1 tbsp. chopped canned hot peppers
¾ c. lime juice
3 tbsp. olive oil
2 tbsp. white wine
Dash Tabasco sauce
1 tsp. salt
½ tsp. pepper
¼ tsp. crushed basil
¼ c. chopped parsley

Note: This recipe requires marinating time.

Discard any liquid from the scallops and put them in a small bowl. Stir in the onions, garlic, tomato and chopped peppers.

Combine in a jar the lime juice, olive oil, wine, Tabasco, salt, pepper and basil. Shake well.

Pour this marinade over the scallop mixture and turn the scallops in it. If there isn't enough marinade to cover the scallops completely, add more lime juice and oil, roughly four parts lime juice to one part oil. (If you're running out of lime juice, you can use a little lemon juice; nobody will sue.)

Cover the bowl tightly and refrigerate at least six hours, stirring once in a while.

Drain before serving, and sprinkle with parsley. Serves six as a first course or 12 as an appetizer.

Here's another raw-meat appetizer or light main-dish item. Unlike seviche, which (my ignorance not to the contrary) has fairly deep roots, carpaccio is apparently a Johnny-come-lately, traced usually to Harry's Bar in Venice about 20 years ago. I suppose that makes it a Harry-come-lately. Anyway, it's paper-thin slices of uncooked lean beef with a tangy dipping sauce.

Several of my guests liked it just fine; a few others had a little of it raw and said that it was OK, but they wouldn't mind a little more of it cooked. That's easy enough, since paper-thin beef cooks in a little oil in almost no time. So you might want to be adventuresome and try it raw but have the old frying pan standing by to turn it into Familiar City if that doesn't work out.

Carpaccio

1 lb. top round steak, all fat removed
½ c. mayonnaise
6 tbsp. Dijon mustard
¼ tsp. crumbled basil
¼ tsp. crumbled tarragon
2 tsp. lemon juice
Wedges of lemon or lime

Slice the meat paper thin. (That's easier to do if you freeze it an hour or two first; not so it turns into a brick, just so it isn't squidgy.)

Meanwhile, combine the mayonnaise, mustard, basil, tarragon and lemon juice, cover and refrigerate.

Once the meat is sliced, put a few slices at a time between sheets of plastic wrap and roll or pound them out until they are even thinner. (Novice carpaccists might want to skip this step, as it is a considerable pain. If it turns out you love the general idea of carpaccio but wish the meat was a bit easier to chew, pound it out like this the next time.)

Arrange the slices prettily on a large platter (you might even want to roll a few up into roses), serve with the sauce and garnish with the lemon or lime wedges.

For those who turn out not to be remotely carpaccoid, sauté the slices ever-so-briefly in hot oil.

An appetizer or very light main course for eight.

More often lately than I care to discuss in the public prints, I find myself admitting either that I hadn't really read a recipe before I started to prepare it, or that I read it but I hadn't fully grasped it.

I am a bad example. Please don't do that.

The next dish was just fine — quite good, in fact — but I realized as I was about to prepare it that it wasn't going to wind up one bit raw. It was simply going to wind up cold. If you're willing to handle that admission gracefully, I'll pass along the recipe.

If you're going to gloat, on the other hand, we'll print it in disappearing ink, and after you cut it out and paste it on one of those cute little cards with the bunnies in the corner it will simply fade away.

So be nice.

Actually, the recipe is based on one in "Good Housekeeping's Best Recipes for 1982," so even if you turn mean on me you could probably find it again if you needed to.

Cold Pasta and Asparagus Salad

1 (7-oz.) pkg. elbow macaroni
4 tbsp. olive oil, divided
1 lb. fresh asparagus
½ lb. mushrooms
2 medium red or green bell peppers
1 small clove garlic
6 or 7 pimiento-stuffed ripe olives
1 lemon
2 tbsp. capers
1 tsp. salt
¼ tsp. freshly ground pepper
½ tsp. sugar
¼ tsp. crumbled oregano
1½ tsp. sesame oil

Prepare the macaroni according to package directions; drain. Toss the drained macaroni in two tablespoons of the olive oil.

Cut the asparagus into one-inch pieces, slice the mushrooms, seed and slice the bell peppers, crush the garlic and slice the olives.

Heat the remaining two tablespoons of oil in a Dutch oven and add the asparagus, mushrooms, peppers and garlic. Cook over medium heat about 15 minutes, stirring occasionally. Drain off the liquid. Stir the vegetables into the macaroni in a large bowl.

Grate about one tablespoon of lemon peel. Add the grated peel, the juice of the lemon and the olive slices, capers, salt, pepper, sugar, oregano and sesame oil to the macaroni-vegetable mixture. Toss well, cover and refrigerate at least an hour. Serves eight.

For dessert, there is one obvious candidate. So I made it. Raw chocolate-chip cookie dough.

You certainly don't need a recipe for it (if you do, it's on the bag of chocolate chips). But how about a Serving Suggestion? (You always see illustrations labeled "Serving Suggestion" on cans and frozen food packages: Soup might be shown in a bowl, for example, to keep you from pouring it into people's hands.)

Serving Suggestion: A scoop of chocolate-chip cookie dough can be plopped in a dish and topped with whipped cream or warm chocolate sauce.

Or not. Any way you serve chocolate-chip cookie dough is deliciously naughty. With every bite you can imagine your mom hollering at you not to do it.

We should have a dessert *recipe*, though, for those who insist on cutting things out and leaving them around the house.

You're never going to actually make most of these things, you know.

Oh, well, if it makes you happy. How about a sort of thin fruit-based mousse? The recipe is based on one in Glorious Desserts, by Carol Bowen.

Banana or Mango Fool

3 bananas (or 2 mangoes and a banana, if you like mangoes and can find them)
Juice of 1½ limes or 1 lemon
1½ c. heavy cream
1¼ c. plain yogurt

Peel the fruit and mash or purée it with the lime or lemon juice. Whip the cream. Blend the yogurt and fruit together; fold in one-half cup of the whipped cream and divide among six serving dishes. Top with remaining whipped cream. Chill.

Serves six.

How about a little something raw for *after* dinner?

When I was growing up skinny, and hating milk, eggs and all the various healthy foods that the American Heart Association is now telling us to cut down on, my mother used to sneak eggs and milk into things that I *would* eat.

To turn one of these child-fatteners into an after-dinner drink might have been difficult a few years ago.

But these days, when Bailey's Irish Cream and other cream-and-booze mixtures are doing so well, it's a snap.

Al's Milwaukee Cream

8 heaping tsp. chocolate malt powder
2 c. milk
1 small banana, sliced
1 egg
½ c. or so brandy
2 scoops vanilla ice cream

Combine all ingredients in blender. Whomp lightly, until ice cream is broken up and mixture thickens.

Makes enough to fill six small drinking glasses.

Little Mystery #10: Pans

Why do those bright, shiny cookie sheets get black no matter how well you wash them? Is there any way to stop that from happening? And while we're talking about cookie sheets, what kind of gunk is that under the label when you buy one? The label has invariably come loose from the gunk, but the gunk won't come off the pan.

Solution: An engineer at Ekco Housewares, Franklin Park, Ill., explained the problem of the discoloring cookie sheet this way:

Standard baking sheets are made of either aluminum or tin-plated steel. Either way, both oven heat and detergents cause the surface to oxidize. That's what the discoloration is — oxides of tin or aluminum.

If you want to work real hard, the panperson said, you can scour the oxidation back off the surface of an aluminum sheet. But if you scour a tin-plated steel sheet, pretty soon you'll have scoured through the tin to the steel. Then when it oxidizes you'll have just-plain rust.

That oxidation would happen, he said, even if you never washed the pan.

If this really bothers you a lot, he said, you can buy stainless-steel baking sheets. But they cost $12 or $14 apiece.

That was pretty depressing, but there was one bright glint among the oxides. Commercial bakers, he said, actually prefer black baking sheets for better, more even heat absorption, and commercial baking sheets (as well as some lines of silicon-coated bakeware) are dark to start with.

Apparently we touched a nerve on the subject of the loose label and the gunk underneath it. The engineer's first remark was "The problem with that damn glue . . . ."

He went on to explain that if the glue is too strong, the label won't come off easily. If it isn't that strong, then if the pan isn't sold within about a year, especially over a winter, the moisture comes out of the glue, leaving just the solids. The label lifts off and solid gunk is stuck to the pan. "We've been through this with glue after glue," the engineer said.

Well, enough of *his* problems; what about *our* problem? How do you get the gunk off your brand-new pan? Simple, he said. It's water-soluble glue. Soak it in hot, soapy water.

That way, you can get your oxidation started.

The Language of Cookies

Not long ago a friend was down in the dumps and I asked her if there was anything I could do to help.

"No."

"Wanna talk?"

"No."

"Wanna drink?"

"No."

I played my trump card. "Want me to make some oatmeal cookies?"

That did it. "Would you?"

I made a batch of oatmeal cookies and brought them to her still warm. She was deeply grateful, and it improved her mood for at least five or ten minutes. (You can't expect a plate of cookies to work miracles, after all.)

You must understand something. I didn't suggest oatmeal cookies because *I* like them. I don't care for them much at all — they are singularly lacking in chocolate. But I know they're her favorites, so that's what I offered.

In that way, cookies are like flowers. A bouquet of carnations is a bunch of flowers to some people but a special thing to those who really love carnations. Getting the right kind of flowers gives the gift extra meaning.

In addition, of course, if you want to really get specific with a floral tribute, there is a whole language of flowers. I don't know where it came from, but reference books and florists have lists of what each flower means.

Some are kind of strange: Azaleas, according to one list, are for transitory passion; red carnations for admiration; dahlias signify treachery (one assumes that it is on the part of the recipient, not the sender, as a treacherous person would be unlikely to telegraph his de-

ceit — even if he did telegraph the flowers). Orange lilies are for hatred; yellow roses speak of infidelity or jealousy, and asphodels mean "my regret follows you to the grave."

Well!

That language of flowers probably comes in handy sometimes. Say a woman has attracted the attention of a particularly obnoxious individual and is having difficulty letting him know that she'd prefer no company at all to his. Saying so outright is difficult, and even a letter to that effect can be kind of cruel. But sending him a mixed bouquet of petunias (anger) and meadow saffron ("let us part"), with a note saying "Look them up, stupid," cushions the blow because the flowers come before their full import is realized.

It occurred to me that, in the same way, a language of cookies might be a good idea. If cookies, like flowers, can be a gift of love, why shouldn't cookies be able to communicate as specifically? There are certainly enough kinds of cookies around that assigning a meaning to each type would provide a very large range of messages.

The only problem I could see was finding some authority to impose the meanings on various cookies, so I began skimming cookbook indexes to see if there were many cookies whose names might already imply specific messages. I found so many that I think we don't need the cookie-meaning czar — a language of cookies already exists.

Date Cookies, for example, mean "Will you go out with me?"

Date-Honey Cookies are a somewhat bolder statement: "Will you go out with me, *honey?*"

Hermits, of course, mean "Leave me alone," while **Molasses Cookies** indicate "I want to stick to you."

Actually, those are fairly general messages, like those conveyed by red roses (love and desire). There are a number of cookies that get pretty specific. If asphodels can go so far as "my regret follows you to the grave" (something you don't hear every day, although you heard it twice already this morning), cookies can do no less.

For example:

Poppy Seed Cookies are for when you want to say "Your father is becoming disheveled."

Cherry Bars mean "You stay out drinking so much that your nose is turning red."

If you send somebody a **Sand Tart** or two, that means "If you wear such a skimpy bathing suit to the beach, people will get the wrong idea about you."

Want your roommate to fork over for half of the groceries? Make some **Toll House Cookies.**

Sugar Nut Cookies mean "I'm nuts about you, sugar," while any of the wide variety of **Refrigerator Cookies** signifies an intention to give the recipient the cold shoulder.

As a reward for those of you who have endured this far without mailing a batch of **Drop Cookies** to the newspaper's Circulation Department, let's stop just chatting about communicative cookies and start making some.

Our first cookie, far easier to make than I would have guessed and really exceptionally good, is for a message of gravity: You deserve to be hit on the head.

Fig Newtons

(Immediate apologies are due Nabisco, as Fig Newton is that company's trademark for a fig bar cookie. I'm sorry.

(It just wouldn't have worked to write "For a message of gravity, send a Fig Bar Cookie.")

---

3 c. sifted flour
½ tsp. salt
¼ lb. (1 stick) plus 3 tbsp. butter or
    margarine
1 c. packed brown sugar
2 egg whites
1 tsp. vanilla
About 1 lb. dried figs
1 c. water
2 tbsp. sugar
2 tbsp. lemon juice

NOTE: This cookie requires a refrigerated rest, so it can't be made in a hurry.

Sift the flour and salt together.

Cream the butter and brown sugar until the mixture is very light and fluffy. Beat in the egg whites and vanilla and then gradually add the flour mixture, beating constantly. The dough is quite thick.

Wrap it in waxed paper and put it in the refrigerator for at least two hours.

Meanwhile, make the filling. Cut off the stems and hard ends of the figs. Chop the figs quite finely (you should have about two cups of chopped figs). Combine the figs, water, sugar and lemon juice and, if you have a blender, blend them briefly to break up the figs even more. (If you don't have a blender, it'll work OK if you just skip that step.)

Pour the fig-water-sugar-juice mixture into a pan and bring it to the simmer (stirring continuously, until it is thickened —

six to seven minutes).

Set the filling aside to cool (don't refrigerate it).

When the dough has chilled, preheat the oven to 350 degrees.

Cut a 2- by 3-inch rectangle from a piece of paper to use as a guide in cutting the dough.

Lightly flour your work surface and a rolling pin. Break the dough into six roughly equal pieces. Leave five of them in the refrigerator.

Roll the dough out into a rectangle about ¼ inch thick. Using the paper guide, cut the dough into 2- by 3-inch pieces (return the scraps to the chunk of dough in the refrigerator). Plop a generous (but not heaping) teaspoon of the filling into the middle of each rectangle and spread it so that it forms a band about an inch wide, running across the rectangle the short way all the way to the edges (the filling should fill the middle third of the cookie).

Use a metal spatula to lift one side of the uncovered dough, and fold it about two-thirds of the way across the filling. Then flip the cookie over onto the rest of the uncovered dough. (The dough should overlap.)

Place the cookies, seam side down, on an ungreased baking sheet and flatten them slightly with the back of the metal spatula. (They don't spread at all while baking, so you needn't leave much room between them.)

Repeat with remaining dough and filling.

Bake them about 12 minutes, until they are just slightly brown and seem to have a bit of firmness — they'll firm up more as they cool.

Cool them on racks.

Makes 30 to 36 cookies.

Next, an old favorite, the Chocolate Chip Cookie, updated by making a sandwich cookie out of two of them, with peanut butter or chocolate frosting in between.

Since this Chocolate Chip Sandwich Cookie has neither top nor bottom, it is the appropriate vehicle for the following message: "Any way I look at it, you seem to have a chip on your shoulder."

Chocolate-Chip Sandwich Cookies

1 c. plus 2 tbsp. flour
½ tsp. salt
½ tsp. soda
½ c. softened butter or margarine
⅜ c. (6 tbsp.) white sugar
⅜ c. (6 tbsp.) brown sugar
½ tsp. vanilla
1 egg
1 (6-oz.) pkg. chocolate chips (1 c.)
½ c. chopped nuts (optional)
      or
1 c. golden raisins (optional)
Filling:
Chunky peanut butter
      or frosting made with:
2 (1-oz.) squares unsweetened
      chocolate
2 c. confectioners' sugar
2 tbsp. milk (approximately)

Make the cookies:

Preheat the oven to 375 degrees. Combine the flour, salt and soda. Cream the butter and beat in the white sugar, brown sugar and vanilla. Beat in the egg.

Gradually beat in the flour mixture, then stir in the chocolate chips (and nuts or golden raisins if you like). (I vote heavily for golden raisins, because they make the cookies chewier, which is the way I like them. If you like 'em crisp, avoid the raisins.) Drop by rounded or heaping teaspoonfuls onto ungreased cookie sheets and bake eight to ten minutes.

Now choose your filling. If you like both peanut butter and chocolate, don't miss the opportunity to try chunky peanut butter in this application.

If you're not such a goober fan, the chocolate filling is quite fine.

Either way, you can't lose. If it were me, I'd make some of each. And since I *am* me, I did.

To prepare the chocolate filling, melt the chocolate in a double boiler or over very low heat in a saucepan. Stir in the confectioners' sugar and gradually stir in the milk until a thick but spreadable frosting is achieved.

Whichever filling you chose, spread a nice thick blob of it on the bottom of one cookie and cover with another.

Makes 20 to 24 sandwich cookies.

To my surprise, the next message unit (as they say in the telephone biz) might require some explanation to some readers.

I made the cookies and brought them to a party (and brought more to work a day or two later), and fully half the people who asked what meaning they were supposed to convey just looked puzzled when I told them.

The message is "I think you're fibbing."

Maybe you have to be a little older, or to have come from east of the Mississippi or something, to recognize the name of this pleasant, soft cookie as the exact equivalent of "baloney," as in "Awww, baloney!"

Some of us do. Trust me. I'm not fibbing.

Applesauce Cookies

½ c. butter or margarine
1 c. sugar
1 egg
2 c. cake flour
½ tsp. salt
½ tsp. soda
1 tsp. baking powder
½ tsp. cinnamon
¼ tsp. allspice
¼ tsp. cloves
1 c. unsweetened applesauce

Preheat oven to 375 degrees. Cream the butter and sugar. Beat the egg and blend it in.

Sift together the cake flour, salt, soda, baking powder, cinnamon, allspice and cloves and add these dry ingredients alternately with the unsweetened applesauce.

Grease cookie sheets well, and drop the batter onto them by rounded or heaping teaspoonfuls. Place the cookies fairly far apart, as they spread.

Bake about 15 minutes. Makes 36 to 48 cookies (depending on the amount of batter you use for each).

Now for a *pleasant* cookie message. (About time, right?) Here's one that's sure to please: "I'd like to be macarooned on a dessert island with you."

And as long as we're about it, let's go ahead and be both coconut macarooned and chocolate-coconut macarooned.

▶

Coconut or Chocolate-Coconut Macaroons

4 egg whites
¼ tsp. salt
¼ tsp. almond extract
½ tsp. vanilla
1⅓ c. sugar
2 c. (less than a 7-oz. bag) flaked
    coconut
2 oz. unsweetened chocolate
    (optional)

Preheat the oven to 325 degrees.

Beat the egg whites with the salt, almond extract and vanilla until soft peaks form (peaks form when you lift out the beaters, but the tops flop over). Add a few tablespoons of the sugar at a time, beating after each addition, and beat until stiff peaks form (the tops no longer flop over).

Fold in the coconut.

If you want the chocolate version, melt the chocolate in a saucepan over very low heat and fold it into the macaroon mixture.

Grease cookie sheets and drop the batter onto them by rounded teaspoonfuls. Leave room, because these cookies spread a little more than one would hope, but they're quite tasty. (The chocolate versions spread somewhat less and have a bit more body.)

Bake 18 to 20 minutes, until they acquire a light golden brown color and are no longer at all mushy when touched. (You'll have to go by feel with the chocolate ones.)

Cool them briefly on the cookie sheets (you'll never get them off otherwise), then put them on wire racks to cool.

Makes about 30 to 36 cookies.

I've saved the most potentially dangerous cookie for last, just to keep hotheads from stumbling across it. You wouldn't want to send this improvement on the oatmeal cookie without thinking about it first, because if you give a lady one of these you're saying "I've just heard about your reputation, so get lost!"

Dropped Chippies

1 c. sifted flour
2 tsp. baking powder
½ tsp. salt
½ c. butter or margarine, softened
1 c. packed brown sugar
1½ c. quick-cooking oatmeal (the dry
    flakes, not the cooked product)
2 eggs
1 tsp. vanilla
1 (8-oz.) pkg. pitted dates

Preheat the oven to 350 degrees.

Sift together the flour, baking powder and salt.

Cream the butter with the sugar and beat in the flour mixture and oatmeal. Beat the eggs lightly with the vanilla, then beat them into the batter.

Chop the dates and stir them into the batter.

Grease baking sheets and drop the batter onto them by rounded teaspoonfuls. Bake 10 to 15 minutes. The cookies should spring back when the tops are touched. Cool on racks. Makes around 40 cookies.

These recipes came from The Doubleday Cookbook and The Culinary Arts Institute Encyclopedic Cookbook.

The writer is sending his boss some butter cookies, hoping that if he butters her up enough she'll send him to do research in the Sandwich Islands.

Little Brother

Well, by now you've had enough of George Orwell to last until 2084, right? It's amazing how much analysis can be wrung out of one work of literature.

Actually, I don't understand what all the fuss is about. I've read *lots* of funnier books.

And, if the truth were told, Orwell kind of missed the boat on the real menace of the all-seeing television camera. In the worst of all possible worlds, as many children know, it wouldn't be Big Brother watching you.

It would be Little Brother.

That's a *really* chilling possibility. "AN-drew! Who said you could play with that? That's MINE! I'm gonna tell Mom!" "BET-ty! You're not doing your homework! Come here and look at what I drew!"

And there would be nowhere to hide.

Little brothers, of course, didn't ask to be little brothers. But once they figure out what Nature has done to them, most of them tend to take their revenge in this classic fashion.

Wise (but possibly foolhardy) is the parent who decides to create a momentary gap in the sibling rivalry by giving Little Brother or Little Sister something special to do. I'm not exactly recommending this, you understand (my degree in child psychology having been revoked by Kay Kyser and the entire Kollege of Musical Knowledge), but if you've already decided to try something of the sort might I suggest a small cooking session?

What follows is a selection of recipes that might entertain a little nipper who has a vague interest in hanging around in the kitchen with you.

These recipes might require some, a little or a lot of help from an older person (depending on the age of the nipper), but none requires any chopping or slicing.

Avoiding knife-work was about my only negative guideline in recipe selection, so some of the recipes involve stovetop cooking and moving things into and out of the oven. If that bothers you considering the size and other peculiarities of your nipper, look over the recipes first.

I did try to choose recipes that have an element that would be kind of fun: One involves making a white sauce, which is kind of remarkable when you first see it; one involves shaking chicken pieces in a bag with potato chips; in one you shape little balls of spinach in your hands like modeling clay; in one you just mix a whole bunch of things and bake them for an appetizer-snack, and for the dessert you have to crush some cookies and scoop ice cream into glasses. Sounds messy but fun, right? Ideal for Little Sibling.

Two of these recipes also have the additional feature of using up some of the Girl Scout cookies/crackers that *other* little nippers sold you. (This is yet another example of the endless cycles of Nature.)

With one exception, I did not have kids actually prepare these recipes. I did an article like *that* once before. It involved three young neighbor kids, who spent as much time giggling and getting in each other's way as I did crying in the corner. I haven't gotten over it yet.

The exception is the spinach balls,

which are either an appetizer or a peculiar vegetable course. The recipe is from my own younger kid, David, who is nine and has prepared them himself on several occasions — once on a recent visit with me. I have no idea where he got the recipe, so my apologies to whomever it is stolen from.

An aside: David's Big Brother, Joe, is an excellent speller. Little Brother David is an excellent logician, card player and reteller-at-length of movie plots, but he is not much, right now anyway, in the spelling department. I mention this because David mailed me the recipe, and his spelling of the name of this dish is so weird that I have to pass it along to you. (I asked him if I could.)

He called it Recepy for Spinich Balls. He added that even Joe loved them, "and he hates helth food."

Spelling, I guess, is like greatness: Some are born spellers and some have spelling thrust upon them.

And some are more equal than others, which brings us back to George Orwell and ties this whole thing up in a nice, neat package.

Except for the recipes.
Which follow.
Starting now.

Here is the recipe that David sent me. I have altered it a tad, to put it into traditional recipe style, and I've added lots of comments, which is my way. I've also fixed the spelling, so that it will make sense years later to those of you who insist on clipping out the recipes without the introductory text. You probably would have had some difficulty, for example, with "½ c. graded cheese."

Spinach Balls

½ stick (4 tbsp.) butter
1 (10-oz.) pkg. frozen spinach
1 egg
1 c. crumb-type stuffing mix (or crushed croutons)
½ c. grated or shredded Cheddar or Swiss cheese
Seasoned salt
Pepper

Preheat the oven to 350 degrees.
Wash your hands.

Melt the butter in a small pan. Prepare the spinach according to package directions, in another pan and drain it well.

(Here's a very important lesson to teach beginning cooks: Open frozen-vegetable packages carefully, so you don't rip through the instructions just to get the stuff out. And don't throw the box away until you have memorized the instructions or cooked the stuff.)

Put the egg in a large bowl. (David points out that you have to crack the egg first.) Now beat the egg a little with a fork. That makes it easier to add other stuff to it, because otherwise the egg white is sort of icky.

Stir the stuffing mix into the egg. Stir in the cheese, melted butter, cooked spinach, seasoned salt and pepper (one or two hearty shakes of each is a reasonable measure). Let it cool a few minutes.

Wash your hands again, just to be sure. Grease a cookie sheet. (That's always fun.)

Shape the spinach stuff into bite-size balls, about an inch across or so (that's even *more* fun if you can get into it) and put them on the cookie sheet.

Now put the cookie sheet in the oven and bake about 10 or 15 minutes.

When the balls are baked, get them off the cookie sheet with a metal spatula and put them on a serving plate or tray.

(These can be frozen before baking, according to David. Add a few minutes baking time if you do.)

When everything is done, wash the dishes — a very important step.

Makes about 24 balls.

Note: Do not allow Little Brother, or anybody else, to attempt to juggle or play catch with the spinach balls. They don't hold up well under impact.

This appetizer-snack mix calls for Golden Yangles, the Girl Scouts' little cheese crackers. You could use other little cheese crackers, too, but why would you? You could also leave out the bacon, if you don't have any or you don't like it or you don't want to have your youngster fry it and maybe get spattered. It'll be fine either way.

Snack Mix

4 slices bacon
2 tbsp. butter or margarine
2 c. thin pretzel sticks (about ⅓ of a
    9-oz. bag)
2½ c. Girl Scout Golden Yangles or
    other small cheese crackers
1 (3-oz.) can French-fried onion rings
About ¾ c. chopped walnuts or pecans
    (about 3 oz.)
1 tsp. Worcestershire sauce

Preheat the oven to 325 degrees.
Wash your hands.

Fry the bacon until it is crisp. Put it on paper towels to drain. Pour off the bacon fat, but save about two tablespoons of it in the pan. Melt the two tablespoons of butter in the same pan. (If you're not using the bacon, melt four tablespoons of butter.)

Break the pretzel sticks in half.

In a big bowl, mix the pretzel sticks, cheese crackers, onion rings, chopped nuts and Worcestershire sauce. Pour the melted fat over and stir up with a spoon.

Spread the mixture out on a cookie sheet and bake for 15 minutes, stirring it around now and then.

Take the mixture out of the oven, let it cool and pour it into a bowl. Crumble the bacon and stir it in.

Wash the dishes.

Serves 10 to 12.

Now for a nice main dish. There's nothing particularly kid-like about this one, but it's awfully easy, and shaking chicken in potato chips is fun.

Chicken in the Chips

1¼ sticks (10 tbsp.) butter or
    margarine
About 4 or 5 oz. potato chips
3 tbsp. sesame seeds (optional)
1 cut-up broiler-fryer chicken

Preheat the oven to 350 degrees.
Wash your hands.

Melt the butter in a large frying pan. Let it cool briefly.

Crush the potato chips to corn-flake size while they are still in the bag. This is not only less messy than other methods, it's more fun. (Poke a small air-escape hole in the bag first; then it will be easy.) Pour the crushed chips into a clean grocery bag. Put the sesame seeds in the grocery bag, too.

Turn a piece of chicken in the melted butter to coat it completely. Then drop it into the grocery bag of potato chips, close the top well and shake the chicken a few seconds. Put the chipped piece of chicken in a 9- by 13-inch baking pan. Repeat with the other pieces of chicken.

Drizzle 2 to 3 tablespoons of any leftover butter over the chicken.

If the chicken was quartered, instead of fully cut up, you probably didn't use up all the chips. You can sprinkle some of the leftover chips on the chicken, or discard them. (Don't eat them. Uncle Al knows best. Cooked chicken is great. Raw chicken is not, and stuff that's been kicking around with raw chicken is not good for you unless it gets cooked, too.)

Put the pan of chicken in the oven and bake about one hour. Put the chicken on a serving plate.

Wash the dishes.

Serves four.

Now a nice vegetable that's very little work but leads into the mysterious ways of the starch granule.

Creamed Peas and Onions

1 (16-oz.) can tiny peas
1 (16-oz.) can or jar boiled whole
    small onions
1 tbsp. butter
1 tbsp. flour
⅔ c. milk
½ tsp. salt
½ tsp. garlic salt
Pepper

Wash your hands.

Drain the peas and onions.

Put the butter in a small saucepan and heat it over low-medium heat until it has melted. Stir in the flour, and keep stirring (use a wooden spoon because a metal spoon might get hot) while it cooks and maybe gets a little brown, for about a minute.

Then add just a little bit of the milk and stir it in. Where did it go? Stir in some more milk. Isn't that amazing.?

Don't add too much milk at once, or you'll have to stir a lot longer before it works its way into the sauce.

When all the milk is in, add the salt, garlic salt and a shake of pepper, then stir in the drained peas and onions. Heat, stirring once in a while, until the vegetables are heated through.

Pour into a serving bowl.

Wash the dishes.

Serves four to six.

Now for dessert. Ice cream parfaits. This might be a little messy, but what the heck?

The final assembly — which is most of the work — has to take place right before you serve them. If you make the parfaits ahead and keep them in the refrigerator, the ice cream melts; if you keep them in the freezer, the peaches freeze. But everybody can wait five minutes after dinner while you and Little Sibling assemble these goodies.

Peach-Cookie Ice Cream Parfaits

24 Girl Scout Thin Mint cookies
1 (16-oz.) can peach slices
1½ quarts vanilla ice cream

Before dinner if you like (but it won't save much time) break up 12 of the cookies into small pieces (something like 6 or 8 pieces per cookie — not tiny crumbs). WASH YOUR HANDS FIRST!

Drain the peach slices and put them in a bowl. Count them to see how many you have. Since this recipe makes six servings, divide that number by six — that's how many peach slices you have for each parfait. It's probably between three and four.

When you're ready to assemble the parfaits, wash your hands again and divide the broken cookies into three equal piles.

Divide the first pile equally into the bottoms of six eight-ounce glasses (regular tall drinking glasses).

Drop a scoop of ice cream into each.

Top with a peach slice or two (about a third of the peach supply).

Sprinkle into each glass the pieces from the second cookie-piece pile. Top with another scoop of ice cream and another peach slice or two.

Put in the last of the cookie pieces, the last of the peaches and one more scoop of ice cream, to fill each glass.

Stick two mint cookies into the ice cream at angles to form a V.

Serves six.

The writer washed his hands before he set the table, too.

Little Mystery #11: Bags

You may have noticed that lots of the waxed-paper or cellophane bags inside boxes of things like cereal and potato chips aren't the same any more. They *look* like waxed paper, but if you try to tear them you can break your hand. What are they, and how are you supposed to open them?

Solution: A spokesperson for Sunstar Foods, Golden Valley, which makes and packages potato chips, among other things, explained that in the past the firm used a "paper-derivative glassine material" for bagging them. That material was a problem because it had to be stored in a humidity-controlled environment to keep it from drying out and tearing.

The replacement product, which suddenly seems to be *everywhere,* is called high-density polyethylene, and it is what the bagperson called "a co-extruded material" — a combination of polyethylene, which provides the moisture barrier, and EVA (ethyl vinyl acetate), which provides the sealing component of the material.

Yeah. Whatever you said. How are you supposed to open it?

Well, the snackperson said, some of this material is provided by its manufacturer with what is called an "easy-peel strip," which pulls apart fairly nicely (except, he said, if the heat-sealing equipment used to close it isn't properly adjusted). But not all of this material is purchased with the "easy-peel strip."

Now we're getting to it. Whether it's a bad or a nonexistent "easy-peel strip," how to do you open the bag with the corrugated seam on top and a flap down the front like a shirt, which gives no hint at all of how to attack it?

Mr. Chips allowed that some of those things are difficult to open, and suggested that the best advice might come from the manufacturer of the material, Crown-Zellerbach.

A spokesman for Crown-Zellerbach, in San Francisco, understood the question perfectly. "Don't try to *tear* it," he said. "It doesn't tear. It *won't.*"

The preferred approach, the Plastic Man went on, is to grab opposite sides of the bag and pull them apart, opening the seam from the inside.

I tried his advice, and it works, but let me pass along a warning: Be careful which seam you're putting the stress on. I managed to pull apart the wrong seam on a bag of stuffing mix; the "shirt front" opened instead of the top, and I got a floor full of croutons. Definitely not my bag.

Foods of the State Fair

There are some foods that are strongly associated with special occasions and are eaten at almost no other time: plum pudding at Christmas, for example; cranberry sauce at Thanksgiving; the traditional Tom and Jerry or champagne on New Year's Eve; the traditional aspirin, raw egg and Worcestershire sauce on New Year's Day; hot cross buns at Easter; stale egg-salad sandwiches for two weeks after Easter, and 24 hours of nothing at all on Yom Kippur.

Nothing stops you, of course, from eating cranberry sauce on the Fourth of July, or from hoisting a few Toms and Jerrys for Labor Day; it's just that almost nobody does it.

And there's no law against making a meal of a Pronto Pup, a pickle on a stick and bunch of tiny donuts when you're at home instead of at the State Fair. But even if there were such a law, who would consider breaking it? The fair is *the* place to eat such stuff.

And anyway, how would you make all that stuff at home even if you wanted to?

You're in luck. Rising to just such pointless challenges is what makes me so peculiar.

In pursuit of this particular challenge, I visited the fair a few days ago and had a good time sampling some of the cuisine that you get almost nowhere else.

This means that I didn't get to eat the hot beef sandwich at the restaurant run by the Jehovah Lutheran Church of St. Paul, for example, or the pork tenderloin dinner served up by the Ramsey County Young Marines, although the food served in such places is very nice.

I concentrated instead on such stuff as fried cheese curds and mini-donuts. And I tried to capture, in my notes, some of the small things that would help you recreate the sense of the fair at home, as an accompaniment to the home-made versions of these fair foods. Here are some suggestions:

■ Eat outside. If it's sunny, wear a hot raincoat. If it rains, eat outside anyway and don't wear a raincoat.

■ Eat standing up. If you *must* sit down, get some neighbor's kids to stand and stare at you all through your meal. One of them can cry, if you like.

■ Do not use plates, nor provide yourself with napkins or anything for cleanup other than waxed paper.

■ Put small pebbles in your shoes and walk around the block before eating.

■ Try to duplicate that elusive State Fair atmosphere. Nothing can match the ultimate State Fair taste sensation — a hot dog eaten at the concession stand just inside the swine barn — but you can get a little bit of Commonwealth Av. in your own back yard if you're willing to work at it.

For example: A day in advance, empty a few cans of beer onto the ground where you'll be eating. At the same time, peel and slice several onions, and scatter them in sunny areas with bits of hot dog. If you must eat inside, pour smaller amounts of beer, onions and hot dog bits onto a kitchen counter or table.

(Now, let me save some of you the cost of a phone call or a stamp. I *like* the State Fair. And a lot of what I like about it is that it *is* hot and greasy and redolent with the perfume of yesterday's Old Milwaukee.)

Back to duplicating the food. My fair-at-home meal consisted of imitation Pronto Pups, deep-fried cheese curds, mini-donuts, fried ice cream and a "health drink." The corn-dog recipe is from the Better Homes and Gardens Cook Book. The donut recipe is from Deep-Fry Cookery, by Mable Hoffman.

My first exercise was the ubiquitous Pronto Pup, also known at the fair as Poncho Pup, corn dog and hot dog on a stick.

If you don't know what this is, your stomach is probably in better shape than mine. It's a skewered hot dog, dipped in a batter containing corn meal, and deep fried.

You can indeed make these guys at home, and very easily if you're willing to use a prepared mix.

Genuine Pronto Pup coating mix is sold in grocery stores, as is pointed out on a sign inside every Pronto Pup booth at the fair. (A sign outside every Pronto Pup booth at the fair defines this item as "A banquet on a stick," and much as I like Pronto Pups I think that gives new meaning to the word "banquet.")

You can also assemble a sort of Pronto Pup batter from scratch. The mix has the advantage of turning out to the proper consistency right off the bat, while the homemade batter must be tinkered with a bit.

And if you make your own you have to come up with the wooden skewers somewhere (the mix has a bunch thrown in). That's not as easy as it

sounds. Despite their abundance at the fair, supporting not only hot dogs but pickles, pizza, steaks, pieces of cheese and slices of pineapple, I couldn't find them for sale at grocery stores. My best suggestion is to ask your butcher for some. This seems to work, but unless you're very friendly with your butcher I wouldn't rely on it if you plan to make enough corn dogs for your church picnic.

Corn Dogs

Oil for deep frying
1 c. flour
⅔ c. corn meal
1½ tsp. baking powder
2 tbsp. sugar
1 tsp. salt
2 tbsp. solid shortening
1 egg, beaten
¾ c. to 1 c. milk
10 hot dogs
Mustard

Heat the oil to 375 degrees.

Mix flour, corn meal, baking powder, sugar and salt.

Cut in the shortening with a pastry blender or a couple of knives, until the lumps are the size of crumbs. Separately combine the beaten egg and three-fourths cup of the milk, add to the dry ingredients and mix well.

Add more of the milk if necessary to achieve the proper consistency. The batter should be mushy — not wet, but liquid enough that it will flow slightly (to coat the hot dogs more-or-less uniformly).

Unwrap the hot dogs, pat them dry, insert the skewers (you can do this after they're fried if you're using a mini-fryer and the skewers won't fit) and dip them into the batter one at a time, getting all sides well coated. Let each drip before inserting it slowly into the oil, and fry until golden brown, about a minute on a side. Drain and brush with mustard.

As with all deep-fried food, fry only a few at a time, and allow the oil to reheat to the proper temperature between batches if necessary.

Makes 10.

Special hint to fair-food lovers: If you don't want to strew the landscape with onion slices, you can achieve a bit of the same effect by frying the hot dogs, or other items, in oil that had been used previously to make onion rings.

Also, beer can be substituted for some of the milk in this batter (and for the water that's added to commercial Pronto Pup mix).

While we're on the subject of hot dogs at the fair, lovers of trivial details might be interested to note that the signs that advertise "FOOT LONG HOT DOGS" have a few words in smaller script above the word FOOT. If you read carefully, the signs really say *"About a* FOOT LONG HOT DOGS." The result of some federal Truth in Hot Dog Act?

Apparently not. The signs that advertise "MILE LONG HOT DOGS" have not been amended.

Onward, to deep-fried cheese curds. I had to do these twice before I succeeded.

With the first batter I tried, the result might be called cheese cruds — they came out soft and eggy, and the effect was like greasy French toast with cheese.

But batter No. 2 worked just fine:

Deep-Fried Cheese Curds

Oil for frying
1 egg
1 c. milk
1 tbsp. oil
1 c. flour
1 tsp. baking powder
¼ tsp. salt
1 (9-oz.) pkg. cheese curds
Salt, if desired

Heat the oil to 390 degrees.

Beat together the egg, milk and the one tablespoon of oil. Add the flour, baking powder and salt and beat until well blended and smooth. Toss the cheese curds into the batter, separating them before they go in. (This works best with large pieces, so don't break up any big ones.) Let the cheese sit in the batter for a few minutes, and stir it around to make sure the pieces are all well coated.

Fry them rapidly, a few at a time, turning once, until they are light golden.

These are a little tricky.

First, because of the odd shapes of the curds, some of them tend to be what NASA used to call, in the days of ocean splashdowns, "monostable" — they will only float one way up. Tough. Just push them around in the oil as best you can and get them out of there.

Because (the second tricky part) if they're in the oil too long, the cheese begins to boil inside and shoot out through the coating. If the surface of the oil begins to get covered by lacy gunk, that's what's happening. You have to cook them quicker, which means raising the temperature, or settle for less brown.

(Fish off the lacy gunk with a slotted spoon and try again.)

Cool a bit and salt if you like.

Makes lots.

If you have a mini-donut cutter, use it to make these mini-donuts — and tell me where you got it: The mini-donuts sold at the fair all get pooted out of machines, and I've never seen a cutter the right size to produce them.

If you don't have one, you can do what I did. Buy a small (5½- or 6-ounce) can of ready-to-drink fruit juice — not frozen concentrate, because those cans, while about the same size, are cardboard and won't hold up. Open the can, discard the top, drink the contents (you'll need your strength) and wash the can. This will serve as the cutter for the outside of the donut. To produce the hole in the donut, I used the cap from a bottle of reconstituted lemon juice. Any similar cap will do just fine.

(I'm using the spelling of "donut" that is favored at the fair. If you prefer "doughnut," you will find yourself offended by the Tom Thumb Donuts," the "Tiny Tim Donuts," the "Tinkerbell Mini-Donuts," and the ones that everyone winds up asking for, "Those Little Donuts.")

Mini-Donuts

Oil for frying
1 tbsp. butter
1 egg
½ c. sugar
2 c. flour
2 tsp. baking powder
½ tsp. salt
⅓ c. milk
½ tsp. vanilla
Sugar for dipping

Heat the oil to 375 degrees. Melt the tablespoon of butter.

In a large bowl, beat the egg until it's lemon colored. Gradually beat in the sugar, and continue beating until the batter is thick. Separately combine the flour, baking powder and salt. Add these dry ingredients to the egg mixture, alternating with the melted butter, the milk and the vanilla. Stir until fully blended.

This is a really tough, sticky dough, and it will make things a lot easier if you refrigerate it for an hour or so, if you have the time. Even if you do, flour your working surface rather well, turn the dough out onto it and flour the top of the dough, too. With floured hands, pat it out, flipping it often on the floured surface so that it doesn't stick. Finally roll it out with a lightly floured roller until it is between ⅛ inch and ¼ inch thick.

Cut the donuts, punch out the center holes, and fry the donuts about 45 seconds on each side. Fry only five or six at a time to avoid cooling the oil excessively. Drain and toss with sugar — put the sugar and the donuts into a paper bag and shake; it's a lot easier and neater than flipping them around in a dish of sugar.

You can fry the holes as a special homemade bonus (the donut-pooting machines at the fair don't produce holes).

As I was cutting donuts, I was reminded of a riddle my father once told me: A bum used to roll his own cigarettes out of butts that he found. It took six butts to make one cigarette. One day he had particularly good luck and found 36 butts. How many cigarettes did he get?

Seven, because he got six cigarettes out of the 36 butts, and when he smoked them he had six butts — enough to make another cigarette.

Anyway, I was able to make 22 donuts out of the dough as first rolled out, nine from the scraps, five from those scraps and two from those scraps, for a total of 38 donuts, 38 holes, and some scraps that I finally threw out but that probably would have yielded a few more holes.

This recipe for fried ice cream is only my guess, but it turns out to taste virtually identical to what is served at the fair.

Besides, under the chocolate, whipped cream and cherry, it's darned hard to tell what you're eating.

Fried Ice Cream

1 qt. ice cream
1 egg
About 1 c. dry bread crumbs
Oil for frying
Canned chocolate sauce
Aerosol can of whipped cream
Maraschino cherries

Shape the ice cream (your choice of flavor) into eight to ten balls. Return them to the freezer for a few minutes, while you beat the egg and put the bread crumbs in a separate small bowl.

Place a cookie sheet covered with waxed paper in the freezer. Roll each ice-cream ball first in the beaten egg, then in the crumbs. Return to the cookie sheet in the freezer. Freeze again for an hour or more, to firm up the coating.

Heat the oil to 350 degrees. "Fry" the ice cream balls, one at a time, for about three seconds, turning rapidly in the oil to crisp all the sides. If you fry them much longer, the ice cream starts to melt and the whole thing falls apart. Remove the ice cream from the oil with a slotted spoon, rapidly drain the oil off the spoon and turn the ice cream into a bowl. Cover with chocolate sauce and whipped cream, and top with a cherry.

Special warning to fair-food lovers: After a night of eating food like this, you wake up very oily in the morning.

While I pondered, weak and weary, what were styled as "Exerps from the Poem 'Why,' by Evel Knievel," painted near the entrance of "The Incredible Show" on the Midway, I realized that I was in need of something not fried.

The fried zucchini (or zuchinni, depending on which sign you read) no longer tempted me, as it had earlier in the day. Nor did "Ice Cream on a Stick," which in my dazed condition I did not realize was simply an ice cream bar.

What I needed, I concluded, was to sit down under the grandstand and watch a health drink being made in the VITA-MIX 3600.

This kind of activity has been an essential part of fairgoing for me since I was a kid and my father wanted to watch all the cabbage-slicer salesmen while I wanted to go on the rides. We watched a lot of cabbage-slicer salesmen.

At the end of the VITA-MIX 3600 demonstration, everybody gets to try a little of the drink. I've never been convinced that the drinks made for these demonstrations are all that healthful, but at least they're not fried. And they're free.

If there is one aroma that, along with the beer, onions and hot dogs, would complete your back-yard simulation of the fair, it is this drink. You never get enough of it in those little paper nut cups to really pin the flavor down, but it seems to combine all the lingering essences of the juice stands that line the fair's sidewalks. (If you don't want to drink it, just slop some of it on the ground.)

I wasn't too sure that I could duplicate the drink with the blender I bought at a garage sale, because the VITA-MIX 3600 is a very powerful machine. Its blades reverse instantly and seem to reduce the ice cubes to slush in nothing flat. But I was willing to take a lot longer to get results than the VITA-MIX man was, and to cut into small pieces the fruits that he threw in more-or-less whole.

By the end, my blender motor smelled like an electrical fire, but I succeeded.

Health Drink

1 orange
½ apple
1 half-inch-thick slice of lemon
1 wedge of melon (Persian or
**   cantaloupe), with seeds**
2 c. ice cubes
⅓ of a banana
2 tbsp. honey

Remove only the zest (the bright orange portion of the skin) from the orange, leaving the thicker white portion. Cut the orange into quarters, holding it over the blender cup to catch any juice. Squeeze the quarters into the cup, then toss in one of the squeezed quarters. Blend at high speed until it is fully liquefied, then add the other three quarters, one at a time, liquefying each before adding the next.

Cut the half of an apple into chunks, without removing the peel or the seeds. (I pitched the stem — I thought that was *too* much, even for a health drink). Add the chunks, one at a time, waiting for each to liquefy before adding the next.

Throughout this process, stop the machine occasionally and probe around with a spatula to make sure there are no hidden chunks. (The drink gets very opaque.)

As you did for the orange, remove only the bright yellow portion of the peel from the thick slice of lemon. Squeeze in the juice, then cut the remaining mess in half and add the pieces one at a time.

Remove the rind from the wedge of melon. Add the seeds to the blender, then throw in pieces of the melon, one at a time.

Now add the ice cubes: Get the blender going at its highest speed and drop the ice cubes into the vortex one at a time, waiting for the awful noises to subside before you go on to the next one. (The VITA-MIX 3600 took all two cups of ice cubes at once with equanimity, and it gave the impression of being up to eating a case of 10-penny nails if anybody wanted to add them.)

Let the blender run for a minute or two after the last ice cube is added, then toss the banana, in chunks, into the vortex. Finally add the honey.

For authenticity, serve in paper nut cups.

Makes one quart, enough for 64 itty-bitty servings.

As a result of this experience, the writer has thought about spending a few days in a degreasing tank at a Standard Oil station, and he is planning to have his kitchen hosed down with live steam.

The Checkerboard Meal

I don't know why I'm on so many mailing lists; I don't buy very much by mail.

I have succumbed occasionally to the blandishments of the New Process Co., of Warren, Pa. (the outfit that sends you five pounds of little pieces of paper every month, each picturing some item of apparel and often accompanied by tiny swatches of crinkle-cut material), and I occasionally buy something from J.C. Whitney in the forlorn hope of sustaining the flickering flame that is my 17-year-old car, but that's really about it.

Still, almost every time I bring in the mail, expecting maybe a form letter from my congressman, an NSP bill or something equally cheering, I get at least one attempt to sell me something.

Some of that stuff is fun — I got one a while back that tried to interest me in furniture designed for "the new way of sitting." Others are merely insistent. "Frankly, I'm puzzled. You have everything to gain and nothing to lose in taking our no-obligation offer [for pantyhose]."

Mostly what I get is catalogs. And that's a real problem for me, because I'm afraid to throw them out. I guess I figure I'll need to look in one for something some day, so I stack them up for a year or so until I can't stand it any more.

Then I throw them out, shortly before I really do need one of them. (I'm not quite to the throwing-out stage yet this year, so if you suddenly find that you need to order ugly salt-and-pepper shakers, publishers' overstock books or a reflecting telescope, I can probably help you out.)

One kind of mailing that is particularly compelling but particularly awful is the fancy-kitchen-accessory catalog. I find it depressing to page through endless arrays of very pretty but outrageously priced cookware and gadgets that might be used once every five years.

How many people in this economy are up to $120 stainless-steel fish poachers or $65 black-aluminum teapots?

One item that is showing up in lots of those catalogs these days is a pan for making checkerboard cake. Checkerboard cake is a two- or-three-layer cake, each layer of which contains two or three concentric rings of different color batter.

You alternate the colored batters when you make the different layers, and the effect, when you assemble the cake and slice it, is a checkerboard pattern.

This is not a new idea. In fact, it's old as the hills.

And when your mother or grandmother made it, she didn't buy any special pan for it, either.

I don't bear any malice toward the kitchen-equipment-catalog folks, but I thought I'd save you the $13 to $20 they're getting for a checkerboard-cake pan by telling you how to make the cake without it.

While we're at it, let's take the theme to our usual ridiculous extreme by making some other checkerboard items.

Check?

Check.

Here's what I made:

Checkerboard sandwiches
Checkerboard pizza
Checkerboard cake
Checkerboard ice cream

I was tempted to take the checkerboard theme past the food itself and into decorations, but I kind of forgot about that until it was too late. All I did was alternate two colors of napkins around the table. A checkerboard tablecloth would have been nice, you could alternate the good dining-room chairs with the plastic ones that are usually on the back porch or in the basement. You could force alternate guests to drink different colors of wine or pop, you could wear a lumberjack shirt with a checkered suit, and you might even prop bags of Purina Puppy Chow, Cat Chow and Camel Chow in the corners of the room.

On second thought, though, all of that geometricity might overshadow the food, and, in these pages anyway, we try to avoid doing that.

Checkerboard sandwiches are sandwiches made on checkerboard bread. Checkerboard bread consists of two loaves of bread — one white, one rye — cut apart, reassembled checkerboard fashion (held together with cheese-butter) and refrigerated until it sets. If the entire idea strikes you as ludicrous, stop reading now because this article gets a whole lot worse.

Obviously you can put anything you want between two pieces of checkerboard bread. Since the opportunity seldom exists to have a sandwich on both white bread *and* rye, you ought to take advantage of it by having something nice. How about ham and cheese? Mustard goes with rye bread and mayonnaise goes with white, so mustardy mayonnaise seemed like a good idea for checkerboard sandwiches. It was.

Checkerboard Sandwiches

Checkerboard bread (enough for 10 to 14 sandwiches):
3 sticks butter or margarine
6 oz. American cheese
1 (1-lb.) loaf white bread, unsliced
1 (1-lb.) loaf rye bread, unsliced
Dressing:
½ c. mayonnaise
1½ tbsp. Dijon mustard
Filling, per sandwich:
1 large slice cooked ham
1 large slice Cheddar cheese

At least six hours (or a whole day) before serving time, begin preparing the checkerboard bread:

Cream the butter and beat in crumbled American cheese. Beat until the mixture is quite soft.

Trim the top, bottom, side and end crusts from both loaves of bread. Cut each loaf into six lengthwise horizontal slices (about three-fourths of an inch thick each).

Spread the cheese-butter fairly thickly on one horizontal slice of rye bread. Don't skip any areas, and go all the way to the edges. Top with a horizontal slice of white bread, butter it carefully, and continue alternating until you have a six-slice alternating loaf, starting with rye and finishing with white.

Repeat, in the same pattern, to make a second loaf. You should have half the cheese-butter left.

Put both loaves back in their plastic bags, press down to help seal the layers together, and chill them at least two hours in the refrigerator.

When the ribbon loaves are quite firm, remove one from the refrigerator and slice it into six lengthwise *vertical* slices.

Spread cheese-butter carefully on one slice. Turn the next slice end over end so that, if the first slice starts with a ribbon of rye and ends with white, the second starts with a ribbon of white and ends with rye. Continue buttering and flipping until the bread is reassembled with half the slices inverted.

Repeat with the other loaf; bag, press firmly and chill again.

Prepare the dressing by combining the mayonnaise and mustard.

The cold bread does hold together fairly well when sliced (although the corner pieces have a tendency to loosen), but it begins to drift a bit when warm. Don't, however, slice the bread thinly, or small defects in the adhesion of checkerboard pieces will cause the slices to fall apart.

You have a choice about how to proceed.

You can cut the bread, assemble the sandwiches and refrigerate them until serving time. But the chill diminishes the rather pleasant flavor.

Or you can cut the bread and assemble the sandwiches 15 minutes or so before serving and allow them to rest that length of time at room temperature (taking a very small risk that you've increased their propensity to explode on impact).

In either case, when you're ready, coat one slice of the bread generously with mayonnaise-mustard dressing, then layer in two half-slices each of cheese and ham (alternating cheese and ham, of course), and top with another slice of bread also well-coated with mayonnaise-mustard dressing. (The dressing helps hold the whole thing together as a sandwich, so don't eliminate it.)

Serve to a crowd of folks, who will probably say something like, "What in the world are *those?*"

In the planning stages, I thought of this next item, checkerboard pizza, as really looking like a checkerboard: red squares of tomato sauce, yellow squares of cheese — surely easy enough to pull off by "masking" parts of the pizza when cheese is sprinkled on.

I decided to make a rectangular pizza rather than a round one, to heighten the effect (a square one would have been even better but I didn't have a wide-enough pan to make a decent-size square), and to complete the image I got slices of pepperoni for the squares at one end and Italian sausage for the squares at the other end.

When the idea was actually executed, it suffered somewhat from the flowing characteristics of the mozzarella cheese, which tended to make the edges of the squares highly indistinct, but the effect was sort of there. Aesthetics aside, the pizza was quite good, and you can skip the checkerboard business if you like. Even the red squares tasted fine, because I blended the Parmesan cheese in with the tomato sauce before I spread it. The thin crust was nice and crisp.

For my taste, there should have been more sauce; others at the table disagreed.

I'll leave it up to you: If you like your pizza reasonably wet, I'd make half again the amount of sauce.

Checkerboard Pizza

(Makes two 15- by 10-inch rectangular, 14-inch round or 12½-inch square pizzas)

Dough:
1 (¼-oz.) env. active dry yeast
1 c. warm water
½ tsp. sugar
3¼ c. flour
1 tsp. salt

Sauce:
2 (8-oz.) cans tomato sauce
1 tbsp. olive oil
2 tbsp. water
2 cloves garlic, crushed
1 tsp. oregano
¼ tsp. basil
¼ tsp. crushed fennel seeds (optional but nice)
½ tsp. salt
½ tsp. sugar
Dash cayenne pepper
1 lb. Italian sausage
3 oz. (½ c.) grated Parmesan cheese
2 (4-oz.) cans mushroom stems and pieces, drained (optional)
12 oz. (3 c.) shredded mozzarella cheese
1 (3½-oz.) pkg. sliced pepperoni

Prepare the dough: Stir the yeast into the warm water; stir in the sugar and let stand 10 minutes.

Sift the flour and salt into a bowl, add the yeast mixture and stir with a heavy spoon, gathering in all the flour, until a stiff dough is formed (if the dough is wet, add up to one-fourth cup more flour).

Knead the dough on a lightly floured countertop for about five minutes, folding, yanking, mauling and pummeling it as necessary to work out your hostilities and to make it smooth and elastic. Add flour only if you must.

Wash and grease the bowl and turn the ball of dough in it to coat it completely. Cover the bowl with a towel and let the dough rise in a warm place about 45 minutes, or until it has doubled in bulk.

After the dough has risen for 10 or 15 minutes, prepare the sauce: Combine tomato sauce, olive oil, water, garlic, oregano, basil, fennel, salt, sugar and cayenne in a saucepan. Cover and cook over very low heat for 20 minutes, stirring occasionally.

Break the Italian sausage into half-inch-or-so chunks. (You may not find the sausage in bulk; if not, squeeze it out of the skins before breaking it up.) Fry until color is gone from the meat; drain and set aside.

When the dough has risen, punch it down and divide it in half. (If you don't want to make both pizzas at once, you can refrigerate half the dough, wrapped, for a day or two.) Grease two pans of the shape you have selected, put the dough in them and stretch it out to fit. You can begin by rolling it with a rolling pin, but in the end you'll probably need your hands. Cut the edge even and fold up a small lip. The dough is very forgiving, so fill any rips or uneven edges with cut-away bits.

Stir the Parmesan cheese into the sauce and cover the dough evenly with the mixture. Sprinkle the mushrooms around.

Preheat the oven to 425 degrees.

If you don't really care about making the pizza look like a checkerboard, you're almost done. Just scatter the pieces of Italian sausage, strew with mozzarella cheese and toss on the slices of pepperoni. Or use whatever other pizza toppings you like.

But if you're going for the checkered flag, this is the tricky (or stupid) part:

Fold or cut 10 or 12 strips of waxed paper about two inches wide. Arrange pieces of Italian sausage in the centers of imaginary two-inch squares at one end of each pizza. Lay strips of waxed paper lengthwise and others crosswise on the pizza, leaving equal-size empty spaces between them. Scatter about a third of the mozzarella cheese on each pizza, leaving a third of the cheese to take care of something peculiar:

You may have thought that this lattice of waxed-paper strips would create a checkerboard pattern, but if you think a little harder you'll realize that it doesn't quite. I didn't figure this out until I got to this point and really looked at what I had: Half the rows are checkered, OK, where the waxed-paper strips cross them, but the rows in between those are completely covered with a strip of waxed paper.

To make it a checkerboard (and to get a decent amount of cheese onto it), the pizza should have cheese not only on the squares that have *no* waxed paper over them, it should also have cheese on the squares that are covered by *two intersecting* strips of waxed paper. If you have a pizza in front of you, are inclined to doodle or are into Boolean algebra, you will probably see what I mean. If not, take my word for it.

Tip the waxed-paper strips, so that the cheese on them falls onto the already-cheesed squares, and remove the strips. Now you can certainly see the areas of missing cheese. Don't bother repositioning the strips. Just drizzle the remaining cheese into those missing squares. If you're really into this, reposition the few shreds of cheese that have wandered where no cheese belongs and neaten up the edges of the squares. It won't avail you much once the cheese start to melt, but some people need to have things just so.

Deal the pepperoni slices onto squares at the opposite end of the pizza from the end with the pieces of sausage. (If the guests don't like the pizza they can play checkers with the pepperoni and sausage.)

Slip the pizzas into the oven and bake 20 to 25 minutes, until the cheese is bubbling and the edges are browned. Cut the pizza into squares and serve to a crowd of folks, who will probably say something like, "What in the world is *that?*"

Because this was supposed to be a piece about checkerboard cake, we'd better make one. It's not hard, and you really could use about any white or yellow cake batter you want, but I have provided here a very stiff pound-cake-like batter that worked quite nicely.

Checkerboard Cake

Cake:

¾ c. (1½ sticks) butter
2 c. sugar
4 eggs
3 c. cake flour
4 tsp. baking powder
1 c. milk
Flavoring for half of cake batter (or use red food coloring):
6 (1-oz.) squares unsweetened chocolate, melted
1½ tsp. cinnamon
½ tsp. ground cloves
1 tsp. vanilla
Dark frosting:
6 oz. cream cheese
4 (1-oz.) squares unsweetened chocolate, melted (or a few drops of red food coloring)
Dash of salt
5 c. confectioners' sugar, sifted
2 tsp. vanilla
3 to 4 tbsp. milk
Contrasting frosting (optional, but what the heck):
2 oz. cream cheese
1⅔ c. confectioners' sugar, sifted
1 tsp. vanilla
2 tsp. milk

Prepare the cake batter: Cream the butter, beat in the sugar and add the eggs one at a time, beating well after each.

Combine the flour and baking powder. Add that mixture to the batter in thirds, alternating with thirds of the milk and beating constantly.

Put half of the batter in another bowl and add the melted chocolate, cinnamon, cloves and vanilla and mix well. (The spices in addition to the chocolate add what I found to be a welcome sense of strangeness to the dark portions of the cake.)

Note: If you're using some other cake batter, prepare one and a half recipes of it. Divide it in not-quite-even halves — one half a little bigger than the other — and add red food coloring to one half. You might be able, instead, to add the chocolate flavoring above to your recipe, but there's no way I can say for sure. The red food coloring is a tasteless but sure-fire alternative. It's up to you.

Grease three eight- or nine-inch cake pans. The idea, in case you've forgotten, is to produce layers of cake, each of which consists of three rings of alternating colors.

The batter I used is so stiff that you might be able to get away without any dividers at all between the rings, but unless you've made this kind of thing before and are not likely to panic as you see batter oozing away from where it belongs, I wouldn't recommend that.

Instead, cut and fold a piece of foil into a strip about two inches high and about 20 inches long. Overlap the ends about two inches. Paper-clip them together and shape the strip into a rough circle a little less than six inches across. Take care that when the ring you've formed sits on a flat surface there are no large gaps underneath it. This is the ring that separates the outer circle of cake batter from the middle one.

Repeat with a strip about twelve inches long, overlapping the ends two inches and forming a ring a little more than three inches across. This is the ring that separates the middle circle of cake batter from the inner one. (For this ring you can substitute a very well washed tuna can or cat-food can with top and bottom removed.)

Preheat the oven to 350 degrees, or whatever is called for by your recipe.

Position the rings in the first pan.

When I made this cake, the batter measured 5¼ cups, and I divided it out for you so that you'd be able to add the batter to the rings with some confidence that you won't come out wrong at the end. This is fairly unusual cake batter, though — there's not much of it and it rises quite a bit — so if you're using a different batter you'll probably have more than 5¼ cups of it. If you're handy with a pencil or a calculator you can figure out similar proportions from mine. If not, guesswork will probably turn out just fine.

Into the inner ring put one-fourth cup of the chocolate batter (or, if you're using a different recipe, a proportionate amount of the larger "half" of your batter). Put half a cup of yellow batter (or proportionate amount of the other batter you've prepared with your own recipe) into the middle ring and one cup (or proportionate amount) of the chocolate batter into the outer ring. Lift out the separators, rinse them off and dry them.

NOTE: This batter, as mentioned, has very little volume until it bakes, so it looks like there won't possibly be enough. There will; just spread it around each ring with a knife or narrow spatula so it's reasonably even and there aren't any gaps.

Put the separators into the next pan, but add batter in reverse order (vanilla, chocolate, vanilla). Repeat with the third pan, using the same order you used in the first pan. Put the pans into the preheated oven.

This batter rises — and dries — quickly. Start checking in 15 minutes. (Or bake your recipe as long as it specifies.)

Prepare frosting:

Cream the cream cheese in the large bowl of an electric mixer.

Beat in the chocolate (or a few drops of red food coloring, if you prefer) and the salt, and add the confectioners' sugar, alternating with the vanilla and small amounts of milk, as needed.

Assemble (with lots of frosting between the layers and top and sides, of course) so that the two identical layers are top and bottom and the other one is between them. When you cut a slice of it, there you are. Checkerboard.

Let's checkerboard the frosting, too, as long as we're at it (although you certainly can skip this if you want to). Let the chocolate (or pink) frosting set on the cake for half an hour or so. Then prepare the small amount of contrasting white frosting by creaming the cream cheese and beating in the confectioners' sugar, vanilla and milk.

Cut a two-inch-square piece out of a brown paper bag and cut a one-inch-square hole out of the middle of it. When the main frosting is set, put one-inch squares of white frosting on it with a spatula and the piece of brown paper as a kind of stencil. If you have enough frosting left, you can pipe a ring of it around the edge of the top.

When you set *this* in front of folks, they'll probably say something like "Enough is enough, already!"

What, dear friends, is checkerboard cake without checkerboard ice cream? I vaguely recall occasionally seeing some ready-made. If you can find that, you're home free. If not, this is the simplest of the bunch of recipes to put together.

Checkerboard Ice Cream

2 rectangular (not cylindrical) cartons ice cream (pints, quarts or half-gallons, as needed) in contrasting colors and flavors. (Vanilla and chocolate seem like reasonable choices, but you could certainly choose cantaloupe and blackberry or whatever else your heart desires.)

Turn your freezer up. That is, turn your freezer temperature down. That is, make it extra-cold in your freezer.

Let the ice cream rest in your cold freezer for at least two hours. Put a couple of wide spatulas where they'll be handy to grab and, if you have them, put on a pair of dishwashing gloves (they insulate the ice cream from your hot little hands).

Working rapidly, open the packages fully and, using a sharp knife, cut each brick into four lengthwise vertical slices. Separate the slices slightly, and rapidly transfer two slices from one brick into alternate spaces in the other one and vice-versa. You now have two bricks, each of which has vertical stripes of alternating colors. Quickly repack and close the packages, then firm them in the freezer for another two hours.

Unwrap one brick and again make four lengthwise slices, only rotate the brick on its side before you cut the slices, so that each slice is four layers of alternating-color ice cream. Turn alternating slices end-over-end, and repackage and return to the freezer. Repeat with the other brick. Let freeze two hours before serving. When you serve checkerboard ice cream with checkerboard cake, your guests will king you.

This has not been the high point in the writer's checkered career.

A British-Mystery Dinner

Some of us who have nothing better to do occasionally find ourselves challenged to really stupid activities. Like rewriting some of the classic passages in literature. For example:

A Tale of Two Cities
By Al Sicherman
It was the becestershire, it was the Worcestershire.

Or maybe rewriting them in the names of others:

A Tale of Two Cities
By David Stockman
On the average, the times were OK.

I don't know how good I'd be at a parlor game like that if it included current important books. For quite some years now, I haven't been able to read anything of substance. The more important the book, the less likely I am even to want to pick it up.

I feel pretty bad about that, as I used to be a serious reader, but I just can't summon up much zeal these days. I think maybe my not wanting to read about Problems is my way of acknowledging that the focus of my life has shifted, along with my center of gravity (in the first case inward, in the second case downward). I'm into brightening the corner where I are, as the song goes, and not very much at that.

Point me to a mystery, though, particularly a British drawing-room mystery, and I'll waste an evening or two with it forthwith. I don't know why British murder mysteries are so much more appealing to me than American murder mysteries, but I am convinced that you haven't been killed until you've been killed by an Englishman.

As you know if you have used these peculiar little essays to piece together my peculiar little life, I worked at an English-language newspaper in France for most of a year some time back. As you probably don't know, I didn't speak any French when I got there.

After a brief stint at a language school (brief both because it met at eight in the morning and I got out of work after midnight, and because I didn't care to discuss at length, with people whose accents were even worse than mine, the matter of Sophie and her cigarette lighter), I decided that what I needed most was not better pronunciation or niftier grammar but a larger French vocabulary.

At the suggestion of a colleague, I began reading books for French toddlers, and I graduated to mystery novels — British mysteries in French translation rather than French mysteries, because I already understood the situations and the manners of speech. That meant that I could make fairly accurate guesses at the translations rather than running to the dictionary every three words. This turned out to be a fairly useful thing to do, and by the time I left France I was able to misunderstand and be misunderstood in a wide variety of circumstances.

While I was acquiring much of the French language by this curious method, I was, of course, getting some parts of it (food and profanity, particularly) by brute force — see a word on a menu, look it up; be called something by an irate taxi driver, don't even need to look it up.

Because I ate more than I took taxis I acquired a pretty comfortable food vocabulary rather rapidly, and I soon stopped using my dictionary when mealtime came.

That food vocabulary often did not help, however, when food was mentioned in the British mysteries, which it frequently is. The British eat lots of dishes that are not widely served in France or the United States. What, for example, would a tarte de mélasse be? From context it's dessert, and the tarte is obvious enough. But what is mélasse? It looks like it could be molasses, but surely there is no such thing as a molasses tart or pie.

Mais oui, friends, there is — although the accurate name is treacle tart.

(The difference between molasses and treacle is not even as interesting as the rest of this discussion.)

I've been back in the good old U. S. of A. more than five years now, and I have forgotten most of my French with far less difficulty than I acquired it, which proves something but I'm not sure what.

In any event, I was reading a British mystery the other night when I was struck again — not from behind with a blunt instrument, but by the number of apparently common things to eat that turn up in British mysteries but that I have never eaten (and in some cases couldn't even describe).

Why not, I thought in my weakened condition, use these foods to compile a British-mystery dinner?

OK, let's say it once here and have it over with. Lots of folks have food prejudices. Scandinavian food, some will say, is all white. German food, others will aver, is all heavy.

And there are those who will say negative things about British cooking.

Not me. If you want to make your own jokes, in the privacy of your own dwelling unit, about what the mystery is in the British-mystery dinner, I can't stop you. But I'm not making them.

Oh, heck. How about if I pass along a remark that is offensive to not one but three or four nationalities? That would sort of even things up, wouldn't it?

A Canadian friend told me this one, and for all I know it's a commonplace observation in that country. "In Canada," he said, "we had the possibilities of American technology, British tradition and French cooking. Instead, what we got was American tradition, French technology and British cooking."

I didn't say that. My Canadian *friend* said that.

Well! If you insist on taking that kind of attitude, we had best push on to the recipes.

The first item to come under our scrutiny is one that is hardly a stranger to our shores, being found in little tins in every supermarket, but I'd venture to say that the average American, asked to assist the police in their enquiries, would say he had never sampled it.

Although in England it is typically tucked into as a breakfast item, I served it as an appetizer.

Reaction was predictably mixed, but three people — *including a 14-year-old kid* — had seconds.

Kippers

3 (3¼-oz.) cans kippered (cured)
    herring
4 tbsp. butter
Salt, pepper
2 tbsp. chopped parsley
1 tbsp. lemon juice
1 lemon, cut into wedges

Cut the kippers in half crosswise.

Melt the butter in a frying pan over low-medium heat, add the kippers and cook gently, turning once, until they are warmed through. Season with salt and pepper.

Garnish with chopped parsley, sprinkle with lemon juice and serve with lemon wedges.

Depending on whether you're presenting them to kipper fans or to colonials who don't comprehend the charm, these will serve from 3 to 12 folks.

Next in my investigation I summoned those little sandwiches that, British mysteries would have us believe, blokes and blokesses are always diving into at peculiar times of the day, having motored down from Elbow Twisting, Herts. (To avoid the possibility of a fortnight in chokey, I will admit that I pinched the name of that village from author Robert L. Fish.)

I must say that I thought the little sandwiches on the bland side, although I always go light on the salt and pepper. H.M. government no doubt suggest heavy seasoning for fuller flavour.

While I'm admitting things, I'll also acknowledge having adapted the recipe for the sandwiches from The Lord Peter Wimsey Cookbook. (If you please, guv'nor! They was so little, and they was like me mum used to make.)

Little Sandwiches

12 thin slices bread
8 tbsp. butter, softened
Salt and pepper
    and
3 medium tomatoes, sliced thin
    or
⅓ c. finely chopped watercress leaves
and 1 tsp. lemon juice
    or
1 medium cucumber
and 1 tbsp. vinegar
and 1 tsp. dill weed

Trim crusts from sliced bread.

Proceed to make six sandwiches of one kind, or by dividing the quantities appropriately, an assortment:

For tomato sandwiches, spread the butter on the bread and assemble the sandwiches with slices of tomato and liberal application of salt and pepper.

For watercress sandwiches, blend the chopped watercress with the softened butter, lemon juice and liberal amounts of salt and pepper. Spread on bread and assemble.

For cucumber sandwiches, peel the cucumber and slice it thinly. Put the slices in a bowl with the vinegar and dill, stir and let sit for 10 minutes. Spread the butter on the bread, and assemble the sandwiches with slices of drained cucumber and salt and pepper.

In any case, cut the sandwiches into quarters or eighths or thin fingers and arrange on a tray, maybe even with a paper doily, and bring them out late in the afternoon, when people are feeling a bit peckish.

Makes six full sandwiches, enough for 6 to 12 people as a teatime snack.

I also prepared potted shrimps, an appetizer that I've seen mentioned several times. They are "potted" in clarified butter.

Depend upon it; people and potted shrimps are much the same everywhere. Even in this small village I have seen the damage caused by mischief and bad recipes. These potted shrimps, now. They remind me of the time young Dora Edwards got into difficulty over a necklace. Old Mrs. Fletcher said Dora had taken a pearl necklace that had been left on the bureau. Dora argued, but old Mrs. Fletcher threw her out.

And that's what I did with almost all of these greasy potted shrimps.

They did have a nice flavor, though, so please allow a person who has learned a great deal about life to suggest that mace goes surprisingly well with shrimps.

Although it is distinctly *not* a British food, I was tempted to serve corn (maize), just so I could introduce a constable on a bicycle who would say: "Ear, ear, ear. Wot's all this?"

It isn't, so I won't. But if I had any fortitude, I would have done.

Instead, I served a vegetable dish (adapted from Farmhouse Cookery, published by the Reader's Digest Association of London) that is so British-sounding that my upper lip stiffened just thinking about it. This is neither fantastic nor terrible, but it is certainly more likely to please if you are fond of celery.

Braised Celery

1 bunch celery (8 to 10 ribs)
4 large carrots
2 medium onions

2 tbsp. butter
1 tbsp. olive oil
1 (10¾-oz.) can chicken broth
¼ tsp. thyme
Salt, pepper
1 bay leaf
2 or 3 sprigs of parsley

Wash the celery and cut into 1½-inch pieces. Peel and slice the carrots. Peel and slice the onions.

Preheat the oven to 350 degrees.

Melt the butter in a frying pan, add the oil and sauté the carrots and onions for 10 minutes.

Transfer the vegetables to a 1½- or two-quart oven-safe casserole. Add the celery, chicken broth, thyme, salt and pepper; stir to combine.

Add the bay leaf and parsley sprigs. Cover and bake 1¼ hours or until the vegetables are tender. Remove bay leaf and parsley.

Serves six.

Let us now concern ourselves with a main dish.

Because I have noted it elsewhere in my journals (it was in the summer of '81, after the curious adventure of the sauerkraut cake), we will not have the odd but quite tasty toad-in-the-hole (sausages in Yorkshire pudding).

Instead, let us have some even better and heartier fare — a pie that features, in addition to steak, an organ meat not commonly consumed on these shores.

There is no need for speculation, for here, unless I am very much mistaken, is our visitor now.

Steak and Kidney Pie

1 to 1½ lb. top round steak
1 veal kidney
1 large onion
4 tbsp. butter
Flour
Salt, pepper
1 (10½-oz.) can beef broth
1 tsp. Worcestershire sauce
1 tsp. dried basil
2 (3¾-oz.) tins smoked oysters,
    drained (optional)
Prepared pastry for 1-crust pie
1 egg, beaten

Trim any fat off the steak and cut it into 1-inch cubes.

Wash the kidney, and use a scissors (a knife, although more elegant, isn't as handy) to trim away the fat and the hard center core and white fibers. Cut or chop the kidney into rather small pieces (smaller than the steak cubes).

Peel and slice the onion.

Heat the butter in a frying pan and sauté the onions until they are translucent. Lift the onions out of the melted butter with a slotted spoon and set them in a two-quart oven-safe casserole.

Toss the steak cubes in a few tablespoons of flour, along with some salt and pepper. (I like to do this in a paper bag, but my origins are humble. Cooks of breeding probably never resort to that.)

Brown the floured steak in the butter, adding more butter if necessary. Remove steak pieces to the casserole.

Shake or toss the kidney pieces in seasoned flour and lightly brown them, too. Transfer to the casserole.

Preheat the oven to 300 degrees. Add one tablespoon of flour to whatever fat and meat juices are left in the pan (if none, melt a tablespoon of butter). Stir flour and fat together over low heat for a minute, then slowly add the beef broth, stirring, and cook until it is slightly thickened. Add the Worcestershire and basil (it was the becestershire, it was the ... no, I did that already) and stir to combine. Pour into the casserole, but don't add more than is necessary to just cover the meat.

Cover the casserole with foil and bake at 300 degrees for 1½ hours.

If you like, you can prepare the recipe to this point in advance, set it in the fridge, then pop down to Brighton for a holiday.

When ready to resume, increase the oven temperature to 450 degrees and have the butler get the casserole back from the pantry. (Keep an eye on him; Bessie, the little serving girl up from the village, says he has been hitting the Port, and he has also been seen in the market town talking with a strange little man with a cast in one eye.)

Add the oysters, if desired (not a bad idea if you're not sure you'll like the kidney, as the smoky oyster flavor tends to predominate).

Roll out the pie crust and cover the casserole with it. Cut a few decorative slashes in it, to allow steam to escape, and brush with the beaten egg.

Bake for 10 minutes at 450 degrees, lower the temperature to 350 degrees and bake another 25 minutes or longer, until the crust is crisp and golden.

Serves six.

Here, as a second side dish (or perhaps an appetizer) is something I liked rather well. It was quite rippin', actually! This recipe, too, is adapted from Farmhouse Cookery, and had I not misplaced my monocle when I went for a punt on the river this forenoon, I should be able to tell you a most interestin' fact from that very volume

Where did I put the dashed thing? Ah! Here we are: "There are 21 species of edible fungi in Britain."

Our late friend would have done well to learn what the others looked like.

Creamed Mushrooms

1 lb. mushrooms
1 tbsp. oil
6 tbsp. butter, divided
2 tbsp. finely chopped shallots
½ c. heavy cream
Salt, pepper
2 to 3 tbsp. sherry
¼ tsp. nutmeg

Clean and slice the mushrooms.

Heat the oil and four tablespoons of the butter in a frying pan. Add the mushrooms and shallots and cook, stirring, about three minutes over medium heat.

Stir in the cream, salt and pepper and cook another five minutes, stirring, until the sauce has begun to thicken.

Add the sherry and boil for one minute.

Break the remaining two tablespoons of butter into four pieces and whisk them in one at a time. Stir in the nutmeg.

Serve with toasts, crackers or crisps (potato chips), or as a vegetable.

Serves four to six.

Do you remember treacle tart?

(The witness is directed to answer the question.)

It is perhaps best to forget treacle tart. One of the eight of us rather liked it, but the other seven of us placed pieces of black cloth on our heads and ~cted that the tart be taken from
⁀e to a cylindrical place and
e morning of the following
collected from that place and

taken to another place and buried.

(If m'lud and Rupert Brooke would forgive a scrap of verse, "Think only this: That there's some corner of a city landfill that is forever treacle tart.")

To be sure, mon ami, what is the treacle tart, after all? It is charming, certainly, but it is nothing more than a pie shell and many bread crumbs soaked in the good golden syrup and molasses, along with perhaps an egg. One bakes the whole of it.

The cells, the little gray cells, my honest friend! They should tell even you that it will taste like bread crumbs, syrup and molasses.

I vowed to prepare another British-mystery dessert, and I insisted to myself that it not be one that is already familiar in these remote provinces.

Trifle, for example, is wonderful, but it has been chronicled countless times.

Then I came across a recipe for Dundee cake, which sometimes turns up when the locale of a mystery shifts toward Scotland.

I will spare the court's time by saying that Dundee cake was not overwhelmingly better received than treacle tart, but that it seemed to have more possibilities.

It can be classified, for purposes of introduction into evidence, as an unmoist fruitcake. It would no doubt benefit from a prolonged association with a wee drap or two (or 500) o' spirits.

In the interests of justice — and of ending this discussion before the moon rises over the windswept moor, revealing a rocky, barren landscape broken only by the twisted trunks of long-blighted trees, their withered branches waving like the gnarled, outstretched fingers of some malevolent warning hand — here's the recipe.

Dundee Cake

About 20 blanched almonds
¾ c. (1½ sticks) butter
¾ c. packed brown sugar
4 eggs
2 c. flour
½ tsp. salt
1½ tsp. baking powder
1 c. raisins
¾ c. fruitcake mix (candied cherries, etc.)
⅓ c. currants (optional)
Juice and grated rind of ½ lemon
Juice and grated rind of ½ orange
2 tbsp. sliced almonds

Grind the 20 almonds finely in a food processor or chop them finely by hand.

Preheat the oven to 325 degrees. Grease an 8-inch round cake pan. Cream the butter and brown sugar until they are light and fluffy. Beat in the eggs one at a time.

Sift the flour, salt and baking powder into a bowl. Stir in the ground nuts. Fold in the butter mixture and add the fruits, rind and juices.

Turn the batter into the cake pan and sprinkle on the sliced almonds. (They are characteristic of the Dundee cake, and without them the cake might be assumed to be traveling on a false identity and could be detained for questioning.)

Bake for 1½ hours, then reduce temperature to 300 degrees and bake an additional 30 minutes. If it is browning too much near the end, drape it with a sheet of foil.

This much baking sounds excessive (and if you was to ask me, your worship, it *was* excessive), but several cookbooks agreed on it. Let the cake cool completely before removing it from the pan. Wrap it in foil to store. It wouldn't hurt to pour some booze over it first.

(One cookbook noted, if this gives you a further hint about Dundee cake, "it will keep for weeks.")

Little Mystery #12: Olives

Olive-can labels carry information about the size of the olives within, but to judge from the names (which seem to have some sort of official status) even the smallest olives have glandular problems: There are "giant," "jumbo" and "mammoth," to name but a few. (I seem to recall seeing one called "Flying Boxcar.") What is the full list of these names, in order, and who made them up?

Solution: Vincent Dole, president of the Dolefam Corp., which cans Old Monk brand olives, acknowledged the question cheerfully. "It *is*," he said, "one of the most ridiculous sets of names I've seen in my life."

The nation's olive growers got together more than 50 years ago, he explained, and set up that list of names.

According to Dole, the exact millimeter sizes that correspond with those names have been changed a few times but the names have remained as standards for the industry. Here is the list, from smallest to largest:

Select
Medium
Large
Extra large
Mammoth (sometimes called Gem)
Giant
Jumbo
Colossal
Super-colossal.

A Halloween Menu

Tomorrow, if all goes well and the world doesn't end tonight, is Halloween.

Normal associations with that holiday run to such things as ghosts and goblins, soap smeared on windows, and bunches of kids dressed up like some cartoon character that adults never heard of standing on your porch holding out pillowcases and expecting large handfuls of amazingly expensive tiny candy bars.

Not the kind of festivity you'd expect to read much about in the Food section.

There is something you don't know about Halloween, though:

It is my boss's favorite holiday.

For that reason, if for no other, the ensuing space will be devoted to an attempt to translate the spirit of Halloween (whatever that is) into a menu.

But before we turn, however awkwardly, to food, may I please tell my favorite Halloween anecdote?

The following is a true story. Only the names, as Jack Webb's important-voiced announcer used to say, have been changed.

Hercule had not been in this country very long, and his command of English was very limited. His wife, an American, had neglected to mention anything about the approaching holiday, and happened to be out that evening.

When she got home, she found a large pile of candy on the table, and Hercule with a happy expression.

Where did all this stuff come from, his wife demanded.

Such a charming holiday, Hercule said. All evening long, little children came to the door, said something I couldn't understand and held up big bags full of candy.

(Imagine how the neighborhood kids felt when this guy opened his door, smiled, took a handful of their candy, said "Thonk you" and closed the door. *That's* the spirit of Halloween.)

That out of the way, we must now talk about things to cook for Halloween. We met this need last year by serving a meal in which every dish was orange and black.

Serviceable (and peculiar) as that was, it's an idea that can only be used once.

Racking what I laughingly call my brain for another way to eke a menu out of a holiday that has nothing to do with food (other than pumpkin), I considered briefly a dinner in which guests would bob for roast beef and mashed potatoes. Too messy, I decided, and it would require an awful lot of gravy.

So I turned to the time-honored technique of looking through cookbook indexes for things that might work.

What I found amounts to a Halloween menu of sorts, but it isn't as tightly conceived a theme as the orange-and-black dinner.

Sorry. But in the words of our nation's foremost philosopher, Richard Nelson, "You cain't please everyone, so you got to please yourself. (La-da dah, lat'n da-da dah.)"

Hewing to the spooks and goblins line, we'll start with a devilishly simple appetizer.

You might be surprised, though, at how many people who cook a fair amount have nonetheless never made some very uncomplicated dishes. So, for those who have lacked the internal fire to look up the recipe, here it is.

Deviled Eggs

9 hard-cooked eggs
¼ c. plus 2 tbsp. mayonnaise
1 tbsp. lemon juice
½ tsp. dry mustard
3 tbsp. finely chopped onion
1½ tsp. Worcestershire sauce
¼ tsp. salt
Pinch of pepper
Paprika

Peel the eggs and cut them in halves lengthwise.

Remove the yolks to a bowl. Mash the yolks and stir in the mayonnaise, lemon juice, mustard, onion, Worcestershire sauce, salt and pepper.

Mound or pipe the yolk mixture back into the whites and dust with paprika.

Chill an hour or so before serving. Serves six or so.

NOTE: It's appropriate at Halloween to hear various awful noises — groans, moans, rattling of chains, and the like.

While I was out in the kitchen after dinner, rattling those pots and pans, I heard a whining noise. It was me.

I will give you a hint that might keep you from hearing that same noise from you:

Even if you want to be very fancy-dancy, don't serve deviled eggs on a silver tray. (Rather instant tarnish!)

I, too, have never made a lot of things that plenty of people make all the time. This next recipe, Parker House rolls, is such an item. The dough is cut into circles and each is folded over onto itself.

I had to try two recipes because the rolls went very oddly awry the first time. I had planned to call them Haunted Parker House rolls, in keeping with this week's very thin excuse for a theme, and you can probably imagine my surprise when every single one of them unfolded during baking.

Heck's bells, I bethought me. What mischief is this? Besides looking funny, which they did, they were very dry and not worth half the effort that went into them.

So I found a recipe that involved about half the effort. Those worked just fine and were, if I say so myself, excellent.

Haunted Parker House Rolls

(Exorcised version)
1 (¼-oz.) env. active dry yeast
¼ c. warm water
1 c. milk
2 tbsp. sugar
2 tbsp. shortening
1 tsp. salt
About 3½ c. sifted flour
1 egg
Melted butter

Dissolve the yeast in the warm water. Set aside.

Scald the milk, stir in the sugar, shortening and salt, then let it cool to lukewarm. (I don't know why this is better than just heating it to lukewarm, but there seems to be universal agreement that this is what you do.)

Sift in one cup of flour and beat well. Beat in the dissolved yeast and the egg. Add remaining flour as necessary to form a soft dough instead of a batter (when you stir, it begins to move with the spoon as one lump). Stir in a bit more flour, then quit.

Brush the top of the dough with a little melted butter, cover and let rise in a warm place until it has doubled in bulk (1½ to 2 hours).

Turn the dough out onto a lightly floured surface and roll it out about ½ inch thick. If it is sticky and hard to handle, work a little more flour into it on the table — even as it's being rolled out — so it won't tear apart when you try to pick up the cut-out rolls.

Cut the dough into rounds with a cutter 2½ inches or so in diameter. Place the rounds on greased cookie sheets. Roll out scraps and cut out more rolls.

Fold each roll in half. Dip a fingertip in water and moisten the bottom front of the fold. Press the dough together there, to make a seal. Brush the top of each roll with a little melted butter, set the rolls in a warm place and let them rise until they are doubled in bulk again (about 30 minutes). Meanwhile, preheat the oven to 400 degrees.

Bake the rolls about 15 minutes. Makes about 20. They're spookily good.

Now we come to a main course of sorts. In fact it was the only thing I could think of right off the bat (flap, flap, flap) when I was reminded of my boss's strange fondness for this holiday. The sauce is a very nice one, which I think allows the main ingredient to hover above its usual location. In addition, the garlic in it keeps vampires away. It may also keep everybody else away, but that's the breaks.

Hollow Weenies

2 tbsp. olive oil
1 onion, chopped
1½ lb. tomatoes (3 or 4 tomatoes)
2 cloves garlic, crushed
Salt, pepper
2 tsp. flour
2½ tbsp. chopped fresh basil or
   parsley
8 hot dogs
8 hot-dog buns

Heat the oil and cook the onions about five minutes, until they are translucent. Quarter the tomatoes and squeeze them dry. (Save the juice if you want to drink it — and if there is any; store-bought tomatoes tend more to transportability than to juiciness.)

Cut the tomatoes into small chunks and add them and the garlic to the onions.

Sprinkle with salt, pepper and flour and stir in the basil or parsley. Cook over medium-low heat about 15 minutes, until the mixture is thick and almost dry.

Meanwhile, cut a notch down the length of each hot dog and scoop out some of the meat.

Add the meat to the tomato mixture and cook the slightly hollowed hot dogs in the usual fashion.

If you like, steam the buns. Here's a painless method: Put half an inch of water in the bottom of a Dutch oven. Put a large metal colander into the pan, making sure the water is below the level of the bottom of the colander. Pile the buns into the colander, cover the whole thing and put over medium heat for a few minutes.

To serve, assemble the hollow weenies in the buns and spoon on the sauce. Makes 8.

I was stuck briefly trying to think of a Halloween-related vegetable (we're saving pumpkin for dessert, of course), and I almost decided not to have one. Then I remembered a dish that I have made before and really enjoyed — green beans, flavored with lots of butter, garlic and vermouth.

Where's the Halloween angle in that, you ask? Boooooo-ze!

Beans with Booooo-ze

2 (9-oz.) pkg. frozen French-cut green beans
¼ lb. butter (unsalted, if you have it)
2 cloves garlic, crushed
Pinch of dried basil
Pinch of dried tarragon
½ c. dry white vermouth

Cook the beans according to package directions. Melt the butter in a frying pan.

Drain the beans and pour them into the frying pan. Add the garlic, crumble in the basil and tarragon and cook over medium-low heat, stirring occasionally, until most of the butter is absorbed (10 to 15 minutes). Raise the heat to medium, allow the pan to heat for a minute, then pour in the vermouth. Cook until most of the liquid is gone, then serve. Serves six to eight.

Comes time now, children, for dessert. On Halloween, though, there should be *two* desserts, so you have something from witch to choose.

First, because it's jack-o'-lantern time, a pumpkin pie. But you can get plain pumpkin pie on Thanksgiving. For Halloween, it ought to be a little different, right?

So I put a layer of chocolate custard under the pumpkin, and to lighten things up, I made it a pumpkin chiffon. You might think this an odd grouping. It was, but it was very, very pleasant.

Chocolate-Pumpkin Pie

(The devil's food made me do it)
Chocolate bottom:
⅓ c. sugar
1 tbsp. cornstarch
½ env. (1¼ tsp.) unflavored gelatin
1¼ c. milk
2 egg yolks
2 (1-oz.) squares unsweetened chocolate
1 baked 9-in. pie shell
Pumpkin chiffon top:
1 (¼-oz.) env. unflavored gelatin
¼ c. cold water
3 eggs, separated
1 c. sugar, divided
1 (15-oz.) can pumpkin (not pumpkin pie mix)
¼ tsp. salt
¼ tsp. cinnamon
⅛ tsp. nutmeg
¼ tsp. ginger
½ c. milk
1 c. heavy cream

Prepare the chocolate bottom layer:

(If you don't trust me that this is a good combination, skip this paragraph, go straight to the pumpkin chiffon and double the amounts of cinnamon, nutmeg and ginger. But don't come crying to me after because your treat is all gone and you didn't get any chocolate.) Combine the one-third cup sugar, cornstarch and gelatin in the top of a double boiler, gradually stir in the milk and heat, stirring constantly, over simmering water until the mixture is steaming. Beat the egg yolks lightly, stir in a spoonful of the hot mixture, then stir the diluted yolks back into the hot mixture. Cook, stirring, about five minutes, until the mixture is quite thick. Add the chocolate and continue to heat, stirring, until it is fully melted. Pour into the baked crust and chill.

Prepare the pumpkin chiffon: Stir the gelatin into the water; let it stand five minutes. Meanwhile, beat the egg yolks and add half a cup of the sugar, the pumpkin, salt, cinnamon, nutmeg, ginger and milk. Cook the mixture over low heat, stirring constantly, until it begins to thicken.

Stir in the gelatin until it is fully dissolved. Cool the mixture in the refrigerator, checking its texture fairly frequently. When the mixture has thickened to the point that it will form soft mounds, take it out of the refrigerator, and beat the egg whites until they begin to foam.

While beating the whites, slowly add the remaining half-cup of sugar to them. Beat until the whites hold soft peaks. Fold the whites into the pumpkin mixture and pour over the chocolate layer in the pie shell.

Beat the heavy cream and decorate the pie. Chocolate curls or something of the sort would make a nice garnish and would hint, to those who are alive to the possibilities, at what lies beneath the pumpkin. Chill until serving time. Serves six to eight.

This meal had been so laden with spooky stuff that it needs something to take the curse off of it. What better than a second dessert — and what better second dessert than this?

Divinity

2½ c. packed brown sugar
½ c. light corn syrup
⅓ c. water
2 egg whites
1 tsp. vanilla
1½ c. coarsely chopped pecans

(Note: Maybe the use of brown sugar instead of white granulated sugar makes this "seafoam" instead of divinity. Maybe it doesn't. I don't care. I like it with brown sugar. If you don't, make it with the same quantity of granulated sugar. It will be divine either way.)

(Another note: Divinity, like fudge and maybe more so, is affected by moisture in the air. If it's a muggy day, you might want to consider making something else. Or reconcile yourself to a divinity that never gets very firm — that's the way some folks like their divinities.)

Put the sugar, syrup and water into a large saucepan and stir over moderate heat until the sugar is dissolved.

With a barely damp paper towel, and watching out not to burn your fingers, wash down the sides of the pan above the mixture. Turn the heat down to low-medium and cook without stirring until the mixture reaches 260 degrees on a candy thermometer. (Wash down again if you see any sugar crystals on the side of the pan.)

As the syrup approaches 260 degrees, beat the egg whites to the soft peak stage.

Once the syrup gets to 260 degrees, beat the egg whites continuously while pouring in the syrup very slowly — in a thin stream. Near the end of the syrup you can speed it up a little.

Add the vanilla, then beat until stiff peaks form. Fold in the nuts. Line cookie sheets with waxed paper and drop divinity on them from heaping teaspoons, or squeeze the divinity from the largest round tube of a pastry bag. Chill at least several hours.

If you aren't lucky and you find that the divinity remains too gooey to pick up comfortably with the fingers, let it air-dry overnight. It won't be quite as creamy that way, but at least you'll be able to get it to your mouth. Or eat it with a spoon.

Dinner at Mom's

I had a particularly unpleasant conversation a few days ago with a friend who has, over time, eaten a great deal of the food I have prepared. We were talking about things parents don't bother teaching their kids, and she said, "You know what my favorite food is? Roast beef, mashed potatoes and gravy, and I don't know how to make it. When I lived at home, my mom used to make the best roast beef in the world."

"ROAST BEEF, MASHED POTATOES AND GRAVY??!!" I rejoined, calmly. "Not chicken breast with vermouth-tarragon sauce, or duck à l'orange or chocolate soufflé, or, or (splutter, splut) . . . . "

I must, despite my calm, reasoned tone, have betrayed a certain tension.

"I love the fancy food you make," she said, in an effort to be placating. "But my very favorite meal is my mom's roast beef, mashed potatoes and gravy."

"OK," I said, my chin stiffening. "I'll *make* roast beef, mashed potatoes and gravy."

"It won't," she replied with triumph, "be like my mom's."

Well, it was a bad beginning but a good idea. There *are* a lot of foods that your mother didn't bother telling you how to make. They were too obvious or too ordinary or something.

(If you're a man, chances are that your mother didn't tell you how to cook *anything*, but that's another story. Part of that same story is that your father probably didn't know how to cook, and that he probably didn't tell your sister how to change spark plugs. But we leave these trembling social issues for the newspaper's Family section. Back to food.)

Some of the same, sturdy, wholesome foods that you didn't get told how to make, as my friend's infuriating remarks suggested, are the ones that are most reminiscent of home.

It is interesting to note that these are also foods that you are almost never served when you're invited to someone else's house for dinner. Quiche, yes, Tournedos Rossini, perhaps. Chicken and dumplings, not likely.

Never one to pass up a challenge, however stupid, I decided to make a bunch of plain good foods of that sort, and to pass along the recipes to the large group of us who never got told how to make them.

Here's what I made:

> Roast beef
> Mashed potatoes
> Beef gravy
> Chicken and dumplings
> Chicken gravy
> Green beans
> Apple pie

Since the idea here is preparing plain, honest food, I decided to avoid any attempts to simplify, modernize or jazz-up the recipes. I was tempted, but I abstained.

In the first instance, roast beef, that abstention was a pleasure. My mother was a fairly decent cook, and a wonderful person, but she did things to roast beef. I believe that the things involved garlic and onion, normally two of my favorite foods, but I didn't know until rather late in my life that roast beef didn't always taste peculiar. (I learned when some neighbors gave me some leftover roast beef to give to our dog. It smelled like the odors that come from restaurant kitchens, and *I* ate most of it.)

What makes good roast beef, in my mind anyway, is a piece of beef roast — and nothing else. (Well, to *get* the piece of beef roast it takes a surprising amount of money, too: Even the comparatively inexpensive rolled roast, which I used, ran up to more than $8 for enough for six people.)

I didn't quite leave it fully alone, either. Following a suggestion in several books, I dredged the meat with flour before slipping it into the oven. But that was it. And it was wonderful. Just like Mom didn't used to make.

Roast Beef

Beef roast
Flour
Salt and pepper

There's lots that could be said, I suppose, about what cut of meat to use, but that really is a matter of personal preference and budget, so I'll leave you to work that out with your butcher. Depending on how much else you plan to serve and how hearty the appetites are likely to be, get between ¼ pound and ½ pound per person.

Dredge the roast (if you like) by putting it into a paper bag with some flour and shaking it a little (the neat way), or by rolling it around in some flour on a counter and patting it in with your hands (the messy way).

Preheat the oven (see below), put the meat on a rack over a shallow pan and roast. That's it. Salt and pepper, if you like, when it's done.

Cookbooks tend to insist that the really old-fashioned way of roasting meat — searing it first and then roasting at fairly high temperatures — dries out the meat, and they recommend roasting at a uniform, relatively low temperature (between 300 and 325 degrees). They're right, the meat does stay juicy that way. And they've been saying that for long enough that your mom probably learned it that way, too. But the tradeoff (there's got to be a tradeoff, you know), is that there's almost no juice in the pan with which to make gravy. More about that later.

The length of time to cook the meat also varies with what kind of meat it is and how well-done you want it, but I really shouldn't beg off giving you *any* information, so here's a little chart:

Standing rib:	
Rare	18-20 min./lb.
Medium	22-25 min./lb.
Well done	27-30 min./lb.
Rolled rib:	
Rare	30-33 min./lb.
Medium	35-38 min./lb.
Well done	40-45 min./lb.
Rump:	
Rare	20-22 min./lb.
Medium	24-27 min./lb.
Well done	28-30 min./lb.

Whether or not you have success with this chart also depends in part on whether we agree on what "rare," "medium" and "well done" mean. The friend whose idea this meal was describes any meat, however gray, from which any juice of any description can be wrung, as "blood rare." I cut off a part of the roast for her and put it in early. It cooked more than an hour a pound, it looked like a piece of leather and she said it was excellent.

Serving a roast to a group of people who like their meat cooked to different degrees of doneness is kind of a problem, even if they all agree (which they won't) on what "medium" is. One way out of the difficulty, and it helps answer the gravy problem, too, is to take the roast out a little early and carve it in the kitchen.

Once you cut into the roast, unless you went for ultra-well done, there'll be juice in the pan. Pour some of it off for gravy, which we'll get to in a minute. Slice most or all of the meat. If too much of it seems too rare for some of the guests, allowing the slices to soak briefly in the pan juices might darken them a little. If that's not enough, slip the sliced meat back into the oven for just a few minutes and it will move quite rapidly toward doneness.

If that's cheating, I'm sorry.

If you're going to have roast beef, you've got to have some kind of gravy. Some folks just serve the pan juices, but flour-based gravy — the kind that comes with hot roast beef sandwiches at diners — is the choice of connoisseurs.

Beef Gravy

2 tbsp. flour
3 to 4 tbsp. beef drippings (fat)
1 c. liquid (see text)
Salt, pepper
Worcestershire sauce (optional, see text)
Coloring (see text)

For about one cup of gravy: In a small pan stir the flour, a little at a time, into the beef drippings. Over low heat stir the flour-dripping mixture constantly until it is smooth and quite hot. Don't quit too soon; give it two or three minutes, or the flour won't accept the liquid you're going to add.

Continue to cook and stir while pouring in a cup of liquid a little at a time. Cookbooks always call for a cup of beef stock; if you're like me and 99.9 percent of other cooks, you don't have a cup of beef stock close to hand. (I usually have veal stock, but I just can't seem to keep beef stock around.) Substitutes, none of which is perfect, include beef bouillon (the best choice; if using canned concentrate, dilute it to normal strength with water — it's quite salty), consommé (dilute this too; it's OK, but doesn't really taste like gravy) and milk (pretty flat).

Cook a while, stirring constantly as it thickens, adding salt and pepper and Worcestershire sauce, steak sauce or anything else you have handy to try and give it the flavor that means gravy to you. Any extra — non-greasy — meat drippings are excellent if available.

Last comes the problem of color. Especially if you used milk, this is going to be a pretty pale gravy. Commercial gravy enhancers like Kitchen Bouquet contain coloring to make the gravy look presentable, but they seem to taste a lot like celery. If you were thinking of adding a little celery anyway, you're home free. If not, you might use some burnt-sugar syrup, made in advance:

Bring a little water to boiling in a kettle. In a small skillet or saucepan, stir a quarter-cup of sugar until it melts and turns dark — keep going until it no longer smells sweet. Then — carefully because it will spatter at first — stir in one-fourth cup of the boiling water. Cook briefly until it thickens a bit. Use a few drops in the gravy and keep the rest around in a jar in your refrigerator — next to the beef stock — or throw it out.

It would be appropriate here to throw in a few quotations from famous people praising mashed potatoes. Food of the people, food of the gods, food of North Dakota, that sort of thing. I don't know any, so the mashed potatoes will just have to stand on their own. (They often do, you know.)

Mashed Potatoes

6 medium-to-large potatoes
3 tbsp. butter or margarine
½ tsp. salt
¼ c. cream or milk

Put four or five cups of water into a Dutch oven and heat to boiling.

Meanwhile, wash and peel the potatoes and dig out the funny-looking parts. Cut each potato into four or five sections and add them to the boiling water. Cover, reduce the heat to rapid simmer and cook about 25 minutes. You should be able to poke a fork through the thickest portions without resistance.

Drain them well but quickly (you don't want them to cool), and return them to the pan.

Mash them in the pan with a potato masher, a pastry blender, a heavy fork or anything else handy.

If you like them *really* smooth, you could put them through a food processor or beat them around a while with your electric mixer, but mashed potatoes are pretty bland, and many folks prefer an occasional lump, just to keep from falling asleep. If you do beat them, do it fast, because they'll cool off in a hurry.

In any case, quickly beat in the butter (cut in small pieces to help it melt sooner), the salt and the cream.

Serves six.

Chicken and dumplings sounds so down-home it's hard to imagine anyone wanting to serve it in places like Edina, but you never know. Edinans had to come from *somewhere*.

It is with this dish particularly that the temptation to fiddle became strong. People just don't stew chickens as much as they used to, and you don't see that many stewing chickens. Also, stewed chicken, left on the bones, is kind of gray and unappealing. But I resisted the modern blandishments of baking the chicken and doing the dumplings in soup.

Sorry, but if I'm making this stuff because Mom used to make it, I'm doing it pretty much the way she used to do it, not the way she learned later in her bridge club.

Chicken to go with Dumplings

1 carrot, cut into chunks or slices
1 small onion, sliced
1 bay leaf
2 or 3 peppercorns
A rib of celery, broken into two or
    three pieces
1 to 2 tsp. salt
1 tsp. parsley flakes
1 (5-lb. or so) stewing chicken (or a
    very large frying chicken), cut
    up

Put three cups of water into a Dutch oven. Add the carrot, onion, bay leaf, peppercorns, celery, salt and parsley flakes and bring to a boil. In a matter of minutes, the kitchen will smell like Mom's — even before you get the chicken into the pot.

Wash the chicken pieces, add them to the boiling water and lower the heat to a simmer. Cover and cook two hours, until the largest pieces seem tender when you poke at them with a fork. You won't need to add any water, but you can check once in a while if you've a mind to.

Remove the chicken and allow it to cool briefly. Fish out and discard the bay leaf and peppercorns, if you can spot them.

I admit it; this next step is a departure from absolute authenticity, but it's not a big one and it dramatically improves the dish's appearance and the ease with which it can be eaten. Remove and discard the skin and tear or cut the chicken meat into bite-size pieces. Skim most of the fat off the top of the broth, putting three or four tablespoons of the fat in a small pan for gravy. Also pour off about 1½ cups of broth for the gravy. Return the meat to the skimmed broth and bring to the boil while you prepare the dumpling batter (see below). Serves four to six.

Since my friend's mother was also alleged to make the world's best dumplings, I called and got her recipe. (These days, she bakes the chicken and drops the dumplings into cream of chicken soup, but we'll ignore that.)

Al's Friend's Mom's Dumplings, to go with Chicken

2 c. flour
4 tsp. baking powder
½ tsp. salt
1½ tbsp. solid shortening
½ c. to ⅔ c. milk

If you're not making chicken with the above recipe, get together about four cups of chicken broth and bring it to the boil. If you *are* making the chicken, wait until you have it cut up so that the dumplings can simmer in the broth, not sit high and dry on the chicken.

In a medium bowl, stir together the flour, baking powder and salt.

Rub the shortening in with your fingers (Mom would surely admonish you to be sure to wash your hands first), breaking it into small flour-coated flakes, NOT smearing it in until there are no separate pieces.

If that process doesn't appeal to you, you can cut in the shortening using a pastry blender or a couple of knives.

Either way, it's just like making pie crust.

Stir in the milk, quickly, just until blended, and using only enough milk to collect the dough so it will stand together by itself.

Drop the batter by soup spoons into the boiling chicken broth. Make no more than one layer of dumplings.

Cover the pot and cook for 20 minutes. Don't take the cover off for *anything*. (I don't know what's supposed to happen if you do take the cover off; I don't think it's anything like warts or rains of grasshoppers. Probably the dumplings get tough.)

When the dumplings are done, arrange them around the perimeter of a large platter (draining each well with a slotted spoon).

Drain the chicken pieces, too, and put them in the center of the platter.

Makes about 12 dumplings. Serves four to six.

Chicken and dumplings need chicken gravy at least as much as roast beef needs beef gravy. The method is the same, but it's easier to do because you don't have to wait until the last minute.

▶

Chicken Gravy

3 tbsp. flour
3 to 4 tbsp. fat skimmed from chicken broth
1½ c. chicken broth
2 or 3 tbsp. milk (optional)

You can do this easily any time after the chicken has been deboned, except you can't get the fat and broth when the dumplings are in the broth because you're not supposed to remove the cover then.

In a small saucepan blend the flour slowly into the fat, stirring and heating over low heat until the mixture is smooth and quite hot. Don't give up too early or the chicken broth won't blend in well.

Continue to cook and stir while pouring in the chicken broth a little at a time. Stir and bring to the boil, adding the milk if you like. Some folks also cook and throw in the chicken giblets.

Makes about 1½ cups.

The vegetable called for in this "Mom's cooking" meal is clearly green beans, because, although there are lots of elaborate ways to make them, they have a plain and wholesome sound.

A standard way to make green beans is to throw in an onion while they boil. That doesn't sound all that interesting, but I was surprised at how nice it turned out to be.

Green Beans

1½ lb. fresh green beans
1 small onion, peeled
3 tbsp. butter, melted

Wash the beans and cut off the ends. Bring about two cups of water to the boil.

Meanwhile, cut the beans in half lengthwise. Drop the beans and the onion into the boiling water.

Cook them, uncovered, about 20 minutes, until they are just tender.

Drain them quickly but well, return them to the pot and stir in the melted butter. Serves six. (Some lucky person gets the onion.)

Even the most chocolate-dependent person would probably say that the appropriate dessert for this kind of dinner is apple pie.

You could cheat and buy a prepared crust, of course, or you could buy prepared apple pie filling.

You could buy both prepared crust and prepared filling.

You could even buy the whole pie already made. But then what would that leave me to write about?

So we're going to make both crust and filling.

First, a very, very brief dissertation on which apples to buy.

If your mom never told you, and especially if you're not all that fond of apples, chances are you'll make the mistake I did not all that long ago, and buy the only kind of apple whose name you recognize, red Delicious.

That, it turns out, is about the only widely available apple that *isn't* good for pies.

Apple Pie

2 c. flour
½ tsp. salt
½ c. shortening
¼ c. butter
¼ to ½ c. ice water
<u>Filling:</u>
7 or 8 medium apples (better too
    many than too few)
⅜ c. (6 tbsp.) brown sugar
⅜ c. (6 tbsp.) granulated sugar
¼ tsp. cinnamon
⅛ tsp. nutmeg
Pinch salt
1 tbsp. cornstarch
1 tsp. vanilla
1 tbsp. butter

For best results, prepare the crust three or four hours in advance. Chilling before the final rolling really improves it.

Sift the flour and salt into a bowl. Cut the shortening and butter (some prefer to omit the butter and use ¾ cup of shortening, others go for lard) into the flour with a pastry cutter, a pair of knives or your fingers until the mixture resembles coarse crumbs. Don't get it too fine. The object is to coat small flakes of shortening with flour, not to make a flour-shortening paste.

Stir in the ice water a little at a time, stopping when the dough holds together without any dry spots. It should not be wet.

Chill, if possible, for three or four hours.

Near the end of the chilling time, prepare the filling:

Peel, core and cut the apples into very thin slices. (If you've never done that before, let me tell you that it's much more work than it sounds like.)

Coring the apple can be done two ways.

One way is to use an apple corer (or, if you're very nimble, a knife), and cut out the center of the apple before you cut it apart. Then cut it in halves or quarters and slice it. If you're not using an apple corer, that sounds easier than it is.

The other way is to quarter the apple and then use a sharp knife to remove the center area of each quarter, which contains the core, seeds, stem and so forth. This usually results in a fair number of quarters that break in half, ruining the shape of the slices, but we're making a double-crust pie, so that's not very important. (There are things worth doing that are *not* worth doing right, and this is one of them.)

Combine the brown sugar, granulated sugar, cinnamon, nutmeg, salt and cornstarch, and stir the mixture into the apple slices. Stir in the vanilla and set the apples aside. Preheat the oven to 450 degrees.

Remove the dough from the refrigerator, divide it in two and lightly flour a working surface. Lightly flour one piece of dough, top and bottom, and roll it out until it is about an inch bigger all around than the pie pan. Roll the dough onto the rolling pin, then unroll it into the pie pan. Let it ease into the bottom, but you may have to adjust it here and there.

If the apples have been sitting a long time, there may be quite a bit of liquid in the bowl. If so, pour most of it off. Fill the pie with the apples, and dot them with the butter. Roll out the second half of the dough just like the first, roll it onto the rolling pin and unroll it over the pie.

Trim the excess crusts. Press the top and bottom crusts together and crimp with your fingers or a fork. Slit the top crust in four or five places (in a nice, symmetrical pattern if your mom was artistic). Some moms brush the top crust with milk and/or sprinkle it with a little sugar.

Cut a few inch-wide strips of aluminum foil and lay them around the outside edges of the crust (which burn easily). It also doesn't hurt to put foil on the bottom oven shelf to catch the drips. Bake for 10 minutes at 450 degrees, then reduce the temperature to 350 degrees and bake for an additional 35 to 50 minutes. Judge doneness by the color of the crust, which should be a nice light golden brown. Remove the foil for the last 15 minutes, to brown the edges.

Follow-Up

After this article appeared, old friend Mildred Holcomb, St. Peter, Minn., wrote to say that she was "appalled and shaken" that the mashed-potato recipe called for draining the potatoes (she inferred, correctly, into the sink).

"I thought it was known throughout all Christendom," she went on, "that one does not pour potato water down the sink. In this case it is used to make the roast beef gravy about which there was so much to-do. In the case of just a random cooking of a kettle of potatoes, you *save* the potato water. You pour it (after cooling) into a washed and stored peanut butter jar (of which we all have enough) and then the next day or two use it in making soup, or as the canful of water that is called for on the soup label.

"It does not matter that at times perhaps a week or two later one finds that potato water forgotten and bubbling in the back of the refrigerator and [that it] must then be thrown out — or rather, in this case, poured down the sink. One still has a warm, comforting glow in the thought that one did Save the Potato Water, as a good cook should."

Words to live by, Mrs. Holcomb, and thank you.

Yet More Follow-Up

Margaret Schlegel, of Lakeville, took me sternly to task for the same infraction and added, "Real moms never use a meat rack. They are for fancy-smancy people, a real mom doesn't have one and you can't get good brown scrapings if you don't let the meat kind of bake onto the pan. Also you can make your gravy in a separate pan if you like doing dishes, but you must use some of your potato water in the roaster to cook up all the good brownings.

"Now I want you to try again, and see if you don't get real good real-Mom gravy."

I'll do that. Thank you, too.

Even More Follow-Up

Then Frances Dixon, of Nevis, Minn., wrote to object to my suggestions for coloring beef gravy:

"SURELY you must know that all you have to do to get that good brown color in your beef gravy . . . is to *brown* your flour in the drippings before adding the water. And really brown it — add the water just before the flour gets to the scorched stage."

Actually, I did know that. And stop calling me Surely. The reason I didn't mention it is the trickiness of stopping just *before* you scorch the flour. First-time cooks usually have difficulty with instructions that tell you to do something just before something awful happens. But it *is* good advice if you can follow it. Thank you.

Touching Follow-Up

The nicest call I got was from a grateful woman who described herself as a new bride. "I know how to make all kinds of fancy things," she said, "but I didn't know how to make anything *he* wanted."

A young marriage saved by a stewed chicken! How romantic!

Food for the Twisted Mind

The quest for the every-more-peculiar theme on which to hang a few recipes takes us sometimes to areas where, some folks might say, only fools rush in.

That I have rushed into those areas is either proof that those folks are wrong or proof that they are right.

In any case I would stoutly maintain that the food that has resulted from these efforts has been pretty decent — and that warm, forgiving individuals like yourselves, who are willing to forget about the strange themes and cleave only to the recipes, need feel no hesitation about adding them to your recipe files/drawers/boxes/heaps.

I would also stoutly maintain that if I didn't write something peculiar at the tops of these articles I wouldn't have anywhere to write down the occasional insight or odd thought that occurs to me, and that these unwritten insights and thoughts would eventually back up and make me ill.

(I maintain things like these even more stoutly since Thanksgiving, when I really overdid it on the gravy and dressing.)

All this is by way of saying that it should not surprise those of you who are keeping scrapbooks based on my life and food that I am prepared once more to boldly go where no man has gone before.

I was feeling a bit Euclidean the other day when it was time to choose a recipe theme — not plane awful, you understand, just a bit on edge — and I decided to venture into an area of geometricity not previously dealt with in this space: spirals.

I was catapulted into making this choice after spending a few minutes contemplating a barber pole, affixed to which was a sign reading "Stylist." The origin of the red-and-white striped barber pole, it is said, is that barbers in years long past were the folks you went to if you wanted to be bled in order to rid yourself of some unpleasant condition. Granted that barbers don't do bloodletting any more (at least intentionally), I still found the notion of a bloodletting stylist a little unsettling.

But the pole started me thinking about spirals. Spirals (or, if you prefer, helixes) (or, if you prefer, helices) (parenthesis fans, please note this stunning collection) (and now back to our regularly scheduled program) are to be found almost everywhere in cooking, so it struck me that I would not have a difficult time at all coming up with a meal's worth of spiral food.

A nonparenthetical aside: Geometry purists may insist that a spiral is a plane figure and that a helix is a three-dimensional figure that circles around a central axis and may change in size (like a screw thread) or may not (like a spring), and that anyone who says a spiral is a helix or a helix is a spiral is clearly a cook. Such geometry purists do not have to deal with Webster's New World Dictionary, Second College Edition, from Simon and Schuster, which insists that spirals and helixes are the same.

I understand that David Guralnik, editor in chief of this dictionary, makes a great peanut butter sandwich.

Anyway, back to spirals. The matter of endless rotation seems to have occupied our thoughts for quite some time. In popular music there are enough examples to make your head spin.

Those of us who are fully over the hill remember "That Old Black Magic" ("in a spin, loving the spin I'm in") and somewhat younger folks may have cut their teeth on Kay Starr's "Wheel of Fortune" (it went spinning around) or "Find a Wheel" (which Perry Como advised went " 'round, 'round, 'round"). There is also "To every thing (turn, turn, turn) there is a season (turn, turn, turn) . . . " and lots more. (If there isn't a stirring march commemorating the discovery of DNA, there ought to be. I'd call it "Under the Double Helix.") And where would we all be without Chubby Checker?

Anyway, if turning and turning is important enough to sing about over the years, a dinner dedicated to the subject shouldn't seem out of the question. So let's begin.

In the words of Major Edward Bowes, "Around and around she goes, and where she stops, nobody knows."

For an appetizer, I made a bunch of those little rolled-up things, sometimes called pinwheel sandwiches, with what I thought was a particularly nice filling.

Blue-Cheese Appetizers

4 tbsp. butter (½ stick), warmed to room temperature
3 oz. cream cheese, softened
½ c. crumbled blue cheese (about ½ of a 4-oz. pkg.)
2 tbsp. Cognac or brandy
6 thin slices bread (pumpernickel makes a nice color contrast)

Combine the butter, cream cheese, blue cheese and brandy. If you do this in a blender, you'll have the treat of seeing a sort of spiral form in the whirlpool or vortex over the blades.

(No, vortex is not a synthetic fiber or a manufacturer of inexpensive men's wear.)

Trim the crusts from the bread and spread the cheese mixture on each slice from edge to edge. Roll each slice tightly and chill for 30 minutes or so, then cut each roll into four or five sections.

Makes 24 to 30 bite-size appetizers.

For a vegetable to accompany the main course, I decided to make some broccoli-filled crepes. See, viewed from the end, a rolled-up crepe is in theory a spiral. It's awfully hard to *see* the spiral, given the rather lumpy presence of the broccoli and the fact that to view a crepe end-on one has to hold it in mid-air. But trust me; it's there. You may observe it when you cut the crepe. So let's cut the crepe ourselves and get to cooking.

Broccoli-Filled Crepes

Crepes:
1 c. sifted flour
2 beaten eggs
¼ tsp. salt
½ c. cold water
½ c. milk
2 tbsp. melted butter
2 (10-oz.) pkg. chopped broccoli
White sauce:
1 tbsp. minced shallots (optional)
½ c. (1 stick) butter
½ c. flour
2½ c. milk
Salt, pepper
2 tsp. dry mustard

I can't tell you how to make the crepes themselves every time we use them. We had one discussion in an article about crepes and things made from a similar batter, and we went over it when we made a flaming meal that included Crepes Suzette, and again in an article about pancakes. So we can't do it again now or we'll never finish the textbook by the end of the semester.

Well, how many want to have crepe-making explained again?

How many don't?

All right, all right, we'll do it again. But this is the last time. I'll do it a tad differently this time, just for the heck of it. It turns out the same anyway.

Those of you who have been paying attention may read ahead. If you have any questions about the new material, just raise your hands.

To make the crepes:

Gradually beat the flour into the beaten eggs and salt. Slowly add water and milk, beating constantly. Finish by beating in the melted butter.

Heat a small iron skillet over low-medium heat and butter it lightly. Add a bit more than two tablespoons of the batter, tilting the pan to cover it with batter.

Cook each pancake for about a minute, until the bottom is lightly browned. (If that takes more than a minute, raise the heat slightly for the remaining crepes or they will be dry. If the pan is too hot, on the other hand, the crepe will start to bake before you can get the batter to cover the bottom of the pan.)

Cook the other side of the crepe briefly.

Cool the crepes, overlapping them slightly, on waxed paper. You'll have about a dozen.

Cook the broccoli according to package directions and drain very well.

Prepare the white sauce: Sauté the shallots in the butter until they are translucent.

Stir in the flour and cook, stirring, about a minute. Slowly add the milk, stirring constantly. Stir in the salt, pepper and dry mustard. Cook until the sauce is thickened.

Preheat oven to 350 degrees. Mix 1½ cups of the white sauce with the broccoli. Spread some of the broccoli mixture over half of a crepe. Roll it up from the filled side and put the rolled crepes in a 9- by 13-inch pan. Pour remaining white sauce over them and warm for 10 to 15 minutes in the oven.

Makes about 12 crepes — enough for six or more folks when served as a vegetable, or for four to six as a luncheon entrée.

For the main course, it seemed to me, there was no choice but to make rouladen — some folks, for reasons I can't imagine, call them birds. The French call them paupiettes. They are rolled up thin pieces of meat with stuffing or something inside.

Having concluded that I had no choice, I changed my mind. A little. I made one big one, based on a recipe in Mastering the Art of French Cooking, instead of a bunch of small ones.

It was lovely.

▶

Giant Beef Roll-Up

4 slices bacon
1 (2 to 2½ lb.) round steak (the full, flat round steak with both top and bottom portions and the little bone)
3 tbsp. Dijon mustard
½ tsp. basil
2 medium onions
1 (10-oz.) pkg. frozen chopped spinach
1 egg
1 tsp. salt
¼ tsp. pepper
Pinch nutmeg
Pinch basil
1 clove garlic
1 slice sturdy bread or 2 slices balloon bread
1 c. (4-oz.) shredded Swiss cheese
Household twine or string
¼ c. or more vegetable oil
1½ c. dry white wine
1½ c. beef stock or 1 (10½-oz.) can beef bouillon
1 tbsp. cornstarch
2 tbsp. soft butter

In a large frying pan, fry, crumble and drain the bacon, reserving two to three tablespoons of the fat. While the bacon is frying, cut the round steak in half lengthwise; discard the bone or do with it whatever you normally do with it. Trim off fat.

Using a long, sharp knife, carefully cut each of the two pieces of steak in half edgewise — so that it is only half as thick. (This isn't really difficult, just kind of tedious.) But don't cut all the way through — leave about ½ an inch uncut along one of the long edges so that each piece of meat can be opened like a tall butterfly.

If you go all the way through, it's no tragedy, nor is it terrible if the wings of the butterfly are of uneven thickness. The idea is just to come up with a lot of meat to roll.

Spread the mustard over the inside (cut) surfaces of the meat and sprinkle with basil. Set the meat aside.

Chop the onions and sauté them in the reserved bacon fat until they are translucent.

Prepare the spinach according to package directions. Drain, cool slightly, squeeze dry and add to onions, stir briefly and remove from heat.

Lightly beat the egg, then beat it into the spinach-onion mixture. Add the salt, pepper, nutmeg, basil and bacon bits. Crush the garlic and add it.

Tear the bread into small pieces and stir it and the shredded cheese into the spinach mixture.

Put the butterflies of steak side by side, overlap them an inch or two and cover the meat with the stuffing, leaving an inch uncovered all the way around the edge. Starting at an edge parallel to the "seam" between the two pieces, roll up the meat and stuffing. You'll wind up with a roll maybe 12 inches long and 4 inches in diameter.

Slip lengths of the string or twine under the roll in the middle and near each end and tie it reasonably tightly. (As the meat cooks it will assume the roll shape all by itself, allowing you to cut away the string before serving.) Preheat the oven to 450 degrees.

Pour a thin layer of oil into a metal 9- by 13-inch pan and put the meat into the pan seam side up. Put the pan on a surface burner and heat gently to brown the meat. Wiggle a spatula under the meat after a few minutes to keep it from sticking. Pour a little of the oil over the top of the meat and put it in the oven, basting every few minutes until the entire roll is browned (about 15 minutes).

Remove the meat from the oven and reduce the oven temperature to 325 degrees. Spoon off most of the oil from the pan. Salt and pepper the meat, and toss a bit of basil on it. Pour in the wine and beef stock. Cover the pan with foil and bake, basting every half hour or so, until the meat is tender (about two hours).

Using a couple of metal spatulas, lift the meat out of the juice, allow it to drip — if it isn't in the process of falling off the spatulas — and put it on a serving platter. Cut and remove the strings.

Pour the juices into a small saucepan. In a cup, combine the cornstarch and two tablespoons of the cooking liquid. Add to the cooking liquid in the saucepan and heat, stirring, until the liquid thickens. Stir in the butter in small bits. Pour some of the gravy over the meat and serve the rest in a gravy bowl.

Serves six to eight.

Obviously one needs to serve something of a potato/pasta nature to sop up all the nice gravy from the giant beef roll-up.

Mashed potatoes would be fine. So would noodles.

I couldn't decide.

So I rolled up some mashed potatoes in some lasagne noodles. (Don't be concerned; it will not harm you. It's only me pursuing something I'm not sure of.)

The result was odd, but likeable. The ruffled edges of the lasagne noodles gave these little bundles a very fancy appearance.

I served them on end, so diners could admire the spiral. Those guests who unroll them and eat only the mashed potatoes should be remembered when it comes time to issue invitations for another evening.

Spirals of Starch

6 lasagne noodles
8 (½-cup) servings mashed potatoes (from 6 or 7 potatoes)
¾ c. shredded Cheddar cheese
1 to 2 tbsp. butter
2 to 3 tbsp. Parmesan cheese

Preheat the oven to 325 degrees. Cook the lasagne noodles according to package directions. Drain.

Meanwhile, prepare the mashed potatoes as you usually do, adding salt and pepper to taste. Stir in the Cheddar cheese.

Working fairly rapidly, lay one of the lasagne noodles flat; spread it thickly with the mashed potatoes and roll it up.

Repeat with remaining noodles and potatoes.

Lightly oil a baking sheet and stand the cylinders on end. Dot them with the butter and sprinkle with the Parmesan.

Bake five to ten minutes, to heat through. (If you worked slowly and the potatoes got cold, you may have to heat them longer. But if you heat them too long, the noodles will get tough.)

Makes six servings.

For dessert, I'm sorry to report, I did not make a chocolate cake roll. I had made one not all that long ago, and it didn't seem reasonable to repeat it, although it would have been very chocolate.

Instead, I made pinwheel cookies. I must say that the guests at the spiral meal liked them a lot, but I found them rather bland.

If you like plain butter cookies, you'll love these. If you like your cookies a bit more flavorful, I'd punch up the chocolate content.

This recipe is adapted slightly from one in a Farm Journal book called Homemade Cookies.

Pinwheel Cookies

½ c. (1 stick) butter
½ c. sugar
1 egg
½ tsp. vanilla
1½ c. sifted flour
¼ tsp. salt
¼ tsp. (or ½ tsp. for more flavor) cinnamon
3 drops red food coloring
½ (1-oz.) square (1 whole square would be better) semisweet chocolate

Cream the butter. Add the sugar and beat until the mixture is light and fluffy. Beat in the egg and vanilla.

Sift together the flour, salt and cinnamon and beat into the butter mixture.

Divide the dough into thirds. Stir the food coloring into one third. Melt the chocolate and stir it into another third. Leave the third third alone.

Lightly flour a sheet of waxed paper and roll out one of the thirds to a rectangle about 6 inches by 12. Repeat with the other colors of dough, each on a separate sheet of waxed paper.

Put another sheet of waxed paper on a cookie sheet. Invert the uncolored dough onto that sheet of waxed paper and peel off the waxed paper that is now on top of it. Turn the pink dough on top of the white dough and peel the waxed paper off of it. Finish with the chocolate dough and remove the paper from it. Chill the stack of dough for five to ten minutes.

Roll the dough up from the 6-inch side, producing a 6-inch-long roll. Wrap the roll in waxed paper and chill several hours. (If you don't chill the dough long enough, the cookies won't stay round when you slice them off the roll. A squashed spiral is not a pretty sight.)

Preheat the oven to 375 degrees, slice the dough into cookies (about five to the inch) and place them on an ungreased cookie sheet. Bake about 10 minutes; cool on racks. Makes 2½ dozen cookies.

Somebody sent David Guralnik a copy of this article, and he replied that although some folks distinguish between the helix and the spiral, most don't. Nobody, he noted, calls it a helical staircase.

He added that he does indeed make a great peanut butter sandwich, using a kaiser roll and banana slices.

Chocolate Dinner

Either you're nuts about chocolate or you're not much interested in it, right? There's no such thing as being merely quite fond of it.

That's what I thought, too, until I started looking for folks to eat a chocolate meal. There were lots of eager hands until I explained that I really meant it: There would a chocolate-laden appetizer, a main course with chocolate, a salad course with chocolate.... Hands started going down.

The office chocolate freak (I should say the other office chocolate freak) had to work that night. Another fellow suddenly recalled that the Legislature was in session. One colleague volunteered, promising to bring a guest, then declined the next day, apparently having thought better of it.

Another volunteer begged off hours before the dinner because of unspecified concerns about his stomach.

I invited a couple, but the woman declined, saying that her husband had to go fishing the next day.

That left me, one somewhat dedicated chocolate eater from the office (on the day before the dinner, she too was registering a possible copout — vague ill health that might force her to cancel at the last minute), my sweetie (who doesn't care all that much for chocolate but clearly felt duty-bound to attend), and her parents. Her mother qualifies as a chocolate eater *sans reproche*, as she eats chocolate every day despite having been told that she's allergic to it. Her father, on the other hand, had to be listed as a doubtful starter — a genial-enough dinner companion but a man lacking an over-whelming interest in dessert.

The idea of the chocolate meal was twofold: First, it would serve as a vehicle to get urgently needed chocolate recipes into the newspaper. Second, it would explore a culinary problem that had been nagging at me — why wait for dessert to have chocolate?

The meal that resulted from serving all of these things at one sitting was not the most elegant I've ever had, but food writing is a harsh mistress.

For the faint of heart I tried to temper the impact of the chocolate as best I could. I served a bland noodle dish and potatoes and peas in cream sauce, as well as lots of sherbet between courses. I also provided a roll of Tums for each diner.

It would be appropriate here, I suppose, to go into the history of chocolate, and to speak knowledgeably of conching, tempering and the differences between semisweet and bittersweet....

Naah.

I'd rather eat the stuff than talk about it, and so, if you like it at all, would you. The menu:

Appetizer: Tache au Chocolat sur Triscuit
Salad: Poires Belle Hélène
Rolls: Chocolate Popovers
First course: Chocolate Omelet
Second course: Chicken Molé
Various non-chocolate vegetables and sherbet, to ease the agony
Dessert: Mint chocolate mousse
With coffee: Chocolate-dipped candied orange peels

The appetizer, blob of chocolate on a

Triscuit (don't things sound more elegant in French?) is a velvety, bittersweet sauce spread on salty, crunchy crackers.

It is extremely nice, but it is not a normal-looking hors d'oeuvre. One guest, regarding her first one with suspicion, demanded, "Did you make this up?"

Yes, I did.

It isn't easy to find a chocolate salad, but I think I came close. Poires Belle Hélène are pear halves cooked in syrup, topped with a rather bitter chocolate sauce and served warm over ice cream. I eliminated the ice cream as a bit much for so early in the meal.

The guests were surprisingly game for this one. It wasn't until after they had departed that I realized that I could have served it on lettuce leaves.

No such improvement could have helped the chocolate popovers, which were deposited in the garbage can before the diners arrived. In the midst of so much other cooking, I didn't notice that the recipe, straight from a book, contained absolutely no flour. I poured the batter into popover tins and watched, horrified, as it shrank, over its allotted 40 minutes in the oven, into dense little ¼-inch-deep puddles.

I suppose that if you really want to do this, a bit of cocoa could be worked into a standard popover recipe without too much difficulty. (Lower the baking temperature a bit, too, to avoid burning.) I no longer have any interest in it.

Moving right along, we came to the chocolate omelet. Wanting to minimize the fuss in the kitchen, I combined in a large pan enough of the mixture to make four small omelets, figuring to cook it a little longer and cut it up at the table. After a few minutes it was clear that it wasn't going to work, so I scrambled it. I'm glad I didn't spend a lot of time with it, as it turned out to be the least favorite item on the menu.

"This reminds me of the U.S. Army," was the father figure's only comment. His meaning was clear.

The chocolate-loving colleague allowed as how it was "real . . . *odd.*" The other diners were silent. Nobody asked for seconds.

The chicken molé turned out to be *very* good. Chocolate plays only a minor role in the sauce, and it was quite tasty, even surrounded by so many desserty items. The sauce goes with turkey (its original Mexican form) as well as with chicken and even ground beef.

After some bland noodles and vegetables and a bit of sherbet, (one diner murmured "Thank God," on the arrival of the noodles) it was time for the chocolate-mint mousse, coffee and the chocolate-dipped candied orange peels.

A word about the choice of dessert is in order. I have made lots of desserts far more intensely chocolate than the mint mousse. But I thought that a deeply chocolate dessert after so many other chocolate dishes would not be much of a treat.

I was right. The mousse went down very nicely, with many appreciative "ahhs" from around the table, but when I produced the orange peels (which are excellent), one guest who apparently had thought she was through, looked at them and said "Blechhh."

Afterwards, instead of finger bowls, we had Stridex pads.

A note about chocolate and moisture: If you're melting chocolate, be very careful not to allow moisture near it, as very small amounts can cause it to thicken, or even to seize up. Carefully dry any pan in which chocolate is to be melted. So small an oversight as a stirring spoon that was rinsed but not dried can cause difficulties.

Don't even boil water near melting chocolate, to avoid condensation on the surface. (Have your tea before you start.)

And a general observation. Even if you are the world's most compulsive chocolate eater (and I'm right up there, suffering from chocolate deficiency anemia if I haven't had at least a Hershey's Special Dark by suppertime), being around the aroma of cooking chocolate all day tends to take the edge off your appetite for it. By the time folks showed up for dinner, I felt as though I had gone through a whole bag of Pepperidge Farm Orleans cookies in five minutes.

But, for country and Tribune, I ate it all.

Tache au Chocolat sur Triscuit

6 tbsp. sugar
1 tbsp. cornstarch
⅔ c. milk
3 (1-oz.) squares unsweetened
    chocolate
3 tbsp. coffee liqueur
4 egg yolks
Triscuits

Combine the sugar and cornstarch in a saucepan and slowly stir in the milk until smooth. Bring to a boil over medium-high heat, stirring constantly. Lower heat and allow to boil for one minute.

Remove from heat and add the chocolate. Stir until it has fully melted into the milk mixture. Stir in the liqueur. Add a bit of the chocolate mixture to the egg yolks and stir until well mixed. Return the yolks to the rest of the chocolate, stirring well.

Blade a blob of chocolate onto each Triscuit with a spatula or knife, but do not spread to the edges. (This allows them to be picked up without getting chocolate on the fingers.)

If you like, refrigerate for an hour or so until the chocolate is firm.

Poires Belle Hélène

1 (29-oz.) can pear halves in syrup
1 tsp. sugar
½ tsp. vanilla
1 tbsp. brandy or Cognac
Sauce:
3½ (1-oz.) squares unsweetened
    chocolate
3 tbsp. sugar
1½ tbsp. butter
2 egg yolks
4 to 6 tbsp. heavy cream

Pour the pear halves and their liquid into a large pan. Add the sugar, vanilla and liquor. Cook slowly, basting the pears, until the liquid has reduced to a heavy syrup. Keep warm.

Prepare the sauce by mixing the chocolate, sugar and butter in a saucepan over very low heat until blended. Add a bit of the chocolate mixture to the egg yolks, stirring, and return the yolks to the chocolate, stirring until blended. Add the cream as necessary for consistency.

Serve pear halves with chocolate sauce.

Chocolate Popovers

Make up your own.

Chocolate Omelet

**(From Juliette Elkon's Chocolate
    Cookbook)**
For 1 serving:
2 tbsp. heavy cream
2 tbsp. sugar
1 (1-oz.) square semisweet chocolate
1 egg, separated
2 tbsp. cherry preserves
1 tbsp. butter

In a small saucepan, combine and heat the cream, sugar and chocolate. Beat the egg yolk. Beat the white separately (until it holds soft peaks). Add half the chocolate sauce and all of the cherry preserves to the beaten yolk, then fold the beaten white into that mixture.

Melt the butter in a small frying pan over medium heat. Pour in the omelet batter and cook in the usual manner. Fold in half and serve with the remaining half of the chocolate sauce drizzled over the top.

(Or scramble it.)

Chicken Molé

**(Adapted from Juliette Elkon's
    Chocolate Cookbook)**
**(This dish is made a day ahead of
    serving time)**
**2 (10¾-oz.) cans condensed chicken
    broth**
1 small onion
½ tsp. ground cloves
2 green peppers, seeded
3 tbsp. sesame seeds
1 (2¾- to 3-oz.) bag slivered almonds
3 corn tortillas, cooked and broken up
3 large tomatoes, seeded
1½ tsp. anise seed
6 cloves garlic, crushed
⅛ tsp. ground cloves
¼ tsp. cinnamon

1 tsp. salt
½ tsp. nutmeg
2 tbsp. chili powder
6 to 8 pieces chicken
4 to 5 tbsp. vegetable shortening
½ c. vegetable shortening
**4 (1-oz. squares) unsweetened
    chocolate**

Simmer together the condensed soup, two soup cans of water, the onion and the half teaspoon of cloves.

Meanwhile, a little at a time, combine in a processor or blender and chop very fine the peppers, sesame seeds, almonds, tortillas, tomatoes, anise seed and garlic. Add dry seasonings. Set aside.

Brown the chicken well in the four to five tablespoons of shortening. Melt the half cup of shortening in a Dutch oven. Stir in the pepper mixture until it is very hot.

Put the chicken pieces into the mixture in the Dutch oven. Cover with the hot broth and bake, covered (aluminum foil will do if the pot cover is not oven-safe), for about 1½ hours in a 350-degree oven, or until meat is tender. Add the chocolate and stir well to melt and blend. Refrigerate overnight. Reheat and serve hot.

Mint Chocolate Mousse

**(From Maida Heatter's Book of Great
    Chocolate Desserts)**
8 (1-oz.) squares semisweet chocolate
⅓ c. boiling water
5 eggs, separated
½ tsp. peppermint extract
Pinch salt
Heavy cream, whipped, for garnish

Break up the chocolate and place it in a saucepan. Pour the boiling water over the chocolate, and stir constantly over low heat until the chocolate is melted. Allow to cool.

Beat the egg yolks for three to four minutes, until they are pale lemon in color. Add the peppermint and gradually stir in the chocolate, scraping the bowl often. Beat until smooth.

Add salt to egg whites; beat (with clean beaters) until they are firm but not stiff or dry. Gently fold in the chocolate mixture until no whites show. Pour into wine glasses or ramekins; chill, covered, three to six hours. Top with whipped cream.

Chocolate-Dipped Candied Orange Peels

**(Dipping instructions adapted from
    Anita Prichard's Complete
    Candy Cookbook)**
2 oranges
2 c. sugar, divided
½ c. water
Chocolate coating:
**4 oz. summer coating (see text),
    broken into small pieces**
**4 (1-oz.) squares unsweetened
    chocolate, broken into small
    pieces**

Peel the oranges carefully. Remove from the peel at least half the thickness of the inner white pith. (Do not remove too much, or the skin will have no body.) Cut into ¼-inch-wide strips about three inches long. If the skin has torn, cut any sizeable fragments into shorter strips.

Cover the strips of peel with cold water in a saucepan, bring to a boil and drain. Repeat twice more, allowing the peel to boil three to four minutes the last time. Drain well and dry on a cake rack.

Dissolve one cup of sugar in the half cup of water. Add the peel, bring to a boil and let boil until the syrup is almost absorbed.

Remove from heat. Quickly remove the peel with a fork or tongs and spread it out on waxed paper to cool.

Put the other cup of sugar into a small bowl. When the peel has almost cooled (but is still warm), roll each piece in the sugar. Arrange on waxed paper to dry.

When the peel has dried (give it at least an hour — all pieces may not be firm, but that's OK), prepare the coating. (Summer coating isn't chocolate but it firms up nicely, so it's good training.) Put the summer coating (available at Maid of Scandinavia, and at Fanny Farmer as "White Pyramid" — do not use imported white candy bars) in the top half of a double boiler. Heat the water almost to boiling and stir the coating until it is melted. Remove the pan from the heat and stir in the chocolate until it melts, reheating if necessary.

Let the chocolate cool to about 100 degrees (a string of chocolate about 1½ inches long dangles from the end of a spatula).

Arrange the sugared orange peel on one side of the pan of chocolate and a waxed-paper-covered baking sheet on the other side. Make a V with two fingers, palm up, and lay a piece of the peel across them with the other hand. Dip the fingers (messy!!!) into the chocolate, making sure the peel is covered. Lift the fingers back out, rubbing the backs of the knuckles against the rim of the pan to drain excess chocolate from the underside of the peel, and invert the peel onto the waxed paper. Don't slide it around once it's down, or coating will be removed.

Keep the other hand out of the chocolate so that it can be used for picking up peels, grabbing paper towels in the event of the inevitable small disasters, and the like.

Do not be concerned if small chunks of the sugar coating come off in the chocolate.

Once all the peel is dipped, refrigerate it until it hardens. Depending on the temperature and your luck, the coating may soften later if it is left sitting out, but it will firm up again if re-refrigerated.

Great Culinary Expectations

When I was attending college briefly in Madison, Wis., many long years ago, I saw a women attempting without success to enter a supermarket.

The door that she was trying to push open was operated by an electric treadle on the inside and had no handles on the outside. It bore a fairly large sign that said "OUT." It was next to a door with a large push handle and a similar sign that said "IN."

I walked up to her, pointed to the other door, and said, "I think *that* is the entrance."

"Oh," she said, smiling. "I'm from out of town!"

I'm not originally from Minneapolis myself, but I have been here long enough that I wouldn't ever think of using that excuse. (Now I say, "I'm sorry; I've been up all night trying to memorize the lyrics to 'Me and Little Ingeborg, We're Going Down to Smorgasbord.'")

In fact, it would be hard to tell, except that I still usually pronounce Milwaukee without the "l," that I am not a native Minnesotan.

Like almost everyone else, if I'm served something that I don't like at a restaurant, I never complain. When the waitperson asks how everything is here, I say "Fine, thank you," and I pay my check and never come back. Who wants a confrontation?

Lots of people, particularly people from large Eastern cities, will never understand this, and most restaurant operators deplore it. They will tell you, if you ask them — and sometimes even if you don't ask them — that they would much rather have you complain

(and maybe they would even rather give you some other food) than have you not come back.

That makes lots of sense, but expecting folks who would never complain about *anything* to overcome their natural tendencies in a public place — and in front of friends or associates — is a real uphill climb (as opposed to a downhill climb). Maybe what's needed is a form that could be presented with the food and quietly collected by the waitperson a few minutes later.

Is your food too:
- ☐ Cold?
- ☐ Warm?
- ☐ Overcooked?
- ☐ Undercooked?
- ☐ Greasy?
- ☐ Soggy?
- ☐ Dry?
- ☐ Soft?
- ☐ Hard?
- ☐ Crunchy?
- ☐ Gooey?
- ☐ Other? _____

On the other hand, it probably wouldn't work. No such list could cover every eventuality (there's hair in the soup, there's not enough hair in the soup).

And no Minnesotan of the sort we are trying here to aid would want to make a scene by filling in anything under "Other." Even were I provided such a card, for example, I don't think I could bring myself to use it to complain about a different kind of restaurant disappointment that happens to me once in a while: What I am served is just fine, but it isn't anything like what I pictured from reading the menu. And what I pictured sounded better.

On the *other* other hand, although I will never be able to jump up on the table, brandishing a laden plate and screaming "*THIS* is Greek chicken?" that doesn't mean the issue has to rest there.

I get to tell *you* about it, for one. And, if you're still listening, I get to tell you how to prepare some of those dishes the way I thought they would be.

Now for an admission more embarrassing than anything that might happen if I tried to send back a dry hamburger:

After I committed myself to writing this article (having immediately thought of two fine examples of such dishes), I couldn't think of any more. So we're going to have those two examples, plus several things I haven't been served but that sounded very good when I thought or heard of them.

Not much of a theme, I'll admit. But you're not likely to complain, so it'll be OK.

To start the meal, a dish that I ordered in a restaurant in Mexico several years ago.

I don't speak Spanish, but even I could figure out Sopa de Lima. (Unless it was lime soap instead of lime soup.) I figured it would be cool, creamy and refreshing — just the ticket on a scorching evening.

It turned out to be a hot chicken broth very lightly flavored with lime. Not bad, but a rude surprise.

I looked at a number of cookbooks later, and if they had lime soup at all that's what they had.

Here's what I wanted:

Cold Lime Cream Soup

2 ripe avocados (good luck finding 2 ripe ones at the same store)
2 (10¾-oz.) cans chicken broth
2 c. heavy cream
1 c. dry white wine
1 c. milk or half and half
1 tbsp. lemon juice
Salt, white pepper
Juice of 4 fresh limes — about ⅝ c.
    — or to taste

Mash and beat or purée the avocados until they have formed a smooth paste. (Peel them first and take out the pits — do I have to tell you *everything*? Some day you're going to be all alone in a great big kitchen, with nobody to help you, and *then* what will you do?)

Slowly add the chicken broth to the avocado, continuing to beat or whomp until the mixture is smooth.

Stir in the cream, wine, milk, lemon juice, salt and pepper. Then add the lime juice, tasting as you go. It will mellow somewhat as it is chilled, so you might go a little stronger than you are first tempted to do. (Ain't it funny how the lime slips away?)

Chill, covered.

Serves eight.

The following peculiar salad dressing is not something I was ever served, but it has lurked in the back of my mind for a long time, ever since I started playing with sauces. And that lurking thought resurfaces almost every time I'm in a restaurant that decorates the plate carrying my cheeseburger by adding a slice of tomato topped with a blob of mayonnaise.

Mayonnaise, I reason each time, in

my own peculiar way, is made by beating oil into egg yolks and mustard. Egg yolk and melted butter, with different seasoning, makes hollandaise sauce, which is widely acclaimed as wonderful because you taste not only the seasonings, but also the butter. So why not make mayonnaise with melted butter instead of oil?

Why not, indeed?

It turns out that the only reason not to do it, unless you count cholesterol as a reason, is that it sets up rather chunkily when you refrigerate it, and it clearly can't be left around for hours unrefrigerated. So if you make it, do so just before you're going to use it, as you would with hollandaise sauce. Or figure on beating it after you take it back out of the refrigerator.

It is yummy enough to elicit oohs and ahhs.

Mayonnoohs or Mayonnahhs

1 egg yolk
½ tsp. Dijon mustard
Salt, pepper
Pinch of sugar
¾ c. (1½ sticks) unsalted butter, melted and cooled to room temperature
1 tsp. white wine vinegar, or to taste

Put the egg yolk in a bowl and stir in the mustard, salt, pepper and sugar.

With a whisk or a sturdy wooden spoon, beat in a very small amount of the melted butter until it is fully bound into the egg mixture. Add a bit more and beat in. Continue adding and beating until it is all absorbed. After half the butter is in, you can begin to add it in somewhat larger increments, but don't get happy and add it too fast — it won't get taken up easily and

you'll have a curdled mess. This is not a rapid process, nor one for somebody with weak forearms.

When all the butter is in, stir in the vinegar. Even if you normally use tarragon vinegar in making mayonnaise (an excellent choice), don't do it this time. The tarragon substantially overwhelms the butter flavor.

Serve somewhere that will allow the flavor to show. Just dolloped onto hard-cooked eggs is a typical French dish, and one that will bring the cholesterol count up to a nice round number.

Makes about a cup.

Back to the restaurant. Not long ago I had lunch with some friends at a local eatery and the waitperson (of course she introduced herself and explained her role in our dining experience when she arrived at the table, but in the intervening months I've forgotten her name; I'm sure she wouldn't remember us either) . . . anyway, she handed out menus and reeled off the several daily specials that were just too daily and too special to write down.

One of them, chicken with a Greek-sounding sauce, rather appealed to me. I can't remember what she said was in it (that's one of the problems of the Talking Menu; also you can't — unless you're from a large Eastern city — call the waitperson over four or five times to ask for another reading of several items as you try to choose among them). I do know it had a Greek sound; lemon and olive oil for sure.

I pictured that in a yogurty sauce much like comes with gyros, with maybe basil too. Wrong.

It was olive oil and lemon juice and, as far as I could tell, that was about all.

Nice, but wrong.

This is what I had pictured:

Greek Chicken

6 to 8 single chicken breasts, deboned and skin removed
3 to 4 tbsp. olive oil
1 cucumber
2 c. yogurt
3 cloves garlic, crushed
2 tbsp. lemon juice
½ tsp. basil, crumbled
½ tsp. crushed anise seed
Salt, pepper
2 tbsp. cornstarch
¼ c. water

In a large frying pan, sauté the chicken breasts in the olive oil, cooking about five minutes over medium heat on each side.

While the chicken is cooking peel the cucumber, cut it in half lengthwise and run a spoon down each half to remove the seeds. Slice the halves.

Combine the cucumber, yogurt, garlic, lemon juice, basil, anise seed, salt and pepper. Heat in a saucepan.

Combine the cornstarch and water and stir into the hot yogurt sauce. Cook five minutes over medium heat.

Pour the sauce over the chicken, lower the heat and allow it to simmer five minutes or until the chicken is done. Six to eight servings.

While I was trying frantically, and unsuccessfully, to remember a dessert misexpectation, I recalled an occasion on which a few orange segments from a salad I had taken out of defensiveness wandered across my plate and mingled with some rice. It was a nice flavor.

You know, I told myself (I *didn't* know, but it all worked out anyway), orange would be a real nice *dessert* flavor, but in something cold and creamy, sort of like I pictured the lime soup.

Orange Pudding

2¼ c. milk
4 tbsp. sugar, divided
¼ c. cornstarch
¾ c. orange juice
1 egg
1 tsp. grated orange rind (optional)
2 tbsp. Grand Marnier (optional)

Heat the milk in a saucepan until it just comes to the boil.

Remove from the heat.

Combine two tablespoons of the sugar, the cornstarch and orange juice and stir into the hot milk. Stir over low heat until the mixture thickens.

It will curdle a bit because of the orange juice, but hang in there. It will get almost fully smooth.

Beat the egg with the remaining two tablespoons of sugar.

Stir in a little of the hot mixture, then return the diluted egg to the hot mixture and stir in. Stir the whole thing over low heat until it thickens again. Remove from heat.

When the pudding has cooled 10 or 15 minutes, stir in the orange rind and/or Grand Marnier.

Pour into serving dishes and chill. Makes six servings.

This second dessert (lucky, lucky!) is one that I had thought of once and forgotten until a friend mentioned that he had seen it in a shop window in a Greek neighborhood in Detroit. What a natural combination — chocolate and baklava!

My first attempt to make it failed because, unbeknownst to me, my oven had quit working.

It was still hot from something else when I put the choclava in for its 1½-hour sojourn, so it wasn't until much later that I discovered that the choclava had been cooling its heels, so to speak.

It had dried instead of baking, and the top sheet of filo dough had curled up and died. It was not pretty.

Thinking it could be repaired, I drove it to a friend's house and baked it there, but it didn't look much better. Hoping against hope that the pouring-on of the finishing syrup would somehow have a resuscitating effect, I drove it home, made the syrup and poured it on.

Not only didn't the syrup do any good, it didn't soak in — it just swam around the pan, threatening to run over at any number of places.

A quick check of other recipes indicated that maybe the baklava should have been hot when the syrup was poured on. (Some say hot syrup, cool baklava; others say hot baklava, cool syrup. This is probably one of the things that ruins marriages in that part of the world.)

The oven was still out, so I did the only thing I could think of: I cleared out the dishwasher, set it to the dry cycle, and ran the choclava through twice.

Nope.

I served it anyway, and there were polite noises from one or two folks, but I decided to make it again after fixing the oven.

That was muuuch better. If I were to make it a third time, I might increase the chocolate level a bit. I haven't tried that yet, because this is a time-consuming recipe. What the world needs is a faster version. We could call it tick-tocklava.

If you don't like the idea of the chocolate and want to stick with the standard version, just omit the chocolate. That way, it's stocklava.

If you like it warm but you don't want to keep the kitchen hot, you could reheat it on your car engine. That's blocklava.

I don't recommend that you substitute margarine for the butter in this very rich dessert. In some things that works fine, but here I'm afraid you'd wind up with shlocklava.

I'll grant that butter is more expensive, but it's worth it in something like this. If you need to borrow a few bucks to make it, it's worth going into hocklava.

If that sounds like a bad idea, and you don't want to go through all the business with the filo dough either, you could try making the whole thing with Ritz crackers. That would be mocklava.

The recipe makes quite a large amount, and given the effort and expense (if you make it the right way) you certainly wouldn't want any of the leftovers stolen, so you'd better check your locklava.

(Slap.)

Thanks, boss. I needed that.

Time to start cooking.

Put on your smocklava and . . . No! I promise! I won't do that any more.

Choclava

1 (1-lb.) pkg. frozen filo dough
1 lb. walnuts
½ c. sugar
1½ tsp. cinnamon
3½ sticks unsalted butter, divided
8 (1-oz.) squares semisweet chocolate
(or 1⅓ c. chips)
Syrup:
3 c. sugar
2 c. water
1 tbsp. lemon juice

Thaw the filo sheets according to package directions. (This takes overnight.)

Chop the walnuts very finely or whomp them in a food processor until they are coarse crumbs. Stop before they turn into flour. We want a little texture. Stir in the sugar and cinnamon. Set aside.

Trim the stack of filo sheets to the size of a large raised-edge baking pan (11 by 17, or 10 by 15 if that's the biggest you have).

Cover the stack of filo with a just-barely-damp cloth, and always keep it covered while working. Melt two tablespoons of the butter in a small saucepan. In a large saucepan, over very low heat, melt the remaining butter with the chocolate, stirring constantly, just until the chocolate is melted. Remove from heat.

Brush the baking pan with the plain melted butter. Lay one sheet of filo onto the pan and brush it thoroughly with the chocolate-butter mixture. Top with another filo sheet and brush with more chocolate butter. Continue until you have built up 10 sheets. Stir the chocolate butter occasionally to keep the chocolate from settling. If necessary, rewarm it gently.

After the 10th sheet is brushed with chocolate butter, sprinkle it evenly with about ½ cup (about four fistfuls) of the nut mixture. Top with two more sheets of filo,

brushing each with chocolate butter, and then sprinkle on another four fistfuls of nuts. Continue until almost all the sheets of filo are used, brushing each sheet with chocolate butter and topping every second sheet with the nut mixture. The topmost two (or three, depending on how it works out) sheets should not have nut mixture (just chocolate butter) between them. Brush the top sheet with chocolate butter.

Preheat the oven to 350 degrees.

With a sharp knife, cut the choclava (yes, before it's baked) into not-quite-diamond shapes, as follows: Make a series of cuts about an inch apart along the length of the pan. Make a series of diagonal cuts about two inches apart.

Smooth out the pieces of the top layer that lifted while you were cutting. If you have extra chocolate butter, have faith that you'll think of something to do with it. If you never have such thoughts, pour it over the top. Bake at 350 degrees for 30 minutes, then lower the temperature to 300 degrees and bake one hour more.

About 30 minutes before the choclava is to be done, prepare the syrup:

In a large saucepan, stir together the sugar, water and lemon juice until the sugar has dissolved. Cook over high heat, without further stirring, until the mixture boils, lower the heat and boil it 20 minutes.

Allow the syrup to cool briefly if it is done before the choclava is. Spoon about two-thirds of the syrup over the hot choclava, allowing it to soak in nicely. An hour later, spoon on the rest of it. Allow it to rest several hours before serving. Makes about five dozen pieces if the larger baking sheet is used.

I am told that baklava will keep for several weeks if merely covered with plastic wrap and not refrigerated. It can also be frozen, I am informed. I don't know; I didn't have that much left.

A Resounding Meal

There is nothing quite so annoying to an adult as to be in a car with a child — even a nice child — who is at the age at which it is fascinating to repeat endlessly some word or phrase.

A few minutes of "Eeio, eeio, eeio, eeio, eeio, eeio, eeio, eeio, eeio," for example, inspired by an unthinking reference to Old Macdonald, can reduce even an otherwise loving parent to contemplating things like tying the happy child to a bench at a bus stop and driving away.

In typical cases, no threat, promise or black glare is enough to silence this performance permanently. There may be a break for a minute or two, but it will be back.

And just when you think it cannot get worse, chances are the little nipper will begin to *sing* the same refrain.

It's not a pretty picture.

You might suppose that this phenomenon — known to people who like to put labels on things as "perseveration" — has nothing whatever to do with food. Regular readers of these effusions know from bitter and painful experience that it is possible to make some connection, however tenuous, between food and almost anything.

Others are about to see that awesome process for themselves.

There are a number of foods, perhaps you haven't noticed them, that exhibit the tendency we have been discussing — repeated sounds.

There is, for example, Lomi-lomi Salmon, the traditional luau appetizer. There are Ho Hos, the traditional Hostess snack cake. There are bonbons, there is steak tartare, there are pu-pu platters — there is more than enough, in fact, if one was silly enough to want to make it, to prepare a whole repast of echoic foods.

Welcome to the Echo Canyon Meal.

If you wanted to do a dinner like this right, of course, it should be served in Walla Walla, Pago Pago, Baden-Baden or Bora-Bora. Or, in a pinch, in Flin Flon. Under duress, you could also do it in Sing Sing. (Oh, all right, nitpickers. You could do it in Ossining Correctional Facility. Happy now?)

Failing to find an echoic location, it would be nice to invite someone with a name like Meyer Meier. Or maybe Nanette somebody (to whom you could spend the evening saying "No, No").

In any case, if we're going to get done before it's time to go night-night, we'd best start talking about some recipes. Chop-chop.

To start things off briskly, let's have a nice, cold spiked punch — the vodka version of a piña colada. Believe it or not, I found this head-knocker in a church cookbook. Here is a smaller version of the original recipe, which could have put an entire congregation out of commission for a week.

Chi Chi Punch

1 (6-oz.) can frozen lemonade
    concentrate
2 c. pineapple juice
1 (8½-oz.) can (the small one) cream
    of coconut
1 c. vodka
2 to 3 qt. 7-Up or similar beverage

Combine the lemonade concentrate, pineapple juice, cream of coconut and vodka. Freeze.

To serve, put a scoop of the frozen punch concentrate in a glass and fill with 7-Up.

Makes about 12 drinks.

(These are stronger than you think, so don't start tossing them down willy-nilly. You don't want to get drunk as a skunk.)

To start the meal itself (once the guests stagger to the table after their chi chi wing-ding), here's a soup that you might run into in a fancy restaurant.

Frankly, I wasn't particularly impressed with the distinctiveness of the expensive canned turtle soup that is one of the ingredients, so the next time I make this soup I would throw authenticity to the wind and instead use a second can of beef broth and a dash of sherry. Not as hotsy-totsy, but still okey-dokey.

Boula Boula Soup

1 small onion
2 ribs celery
6 tbsp. butter
1 (17-oz.) can plus 1 (8½-oz.) can peas
Salt
White pepper
2 tbsp. flour
1 (10½-oz.) can beef broth
1 (14½-oz.) can turtle soup (or a
    second 10½-oz. can beef broth
    plus 2 tbsp. sherry)
1 c. heavy cream

Chop the onion finely. Chop the celery finely.

Melt the butter in a Dutch oven. Add the onion and celery and cook over low heat, stirring, several minutes. Drain the peas, reserving one-fourth cup of the liquid. Add to the contents of the Dutch oven the peas, the reserved liquid and salt and pepper. Cover and cook until the peas are soft.

Remove from heat, sift in the flour and stir in the canned soups. Bring to the simmer, stirring, over low heat, and continue to simmer two minutes.

Pour the soup, in batches if necessary, into a blender and purée. (Taste for texture. The pea skins should not be gritty. Blend longer if necessary.)

Return soup to the cooking pan over low heat.

Whip the cream and stir all but about one-fourth cup of it into the soup. Top each bowl with a dollop of whipped cream and serve.

Serves six to eight.

For the main course, let's have a big platter of couscous.

Not only does couscous fit the theme of this meal, it also has the peculiar property of being the name of both the completed dish and one of the ingredients of that dish.

The ingredient couscous is a grain that, when cooked, is somewhere between oatmeal and rice, over which the rest of the dish, a kind of chicken and lamb stew, is served.

Actually, the couscous grain is semolina, a wheat product made famous in two songs.

One is from a Danny Kaye movie: "Semolina, Semolina, tiny little thing . . . ."

The other was a hit by Doris Day and Les Brown (and his Band of Renown): "Gonna take a semolina journey . . . ."

Couscous

Stew:
2 large onions, chopped
2 tbsp. oil
1 clove garlic, chopped or pressed
1 (3 lb. or so) cut-up broiler-fryer
1 lb. lamb, cut into cubes as for stew
3 c. water
4 carrots, peeled and cut into 1-inch
   chunks
1 bay leaf
1 tbsp. salt
¼ tsp. pepper
¼ tsp. ground ginger
1 piece stick cinnamon
2 medium tomatoes, chopped
1 (16- to 20-oz.) can garbanzo beans
1 green pepper, cut into strips
1 c. raisins
Couscous grain:
1 (1-lb.) box (2½ c.) couscous
2½ c. water or 2 (10¾-oz.) cans
   chicken broth
1 tsp. salt (omit if using broth)
2 or more tbsp. butter

Sauté the onion in the oil in a large frying pan, adding the garlic after two or three minutes. Continue to sauté two or three more minutes, until the onion is beginning to turn golden. Transfer the onions and garlic to a Dutch oven.

Adding oil if necessary, brown the chicken pieces and the lamb in the skillet that was used for the onions, and transfer them to the Dutch oven.

Put the water in the skillet and bring it to boiling, using a wooden spoon to scrape up bits of meat that had stuck to the pan. Pour the water over the meat. Stir into the mixture in the Dutch oven the carrots, bay leaf, salt (yes, that's a lot, but this is a lot of stew), pepper, ginger and cinnamon. Simmer 40 minutes.

Stir tomatoes, garbanzo beans, green pepper and raisins into the stew and simmer about 30 minutes more, until the meat and vegetables are tender. Remove bay leaf.

A side note about the couscous grain. It's available in lots of supermarkets, and almost invariably it is an "instant" or "quick-cooking" version (although it is not always labeled that way). Non-instant couscous has to cook for something like 30 or 40 minutes; the kind you're likely to find cooks in five minutes or less.

If you can't find couscous, substitute brown rice or kasha, cooked according to label directions.

In any case, starting when necessary to get the couscous and stew done simultaneously, prepare couscous according to package directions — something like this for quick-cooking versions: Bring to the boil a volume of salted water (or broth) equal to the volume of the couscous. Add the couscous, cover and let stand five minutes.

(If there's lots of liquid in the stew, you might want to substitute a cup or so of it for some of the boiling water or broth used to prepare the grain.)

When the couscous grain has been thus cooked, put it in a strainer and suspend it over the bubbling stew for five minutes (with the cover over all). Then turn the grain into a bowl, toss it with the butter and spread it onto a large platter. Spoon the stew over that and serve.

Serves eight.

If you like, spoon off another cup of the stew liquid at some point and use it to prepare the traditional hot sauce.

In terms of echoic titles, this isn't so strong as to be Hot-Hot Sauce, nor is it mild enough to be Not-Hot Sauce. I wouldn't want to call it So-So Hot Sauce, because that gives the wrong impression. So let's just call it Hot Sauce.

As Doris Day (we called her Dodo) would point out, "Que sera sera."

Hot Sauce (for Couscous)

1 c. stew liquid
2 tbsp. tomato paste
1 tsp. paprika
1 tsp. (or more) crushed dried hot red
    peppers
¼ tsp. coriander
½ to 1½ tsp. cumin
1 tsp. black pepper

Combine all ingredients and warm over low heat.

When I made the couscous for the Echo Canyon Meal I didn't make the hot sauce; I made it later and tried it with the leftovers. Instead I made Chow-Chow Relish, something I'd never heard of but that is apparently quite widely known. (Actually I didn't make the relish *instead* of the hot sauce; I simply forgot to make the hot sauce.)

Chow-Chow Relish is normally made in large batches and canned. I made a small batch, which would be excellent for getting rid of some left-over vegetables.

Chow-Chow Relish

1 c. chopped cabbage (about ¼ head)
¾ c. chopped cauliflower (about ¼
    head)
1 small onion, chopped (about ½ c.)
1 tomato, chopped
½ of a sweet red pepper, chopped
1 medium green pepper, chopped
2 tsp. salt

½ c. plus 2 tbsp. cider vinegar
¼ c. plus 2 tbsp. sugar
¾ tsp. dry mustard
¼ tsp. turmeric
⅛ tsp. ginger
½ tsp. celery seed
Dash white pepper

Note: To make a canning-size batch, quadruple this recipe.

In a bowl combine the chopped cabbage, cauliflower, onion, tomato and red and green pepper. Sprinkle with salt and let stand in the refrigerator four to six hours. Drain well.

Combine vinegar, sugar, mustard, turmeric, ginger, celery seed and pepper. Simmer 10 minutes, add vegetables and simmer 10 minutes more.

At this point, if you're making a larger batch to can, pack it, boiling hot, into hot jars, leaving ¼ to ½ inch headspace. Process 10 minutes and adjust caps.

If you're not canning but just making this small batch, boil it gently, covered, 10 to 15 minutes, until most of the liquid has evaporated. Keep it refrigerated. This recipe makes two cups.

For an odd vegetable with this meal, I decided to prepare some seasoned lentils.

This legume, as you may or may not know, is referred to in the Middle East and on the Indian subcontinent as dal or dhal.

Cooked lentils are kind of mud-brown and rather bland. When perked up with my favorite seasoning they are still rather unattractive, but they are quite pleasant to the taste.

▶

Dill Dhal

2 c. dry lentils
6 c. water
3 tbsp. oil
1 onion, finely chopped
1 clove garlic, minced or crushed
3 tbsp. flour
Salt, pepper
1 tbsp. honey
1 tbsp. dill weed
1 c. shredded Cheddar cheese

Boil the lentils in the water, partly covered, 35 to 40 minutes, until they are tender. Drain and purée in blender or food processor.

Meanwhile, heat the oil and sauté the onion for a few minutes, add the garlic and continue to sauté until the onion is golden. Stir in the flour and cook briefly, then stir in the salt, pepper, honey, dill and puréed lentils.

Turn the mixture into a greased casserole, top with the cheese and run it briefly under the broiler. Serves six. (Or 150, if they don't care for lentils.)

For dessert, I wanted to serve paw-paw melon. Yes, you have *too* heard of paw-paw melon. Remember "Way Down Yonder in the Paw-Paw Patch"?

It turns out that paw-paw melon is only grown in the American South, and that even there it is not highly prized. However, in some places, according to several cookbooks, the fruit commonly called the papaya is known as a pawpaw. That gives us the opportunity to prepare a very tasty papaya mousse and call it something resounding. This recipe is based on one in The Gourmet Cooking School Cookbook, by Dione Lucas.

A linguistic side note (don't you just love side notes?): Should you wind up unexpectedly in Havana some time, and should you, while there, desire a papaya, ask for a "fruta bomba" because "papaya" is not a very nice word at all in Cuba. It is, however, a fine word in other Spanish-speaking countries.

Don't ask.

"Pawpaw" (Papaya) Mousse

5 eggs plus 4 egg yolks
½ c. plus 1 tbsp. granulated sugar
2 (¼-oz.) env. plus ½ rounded tsp.
** unflavored gelatin**
2 tbsp. lemon juice
6 tbsp. water
3 ripe (yellow-orange) papayas (2½ to
** 3 lb. total)**
2½ c. heavy cream
1½ tsp. vanilla
2 heaping tbsp. confectioners' sugar
3 tbsp. Grand Marnier or other
** orange-flavored liqueur**
<u>**Optional decoration:**</u>
9 to 10 strawberries
¼ c. red currant jelly
1 tbsp. Grand Marnier or other
** orange-flavored liqueur**

Put the eggs and egg yolks and the granulated sugar in the large bowl of an electric mixer.

Beat until the mixture thickens enough that, when you lift out the beaters, what falls off of them does so as a single wide ribbon that folds over onto itself on the surface and dissolves slowly.

While the eggs are getting to that stage (it will take a while), put the gelatin, lemon juice and water in a small pan; stir over very low heat until the gelatin is fully dissolved and no grains can be seen in a metal spoon. Set aside to cool.

Halve the papayas, remove the seeds and the stringy part and spoon the flesh of the fruit (leaving the skin) into a blender or food processor. Purée the fruit. Set aside.

In another mixer bowl, beat the heavy cream until it begins to thicken. Add the vanilla and the confectioners' sugar and continue beating until the cream is thick and stiff.

Stir the puréed papaya into the egg mixture with a spatula. Fold in the three tablespoons of Grand Marnier and three-fourths of the whipped cream.

Carefully stir in the gelatin, being sure it is well blended throughout the mixture.

Pour this mousse into a clear-glass serving bowl and chill for several hours.

If you like, decorate with strawberries: Cut each berry in half and place the halves, cut side down, on top of the mousse around the rim of the bowl. Warm the currant jelly slightly in a small pan with the tablespoon of Grand Marnier, stirring, until it is somewhat liquid. Carefully brush the tops of the berries with this mixture to give them a bright glaze.

Pipe or mound the remaining whipped cream in the center of the mousse.

When your guests get a load of this beautiful dessert, they'll say "Hoo-Ha!"

After dinner, guests who had expected a chocolate dessert were given Ding Dongs. The writer couldn't find any Sen-Sen, so when all the food was consumed he passed around some Tic Tacs.

Bye-bye.

The main text of this book is set in 11-point Century Schoolbook on 13-point leading. Recipes are set in 10-point Century Schoolbook on 13-point leading.

Typesetting and pagination formats by Brian Cravens.

Keyboarding by Wendy Erickson.

Index